I0810398

IMAGES
of America

THETFORD

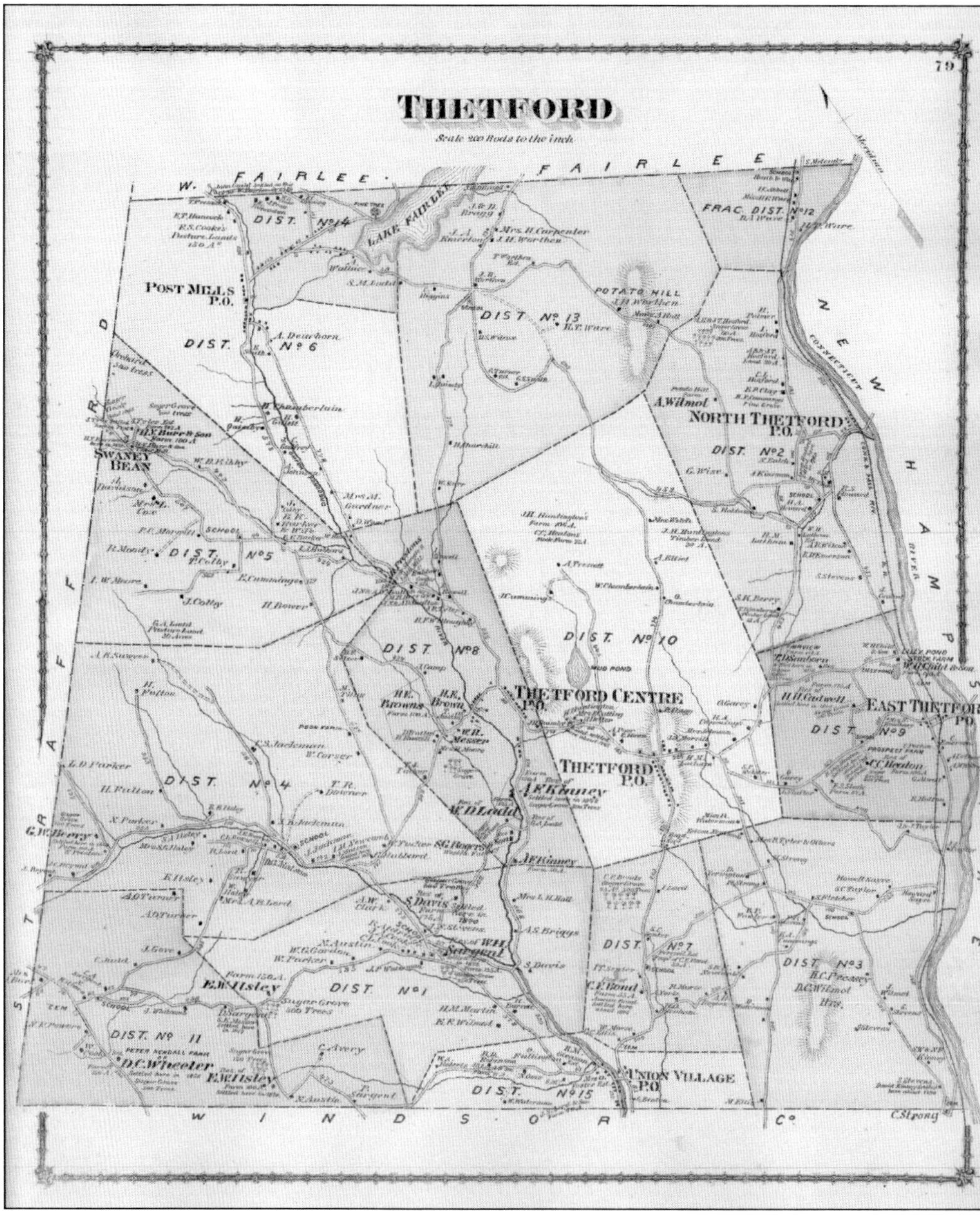

This 1877 map of Thetford comes from the F.W. Beers atlas. In the 19th century, Beers atlases were very popular because of their level of detail: they showed all the usual roads and landmarks, as well as property owners' names, building locations, and sometimes even their occupations. The Beers family produced more than 80 county atlases, local maps, and local histories. (Courtesy of Middlebury College.)

On the Cover: Campers from Camp Hanoum in Thetford Hill bring a canoe to the Connecticut River. It was common to see Hanoum campers all over Thetford in the summer hiking, canoeing, camping, and participating in the town's annual summer fair. (Courtesy of the Thetford Historical Society.)

IMAGES
of America

THETFORD

Susanna H. French

ARCADIA
PUBLISHING

ISBN 978-1-4671-2290-0

Published by Arcadia Publishing
Charleston, South Carolina

Printed in the United States of America

Library of Congress Control Number: 2014945980

For all general information, please contact Arcadia Publishing:
Telephone 843-853-2070
Fax 843-853-0044
E-mail sales@arcadiapublishing.com
For customer service and orders:
Toll-Free 1-888-313-2665

Visit us on the Internet at www.arcadiapublishing.com

To my daughter Caroline and to all of Thetford's children. Here is a bit of your history.

CONTENTS

ACKNOWLEDGMENTS

I am deeply grateful to the Thetford Historical Society for the use of its resources, without which this book could not have been written. I also wish to thank those on the board of the historical society who took the time to read my manuscript.

Thanks to Frank J. Barrett Jr. for your guidance.

I am beholden to Thetford's past historians Charles W. Hughes, Mary B. Slade, and Charles Latham Jr. Their knowledge has proven invaluable to the creation of this book.

Unless otherwise noted, all images appear courtesy of the Thetford Historical Society. I wish to thank University of Vermont Special Collections, the Vermont State Archives and Records Administration, Frank J. Barrett Jr., the Norwich Historical Society, Lyme Historians, the Aloha Foundation, Middlebury College, Thetford Academy, the Vermont Historical Society, Lochearn Camp, and the West Fairlee Historical Society for the use of their images as well.

Sincerest thanks to my unfailingly positive and patient editor, Caitrin Cunningham. I am deeply indebted to Bob Parke, who got me writing in the first place.

I cannot express enough heartfelt gratitude to my husband Jeff, daughter Caroline, and mother Anne, for their solicited editorial input and unsolicited encouragement. You made every page of this book possible. I love you all so much.

INTRODUCTION

Thetford was, in a way, the creation of New Hampshire governor Benning Wentworth. After the French were defeated in 1759, wide swaths of land in modern-day New Hampshire and Vermont opened up for settlement by other European colonists.

Wentworth signed charters for a slew of new towns that pressed beyond existing borders. He named them after nobles back in England as a means of currying favor with his superiors. In this case, the town of Thetford was likely named for Augustus Henry Fitzroy, Duke of Grafton, Earl of Arlington and Euston, Viscount of Thetford and Baron of Sudbury. In 1761 alone, Governor Wentworth granted charters for 60 towns. Thetford was one such frontier town, laid out on paper and offered to 62 speculators, most of whom were from Hebron, Connecticut. All they knew about Thetford was that, like most new towns in the area, it was six miles square.

Between the ravages of smallpox and the loss of their French allies, the Abenaki who had lived in the region for millennia could no longer hold back the settlers. First among them was John Chamberlain in 1764, the only one of Thetford's original landowners to settle here. He chose a site by the Connecticut River, a shoreline still densely forested but with the promise of farmland. Future settlers tended to stay low in the valleys, near workable land, and set up sawmills on the Ompompanoosuc River. As more settlers arrived, it became necessary to lay out roads and choose a cemetery site, which is in East Thetford.

The Revolutionary War came as close as Royalton, which was burned in 1780. Thetford's first pastor, Clement Sumner, was accused of being a Tory; he decamped to friendlier lands. Rev. Asa Burton, passing through the area, had a poor first impression of the people of Thetford: "They appeared to me to be very litigious, quarrelsome, intemperate, immoral, clownish and vulgar; and in view of towns around, they stood lowest in public estimation. I felt as though I could not live among a people so degraded."

Burton saw room for improvement and stayed to be Thetford's second minister. He was ordained in 1779 and became one of the town's most dominant forces. He served for 56 years, continuing to fight for his vision of piety and temperance.

Burton also helped to found Thetford Academy, Vermont's oldest and first coeducational secondary school. It accepted girls from the very start, in 1819. As it is today, the academy was also a private high school for those living outside Thetford. The academy had a large number of boarding students who stayed with townspeople until a dormitory was built in 1846. As it became more common for girls to enter college, their curriculum was integrated with that of the boys. Mary Hosford, an Academy alumna, became the first woman in the country to receive a college diploma when she graduated from Oberlin College in 1841.

It is hard to describe how rapidly Thetford changed in the early years of the 19th century. At first, each farm was virtually self-sufficient. Then, as the mill villages developed and small industry grew more robust, farmers relied on the local blacksmith and the woolen mill instead of having to do everything for themselves.

With the Louisiana Purchase and the opening of the Erie Canal came rapid westward expansion. Even by the 1820s, some Thetford families had already moved out seeking greener pastures. But the town continued to grow, especially with the arrival of the railroad in 1848. It was a development that would eventually give the small business owner unprecedented access to markets across the United States and into Canada. The formerly sleepy villages of East and North Thetford boomed, with bustling depots, stagecoach hotels, and shops.

With its forests rapidly becoming depleted, Thetford had less lumber to cut, but it diversified into industries such as textiles. New England experienced something of a merino sheep craze in the early 1800s, after Spain lifted its export ban. In the 1830s, there were more than one million merinos in Vermont. But soon thereafter, the price of merino wool plummeted due to international and western competition and changing tariffs, and the Vermont merino industry collapsed.

After the Civil War, Thetford experienced a period of both industrial and population decline. Rural farmers and manufacturers in New England found it hard to compete with the lower prices and increasing volume of goods coming from the West and southern New England. Many young people and restless veterans moved west or into the cities in search of more fruitful prospects. Between 1860 and 1890, Thetford's population declined by 32 percent. The population would not increase again until the 1950s.

At the same time that business in Thetford started its slide, Thomas H. Chubb arrived from Galveston, Texas. Chubb bought a factory on the Ompompanoosuc River. After an unremarkable stint making rake handles, he discovered enormous success with bamboo fishing rods. At one point, the Chubb Rod Company was the largest manufacturer of fishing rods in America. It continued until the Depression shut its doors; it later reopened as the Malmquist Wood Products Company, which closed in the 1990s.

Starting around 1900, tourists began to arrive en masse in northern New England. Newcomers bought up abandoned homes and farms and started camps on the shores of Lake Fairlee. While still rare in the rest of the country, summer camps were opening all across New England. By the 1920s, more than a million children journeyed by train and automobile each summer to spend several weeks canoeing, singing, learning new skills, and swatting mosquitoes.

Thetford's camps were, at first, primarily for girls, a fact that is striking because most camps in those days were for boys. Indeed, Camp Fire Girls, the nation's first scouting organization for girls, got its start here in Thetford.

Thetford was battered by floods in 1927 and 1936 and a massive hurricane in 1938. The damage across New England from these disasters was so severe that the federal government built 16 flood control dams in the Connecticut River watershed, dams capable of holding back vast amounts of water. The Ompompanoosuc River at Union Village was one such location. Roads were rerouted, and many homes—and three covered bridges—were demolished to clear the area that might be needed in case of flood.

The federal government made its presence known again in the 1960s when the construction of Interstate 91 reached Thetford's borders. Once again, homes were demolished and maps redrawn.

Today, Thetford's citizens work throughout the Upper Valley in an interdependent web of livelihoods. Meanwhile, just as before, maple trees sprout buckets in the spring, and Lake Fairlee's camps fill with energetic children each summer.

This book is not a comprehensive history of Thetford. It is, however, a photographic mosaic of many of Thetford's people and places. If, after reading it, you drive Thetford's roads or use its public spaces, perhaps an image will come back that reminds you how Thetford got where it is today.

No matter where I have lived, I have always been driven to know the history of my environment. Writing this book has been as fascinating for me as I hope reading it will be for you.

One

Thetford Hill

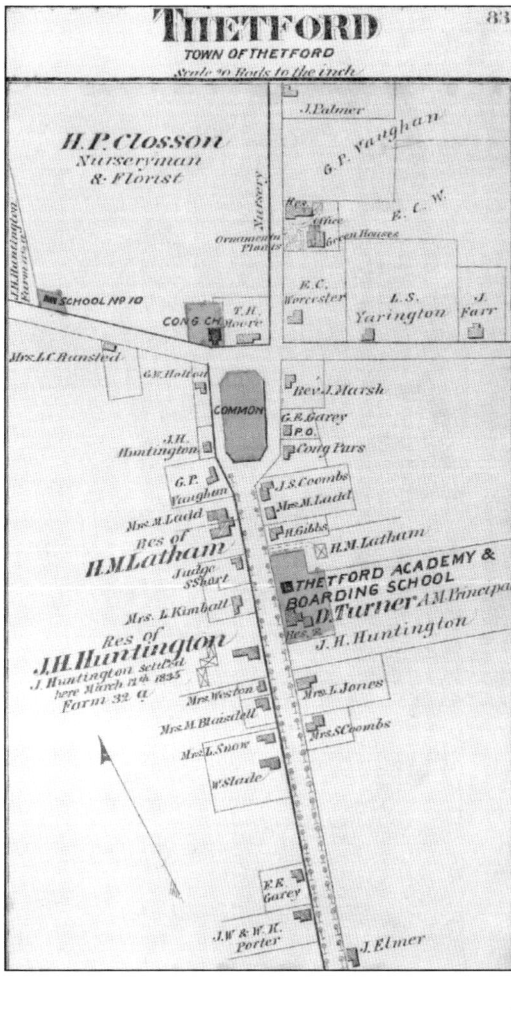

This map shows Thetford Hill as it was in 1877. Thetford Academy was established early in Thetford Hill's history, and so, the village drew doctors, lawyers, and educators. Vermont's first commercial nursery, established in 1852, was at the northeast corner of the intersection of Academy Road and Route 113. A century later, ornamental plants and fruit trees could still be found in that area. (Courtesy of University of Vermont Special Collections.)

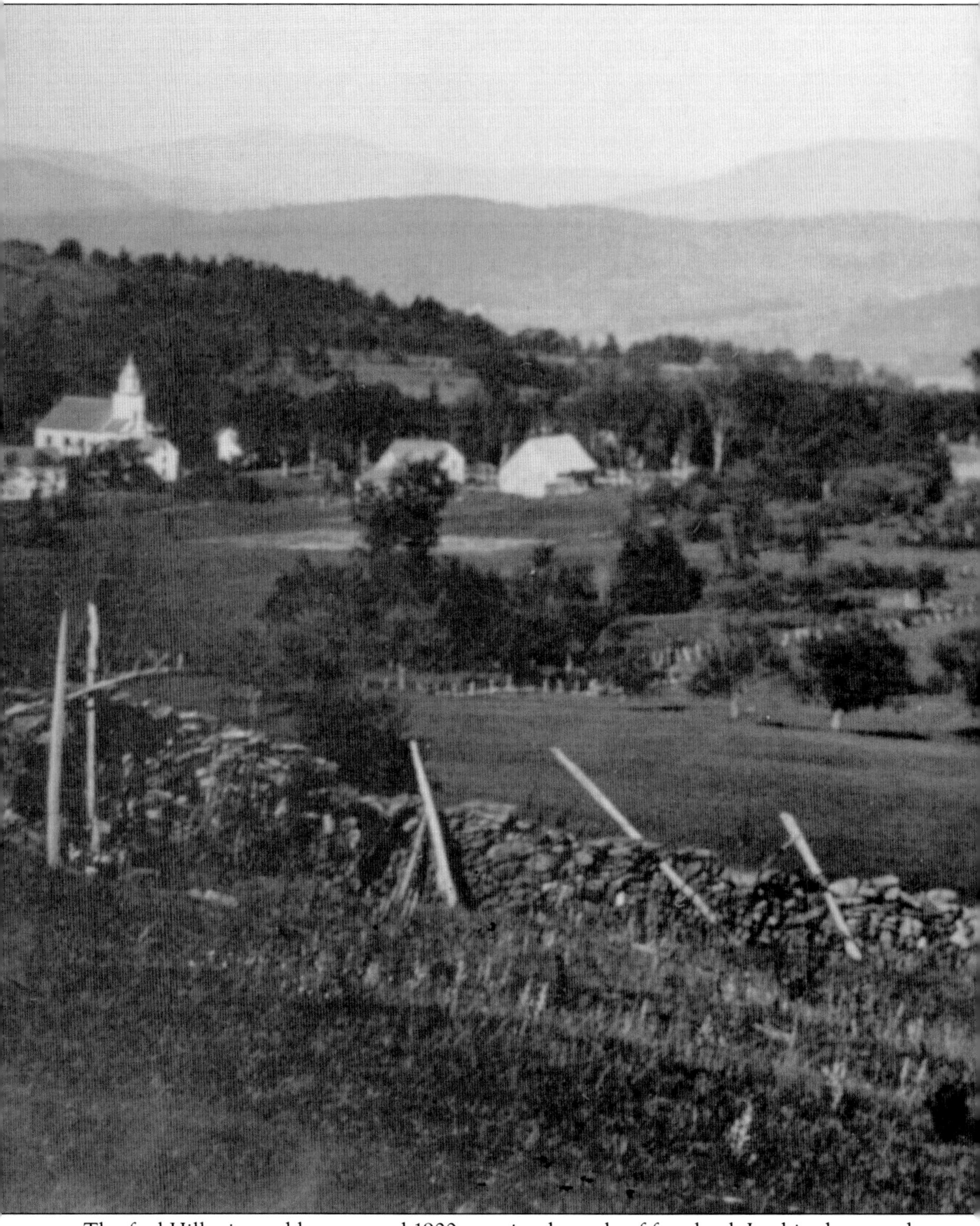

Thetford Hill, pictured here around 1900, consisted mostly of farmland. In this photograph, Thetford Academy is at right. Thetford Hill was born with the construction of the meetinghouse

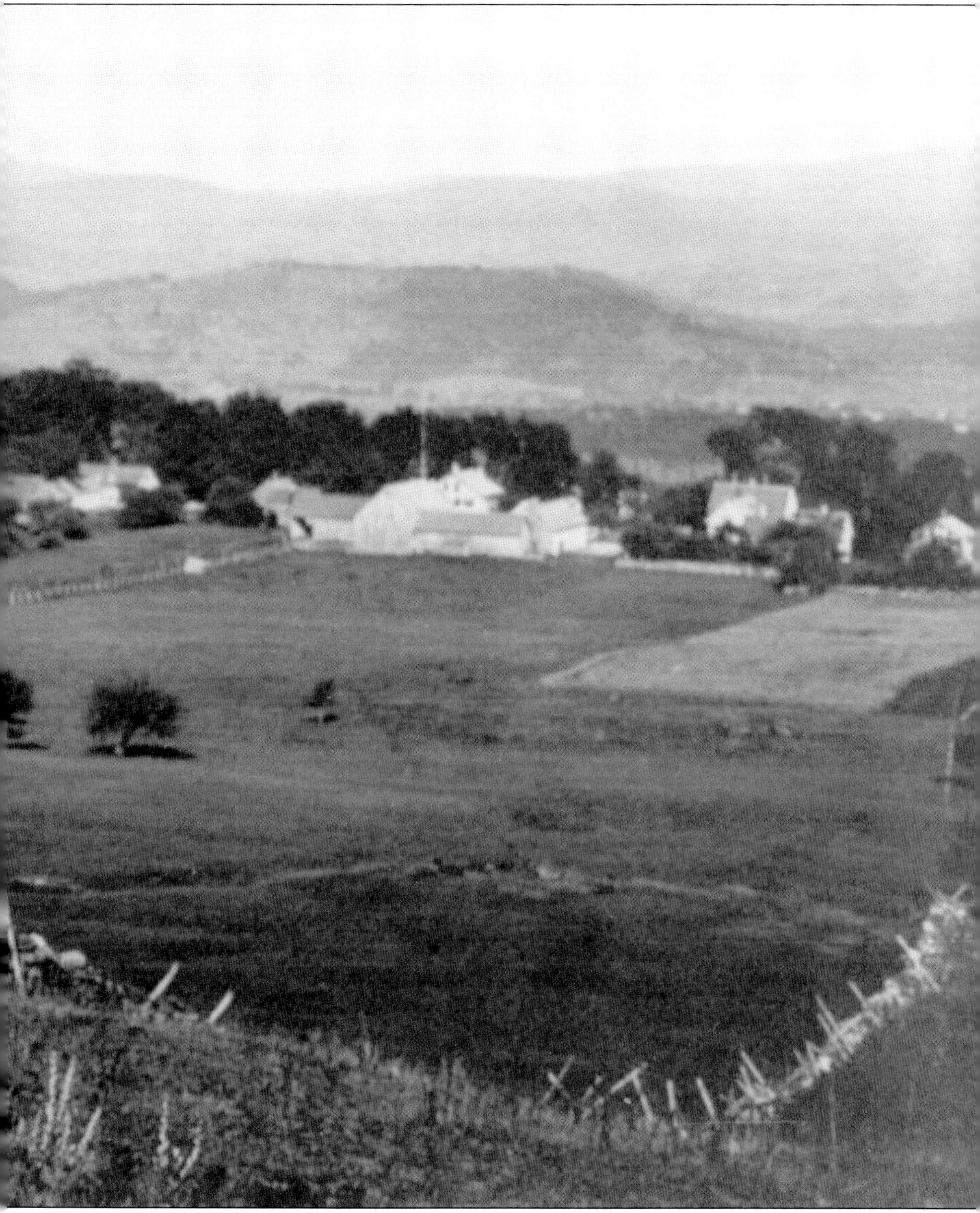

that became the First Congregational Church.

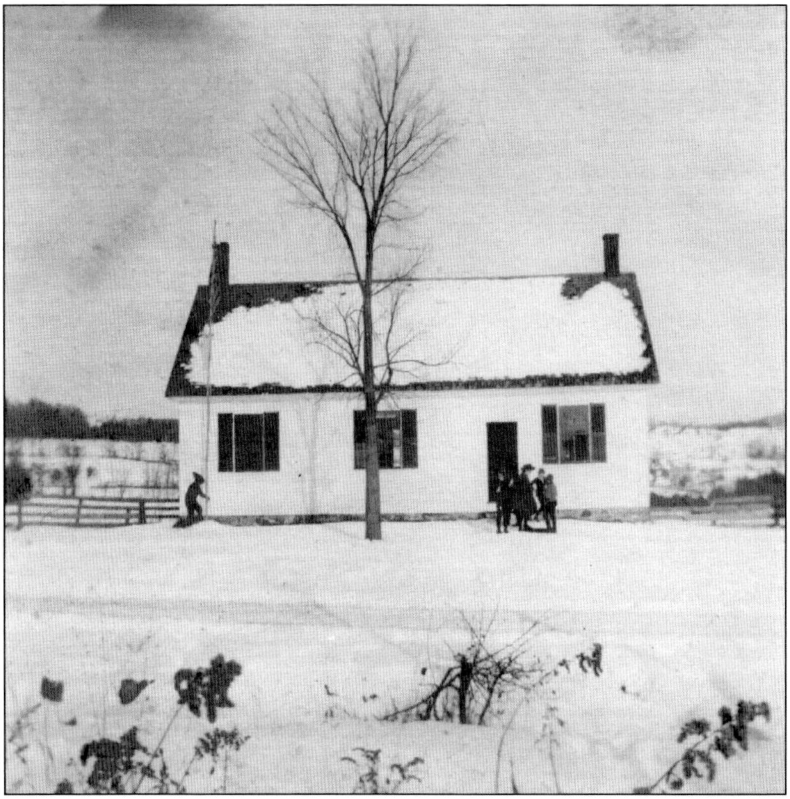

The first schoolhouse in Thetford Hill was built in 1798 near the meetinghouse. The second (left) was built in 1819, and the third (below) was constructed in 1910. It was discontinued as a school in 1945 and sold to the American Legion in 1952.

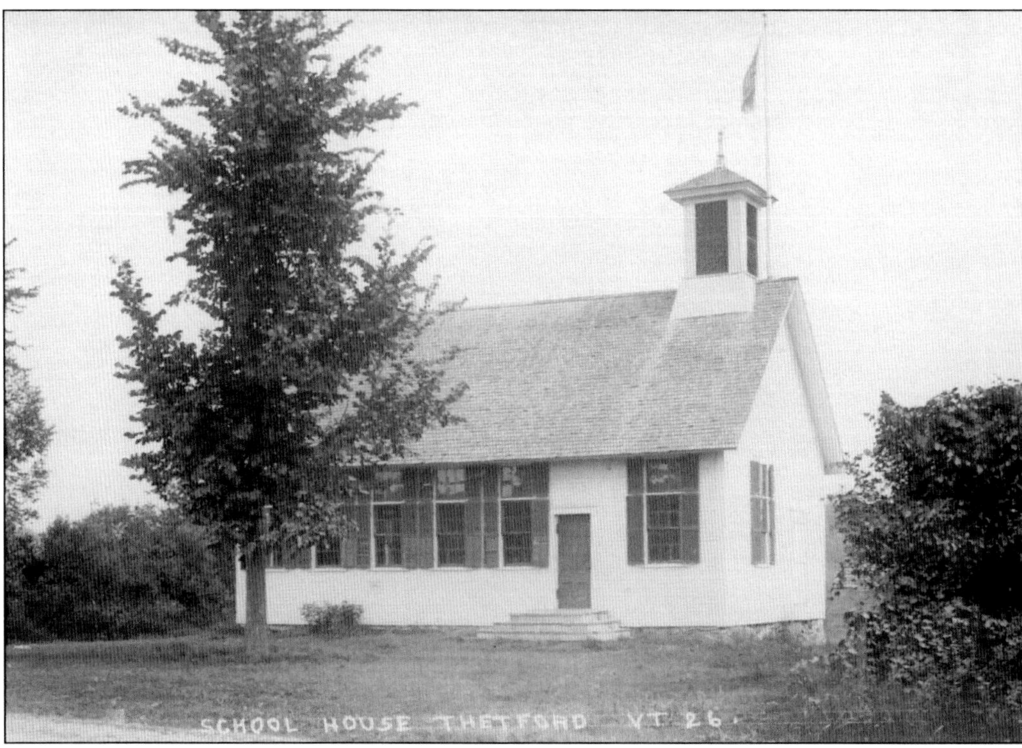

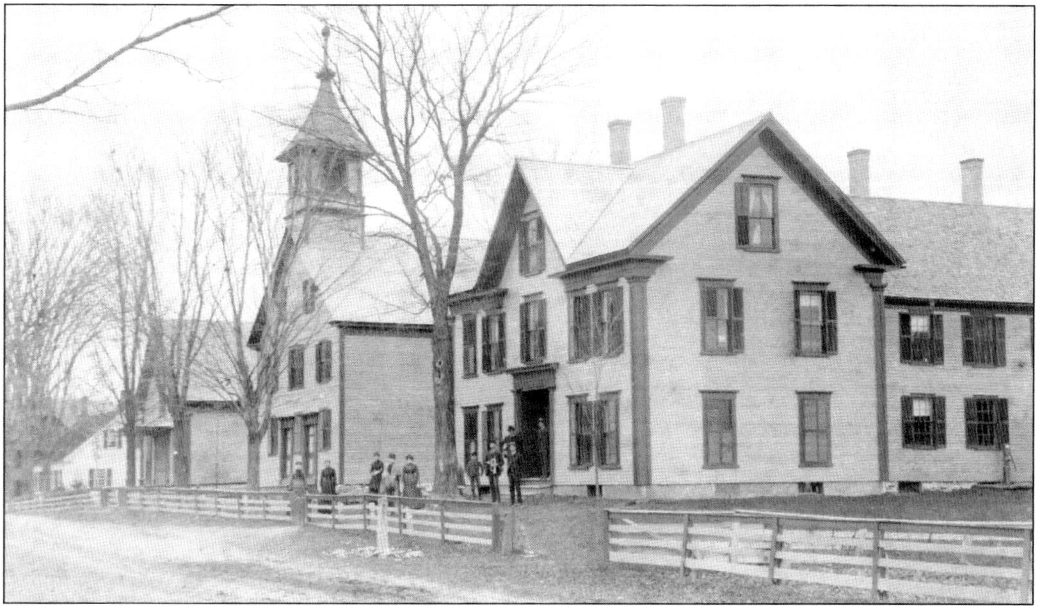

The original Thetford Academy was situated just north of the Eclipse Grange. Although founded to prepare boys for college, it educated girls from the start, becoming Vermont's first coeducational secondary school. The central building was erected in 1818; the dormitory at right was added in 1845. (Courtesy of University of Vermont Special Collections.)

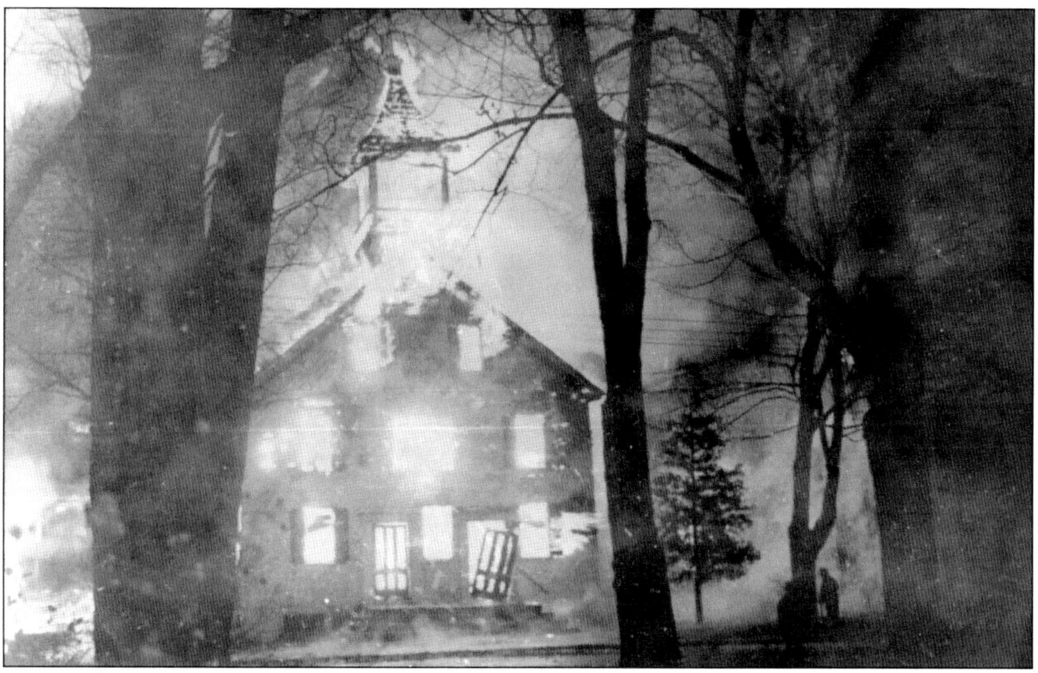

The academy burned down in 1942. The fire also destroyed the dormitory, the town library, and a building next door as Thetford residents and students scurried to save books and furniture. There were no fatalities. Coal in the academy's cellar smoldered for months, even as students returned to school in borrowed quarters just one week later. In 1949, the new school opened on land donated by Porter Adams's widow.

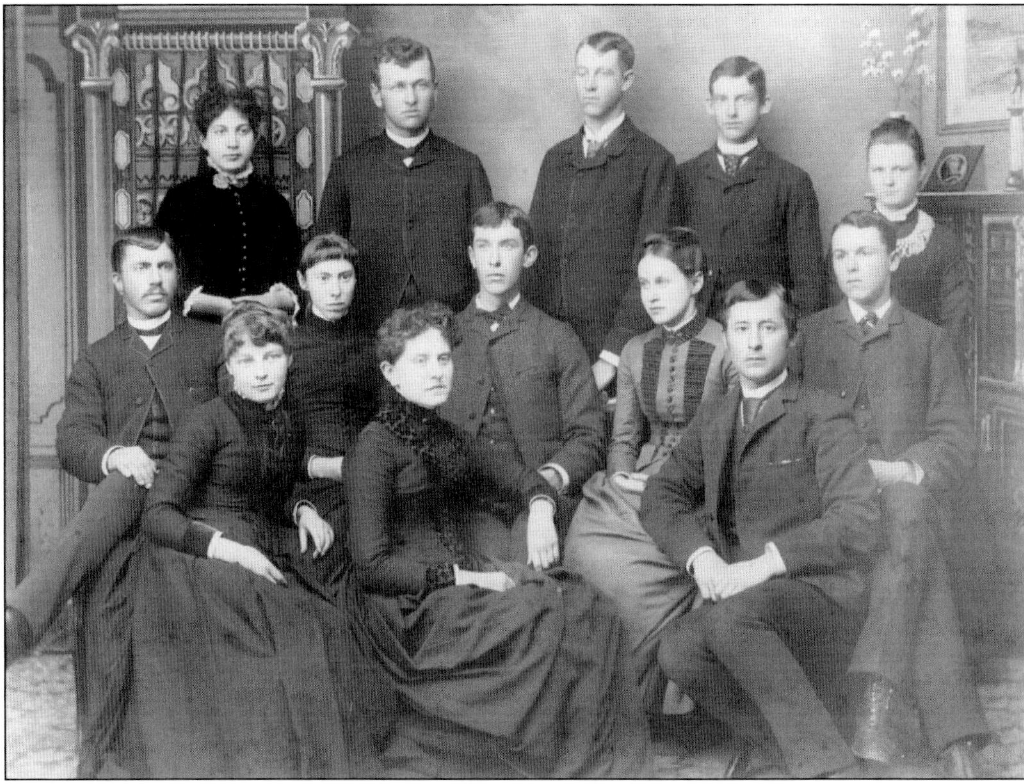

Past graduating classes of Thetford Academy, such as these of 1888 (above) and 1935 (below), were significantly smaller than they are today. It became more common for girls to go to college by the late 19th century, and their curriculum was fortified to more closely match that of the boys. Girls were originally not eligible for financial aid, however.

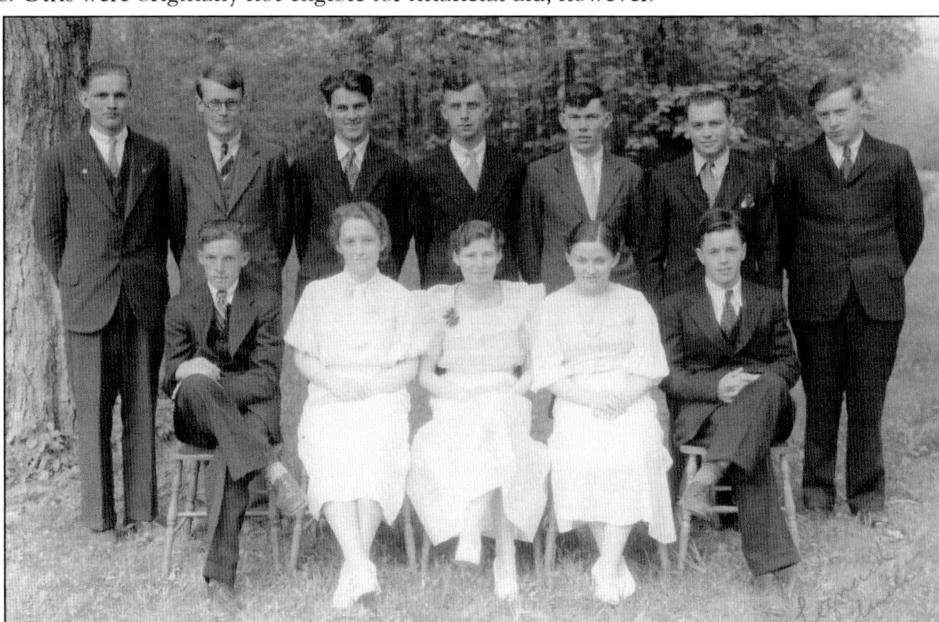

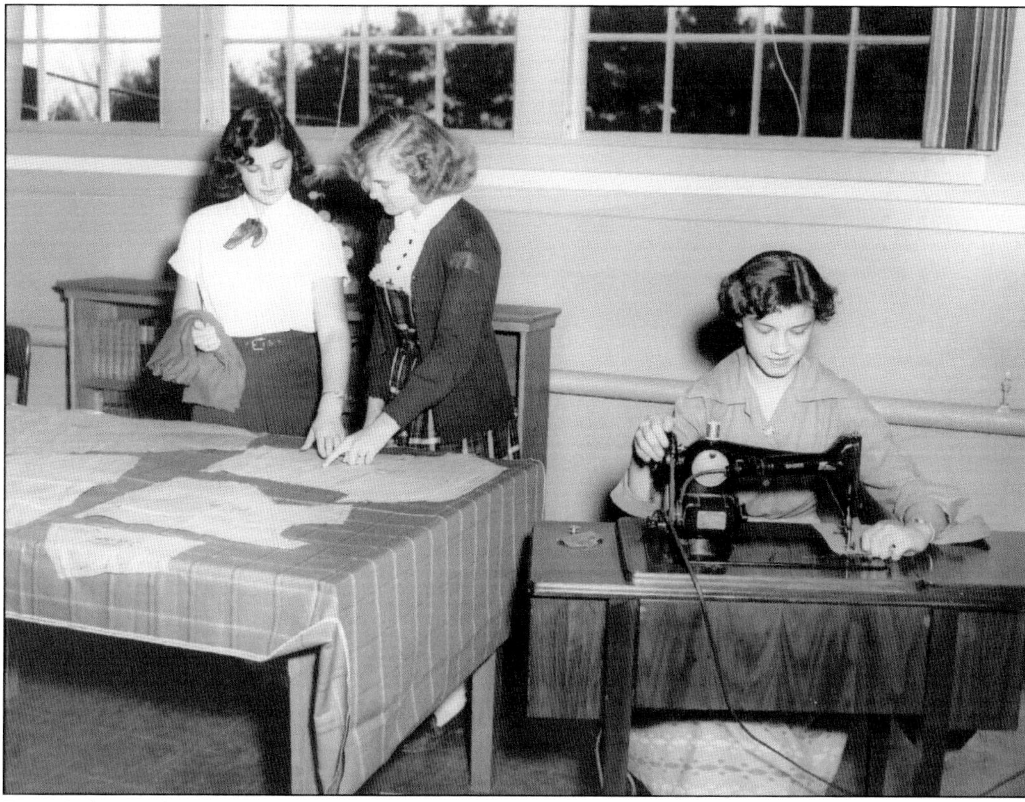

From left to right, Roberta Bailey, Mary Fifield, and Barbara Mobus sew during home economics in 1955. Thetford Academy had the first full-time home economics program in the country.

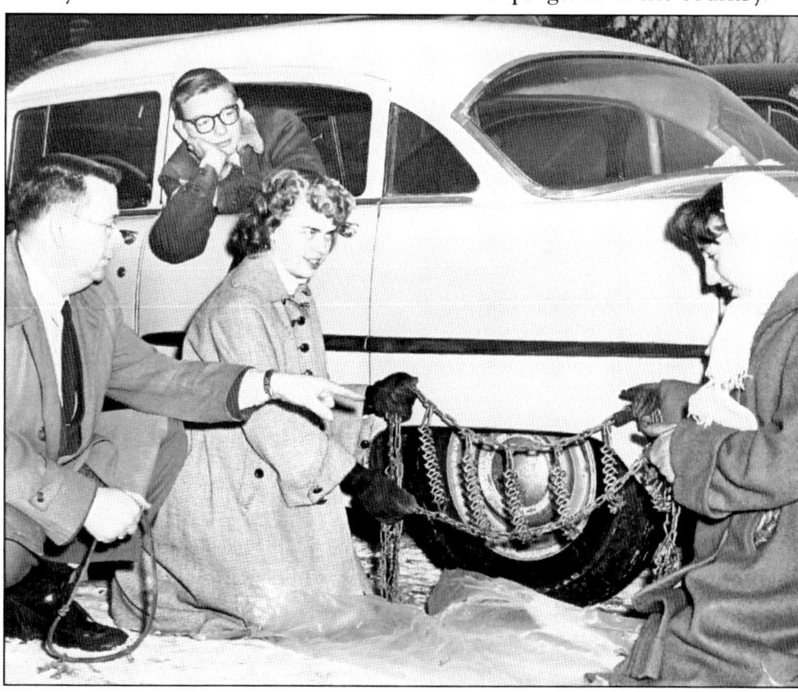

From left to right, Robert Bacon teaches the class of 1958's James Crowley, Carolyn Kelley Porter, and a classmate a valuable skill in Vermont: putting chains on tires.

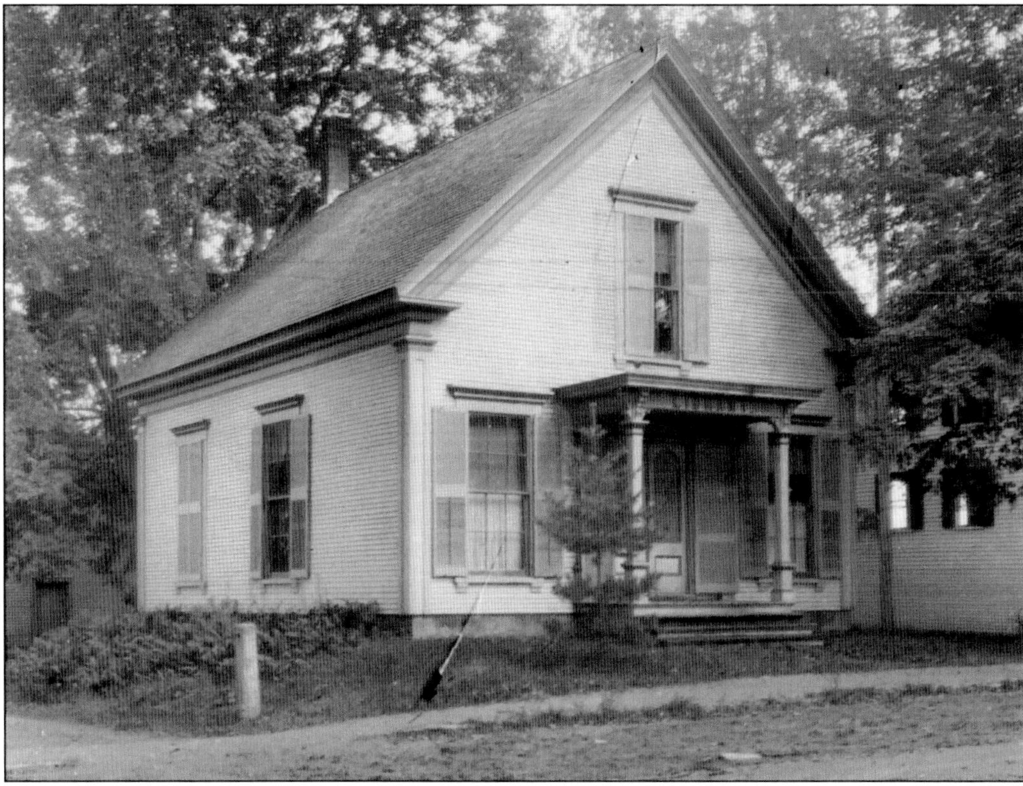

The first Thetford Hill library (above), next door to Thetford Academy, burned in the 1942 fire. Emma Thurston donated the second library building (below) to the town in 1950. The building was used until 1975, when the new structure opened on Library Road to house both the library and the Thetford Historical Society.

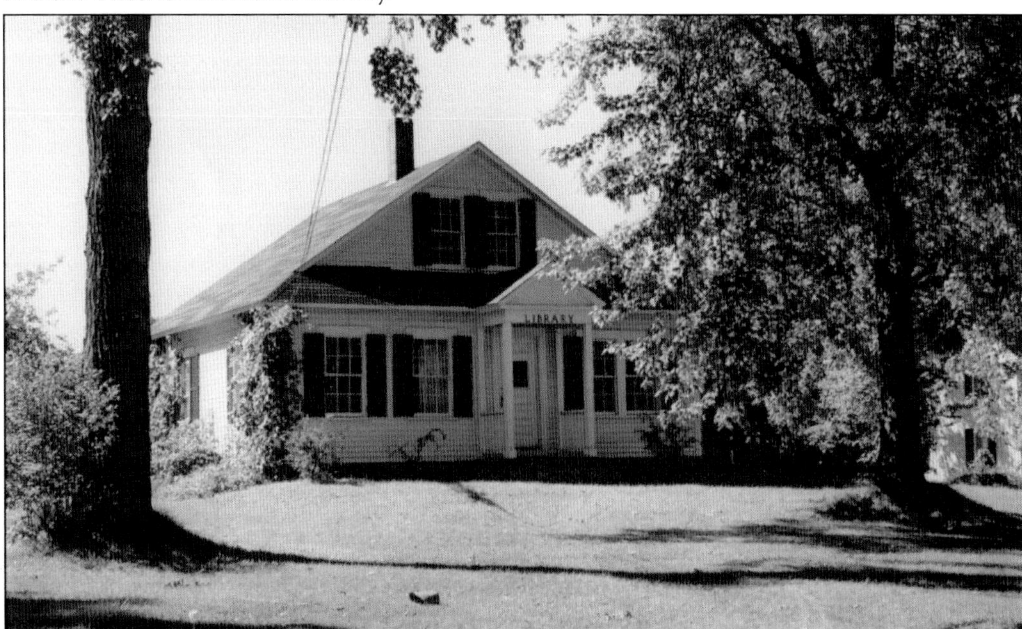

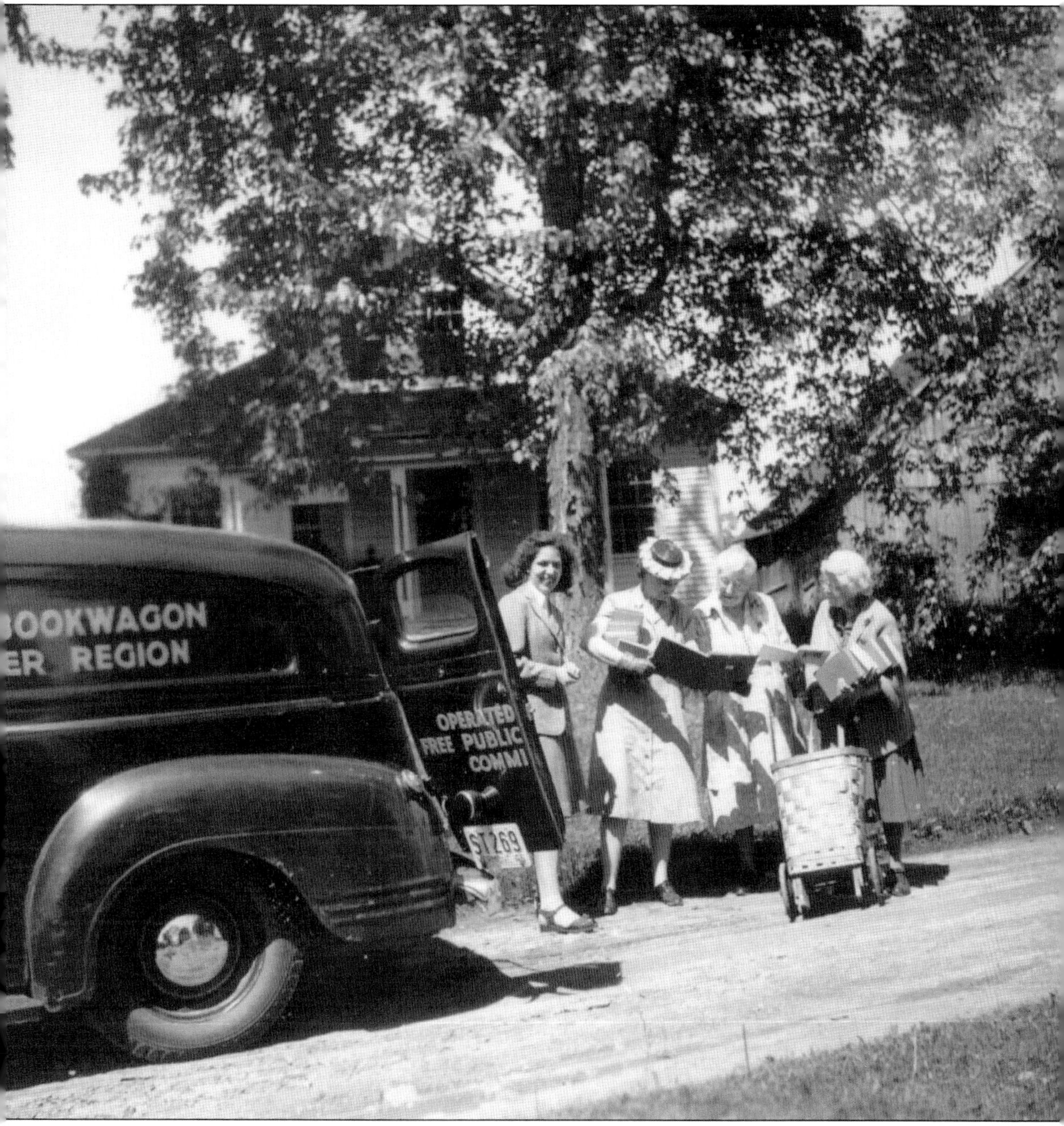

The Federation of Women's Clubs donated book wagons for each of five regions in Vermont. In 1965, Vermont's five book wagons had 62 regular stops at schools, libraries, homes, and farms, reaching more than 57,000 people. The book wagon was regularly seen in Thetford, as in this picture taken at the Latham Library around 1950.

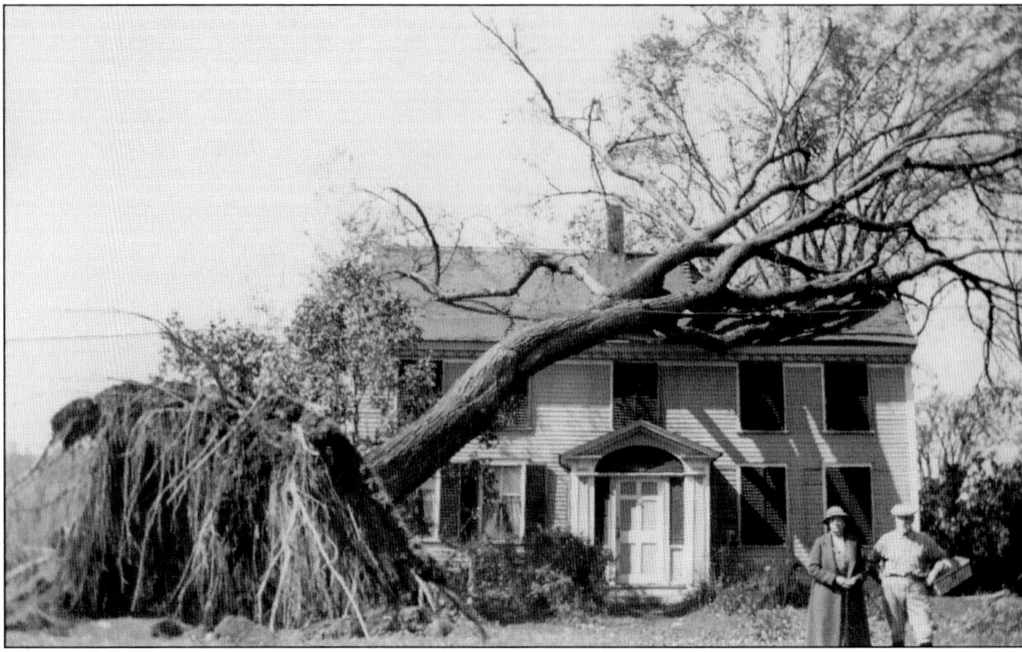

The hurricane of September 1938 ripped out many of the enormous trees ringing the green on Thetford Hill. The Farnsworth house (above) and Slade house (below) both sustained severe damage. Thetford resident Rosetta Estabrook reported in a letter to her sister Gladys that she counted 42 fallen trees along the road between Route 113 and Thetford Academy (from its original site, a distance of two tenths of a mile).

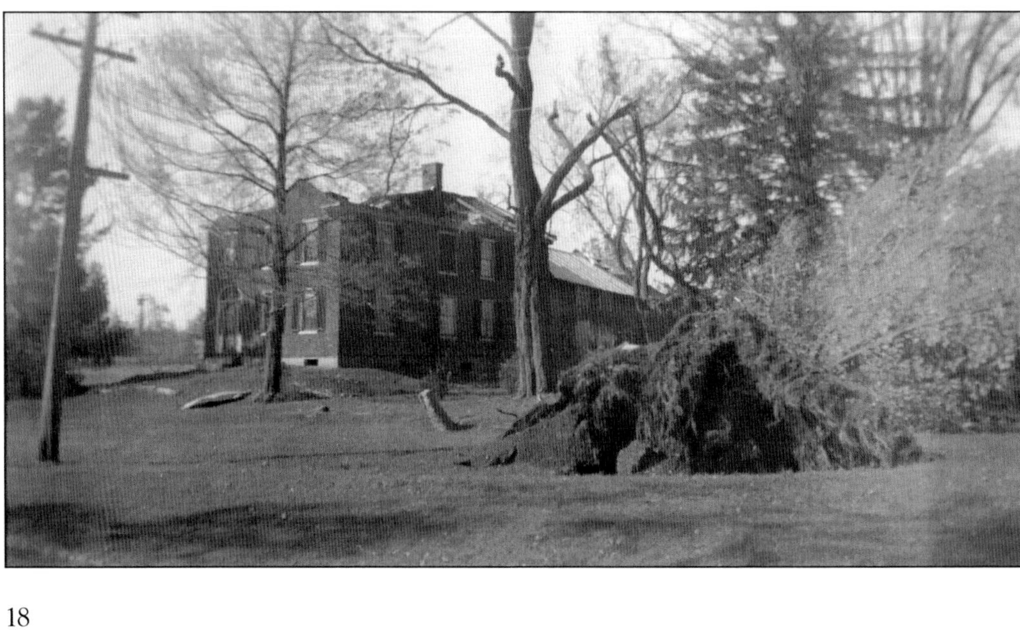

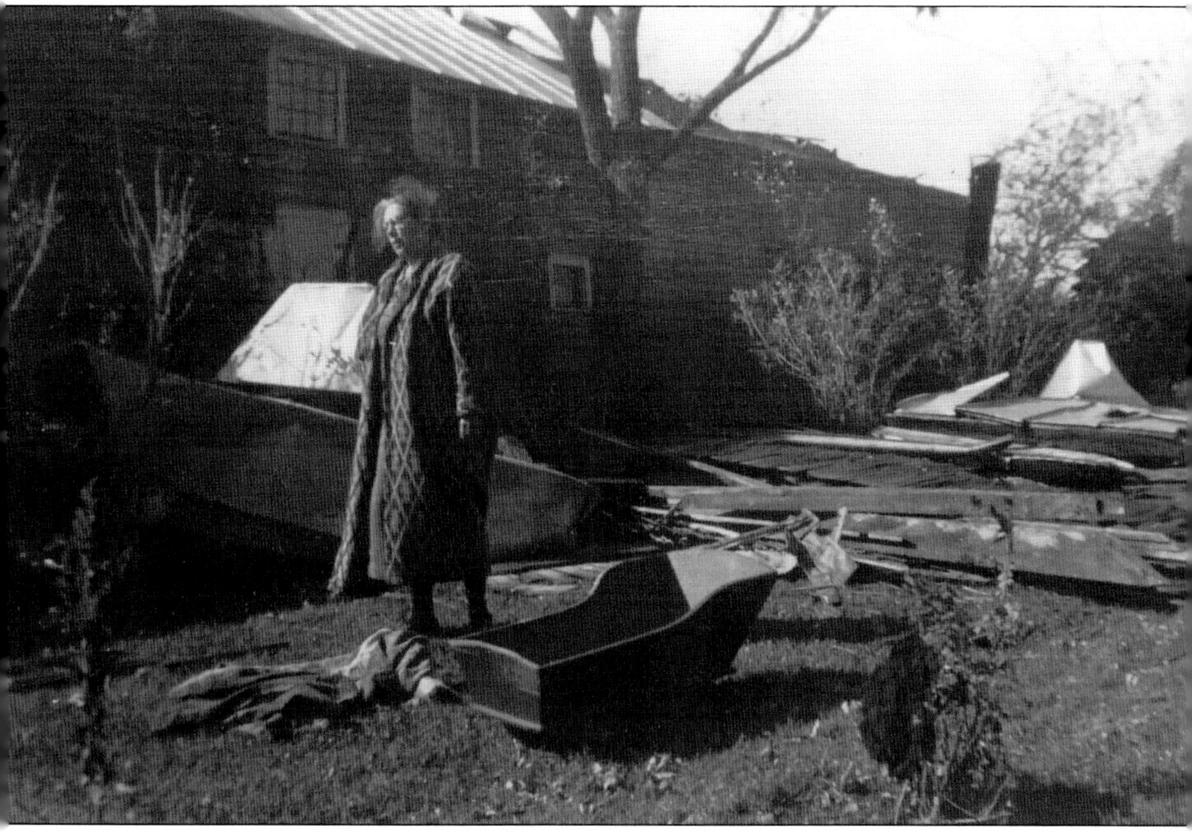

Thetford historian Mary Slade stands in her yard next to the cradle that blew out of her attic. "It's a wonder they are alive to tell the tale," recalled Estabrook. "Mrs. S. realized the fury of the gale . . . She heard the chimney fall . . . Our greatest fear now is that some of us may have defective chimneys, or that the least wind will take trees that have already been weakened."

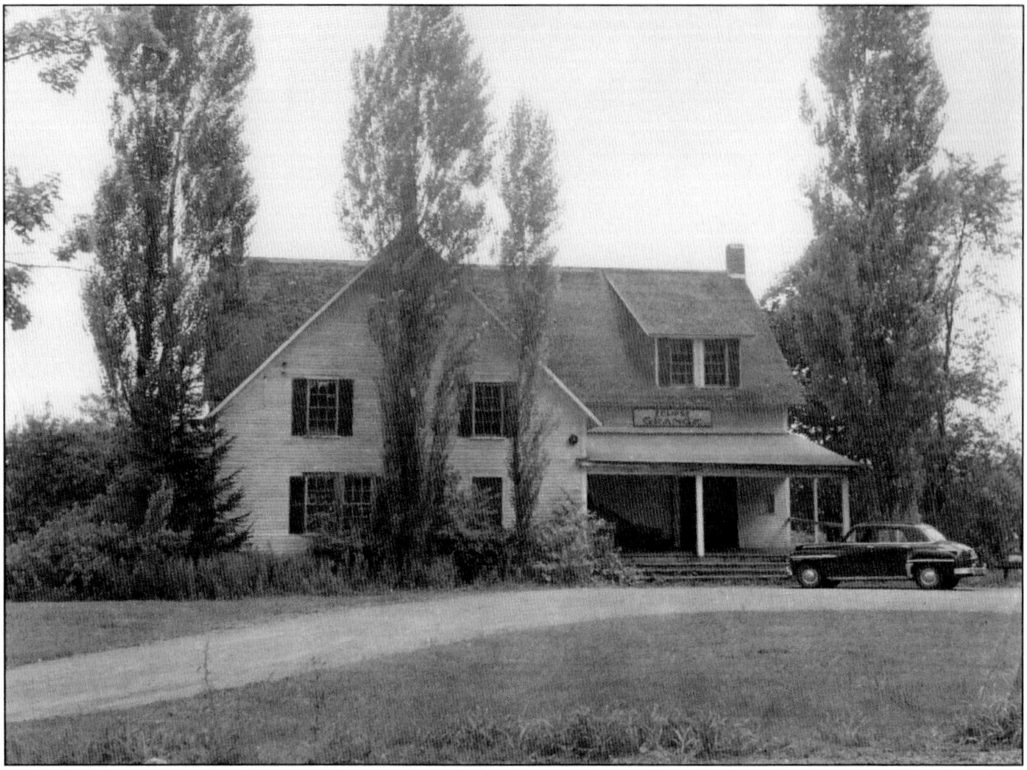

Originally a barn, this building housed activities for nearby Camp Hanoum in the early 1900s. In 1920, the Eclipse Grange bought the building from Camp Hanoum. The Grange let Thetford Academy use the space from 1943 to 1950 while Thetford Academy recovered from its devastating fire. The Parish Players theater group began using the building in the 1970s.

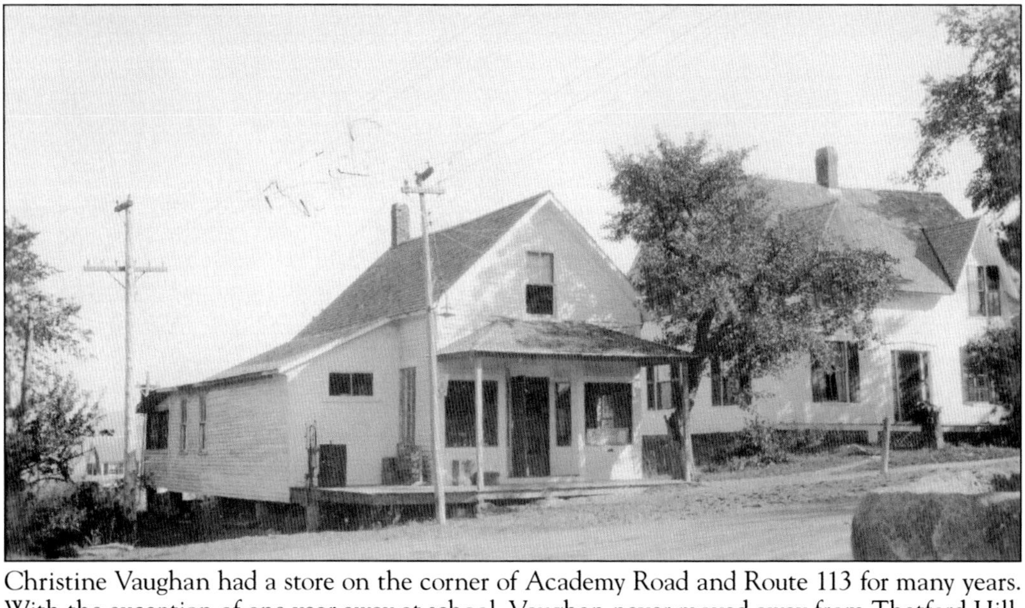

Christine Vaughan had a store on the corner of Academy Road and Route 113 for many years. With the exception of one year away at school, Vaughan never moved away from Thetford Hill. Note the stone horse trough at lower right; it still stands on the common today.

Vaughan's store kept going, under reduced inventory, during World War II. Using ration books, Thetford residents could buy some of what they needed, including war bonds, at the store.

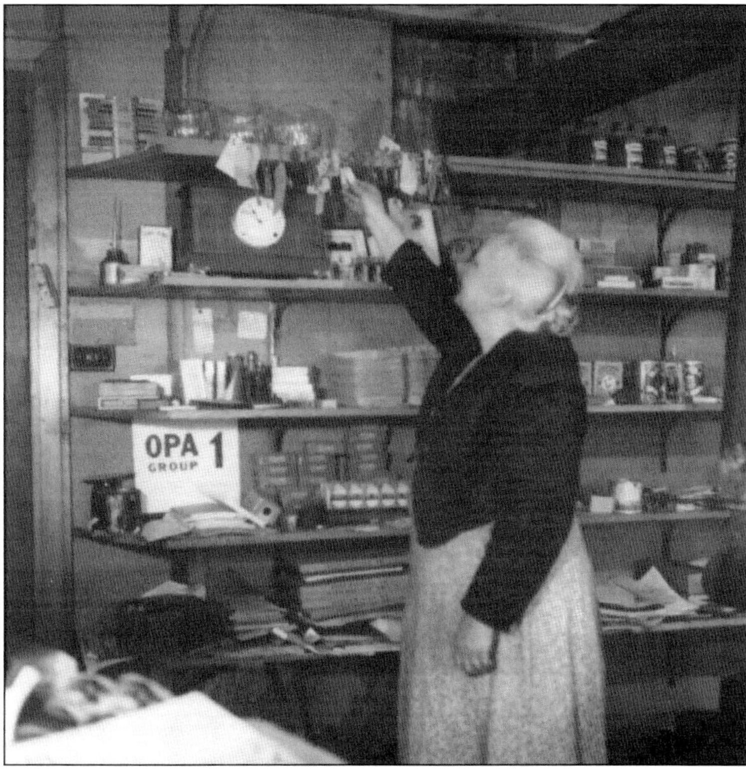

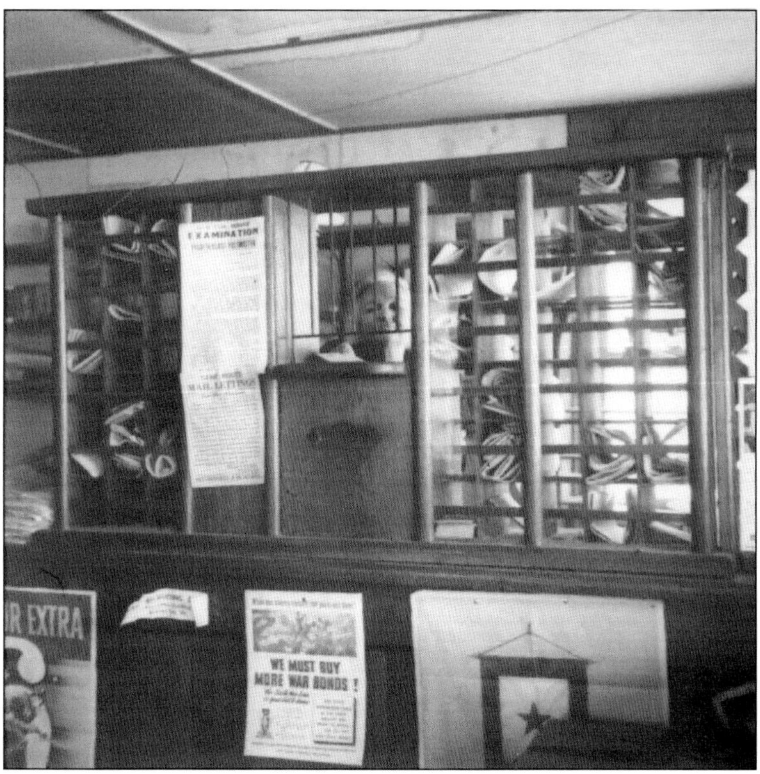

Vaughan was town postmistress for 30 years. The blue star banner hanging at lower right was seen in the windows of many servicemen's homes, each star symbolizing one family member serving in the military. A gold star represented a family member who died in the war.

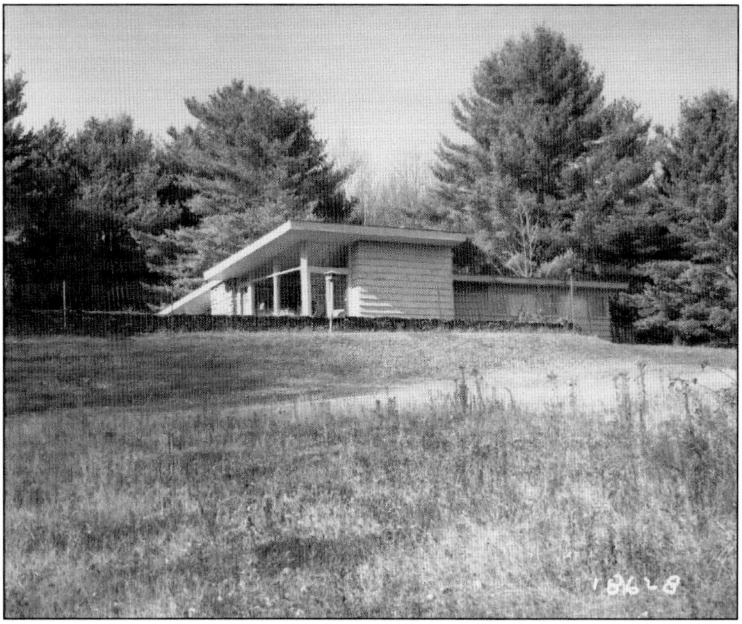

The Henry P. Dart house on Godfrey Road was on the leading edge of architectural design when it was built in 1949. The first project of modernist architect Edward Dart, built when he was just 25 years old, it was torn down in 2005. (Courtesy of the Vermont State Archives and Records Administration.)

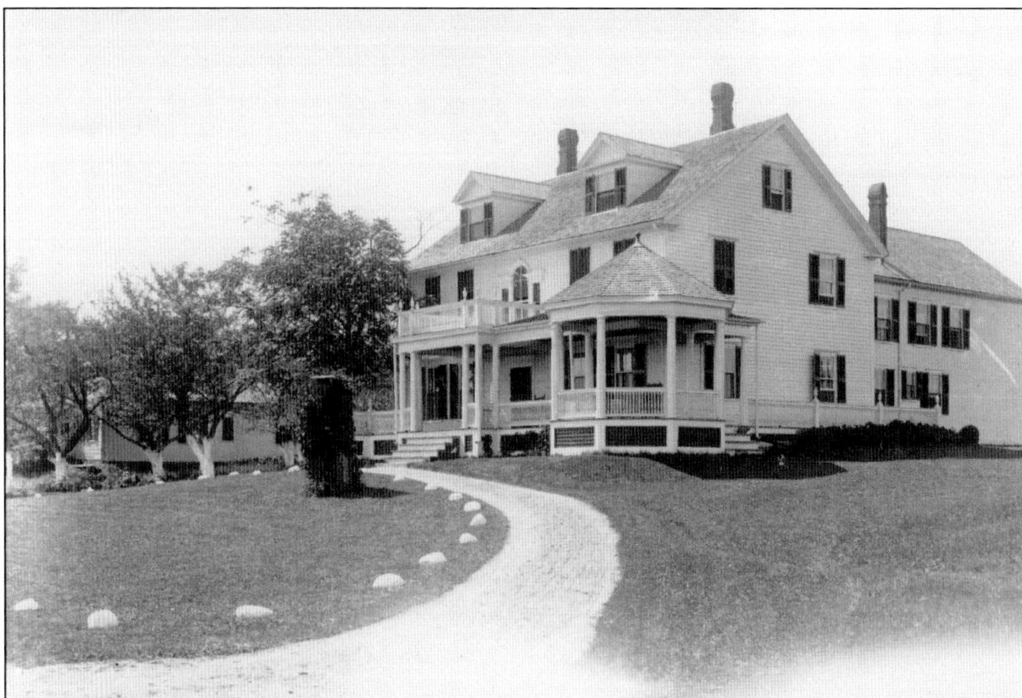

Porter Adams, one of Thetford's more famous (if seasonal) residents, lived in a large house, Aero Acres, on Thetford Hill in the 1920s and 1930s. Adams was the former president of the National Aeronautical Association and would go on to be president of Norwich University. Aero Acres was notable for its wind tunnel and the word "THETFORD" spelled out in large letters on the roof for the benefit of passing airplanes. When the house burned in 1933, Adams did not rebuild, but after Thetford Academy burned in 1942, his widow donated the land for the new campus. Anderson Hall now stands on the site of the home.

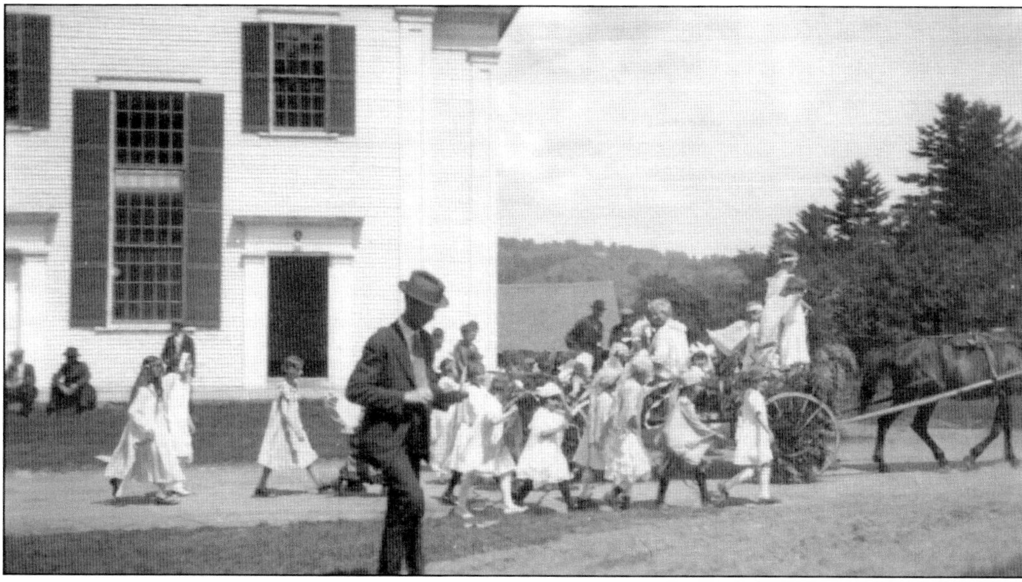

Young people have been part of the Thetford Hill Fair every summer since it began in 1905. Campers from nearby Camp Hanoum often took part in this event, as well as in the 1911 pageant in North Thetford.

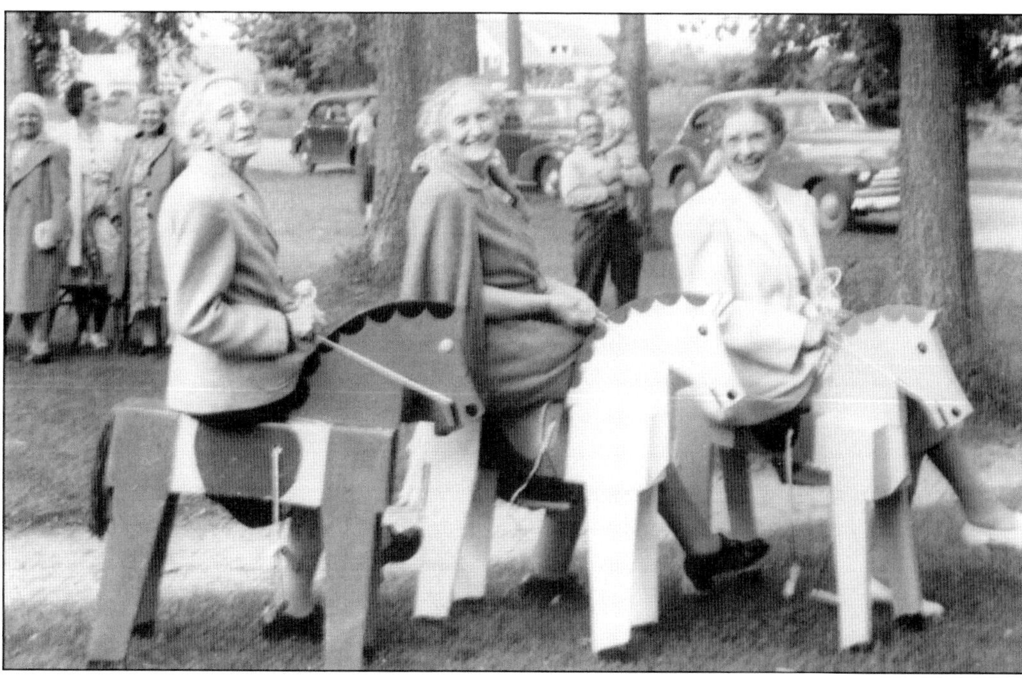

From left to right, sisters Ellen Farnsworth, Harriet Farnsworth Gulick, and Charlotte Farnsworth Little ride the Thetford Hill Fair's ubiquitous wooden horses. Their brother Charles Farnsworth and his wife, Charlotte, founded Camp Hanoum in 1909. Harriet and her husband, Edward, founded Camp Aloha in Fairlee in 1905.

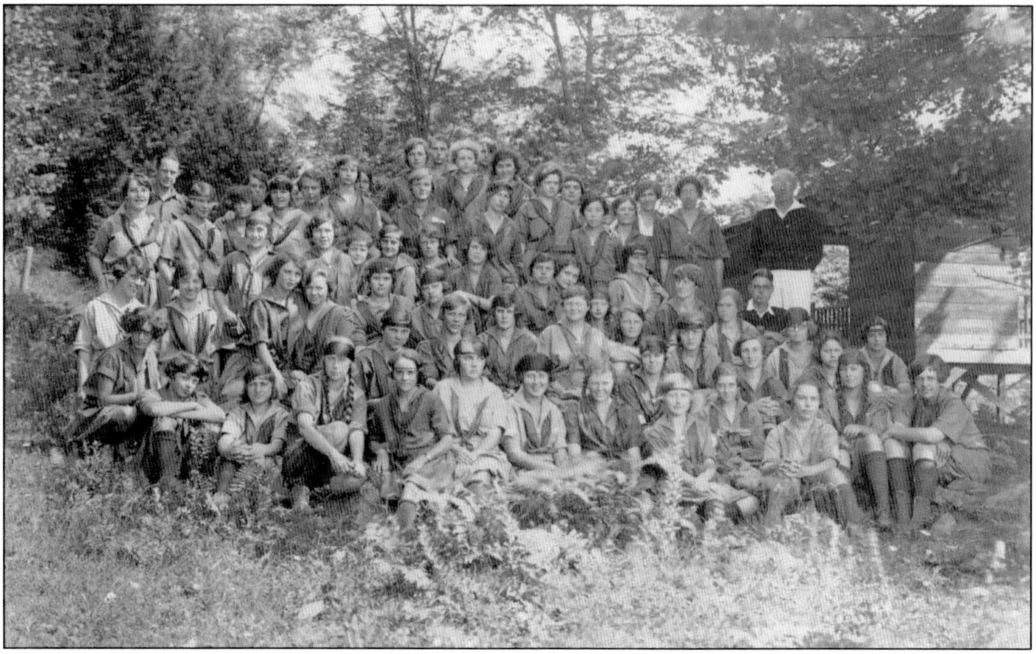

The girls of Camp Hanoum gathered for a group photograph in 1922. Camp Hanoum had a decidedly Turkish take on camp life. The son of a missionary, founder Charles Farnsworth had been brought up in Turkey and was known to campers as "Chelebe" (Master). Charlotte Farnsworth was known as "Madama" (Mistress).

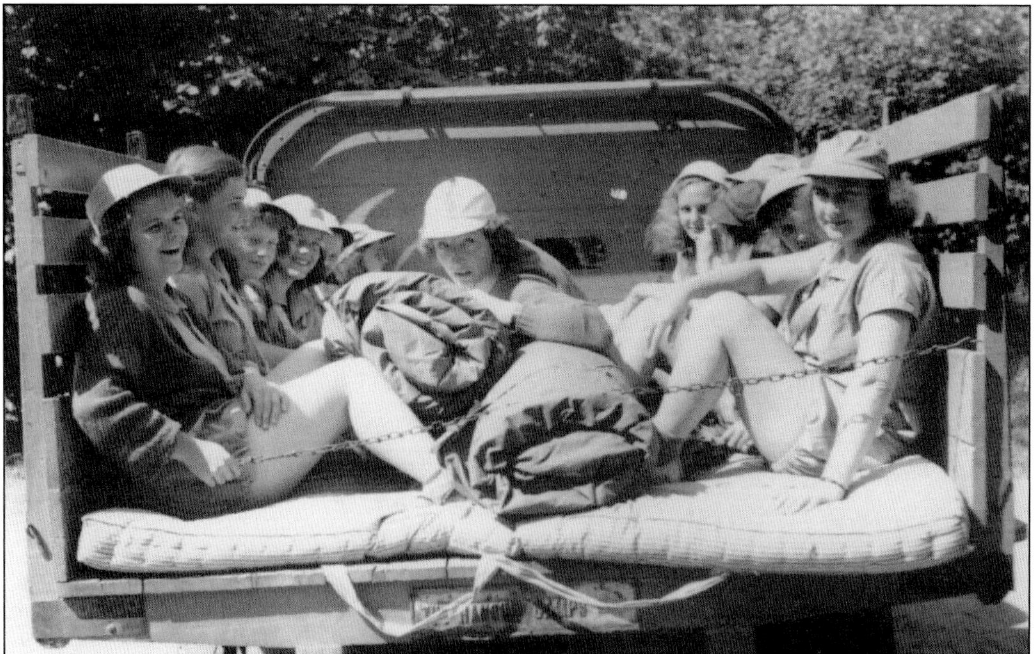

Twenty years later, the uniforms had changed, but the traditions were still going strong. During World War II, campers grew victory gardens, and some of the camp's staff served in the war. Campers also hosted girls from Europe and raised money for war refugees.

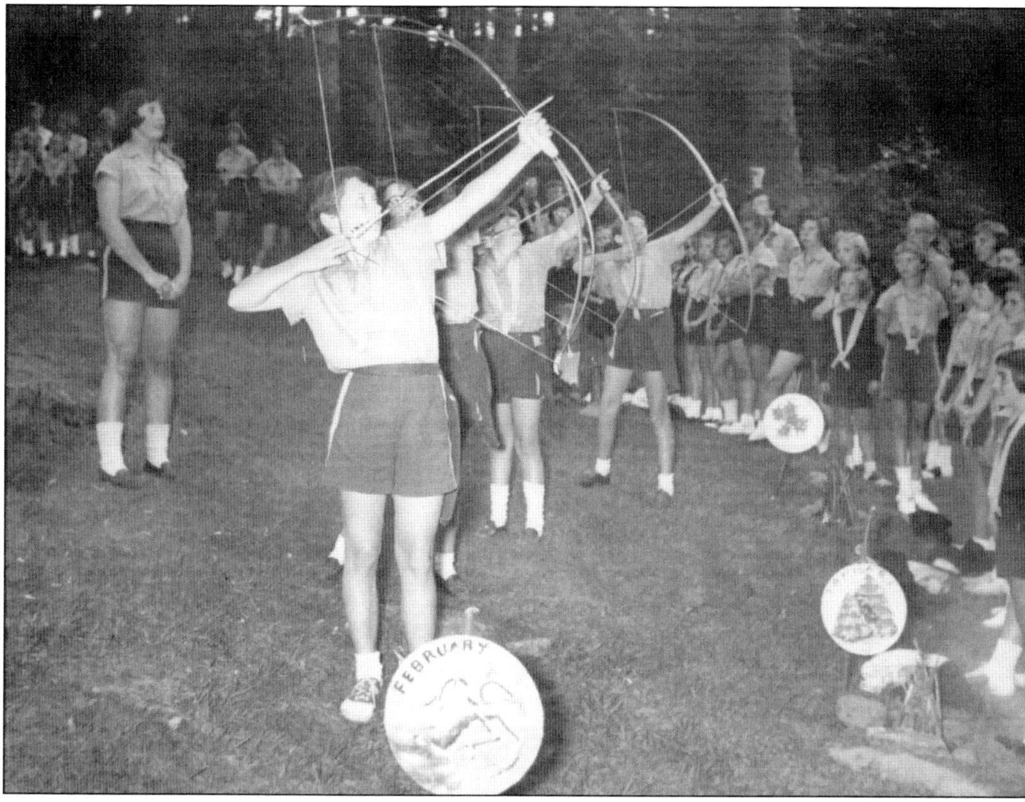

The archers in this picture are in Birthday Grove. All of the campers' birthdays were celebrated on Charlotte Farnsworth's birthday, as campers gathered around each of 12 birthday fires.

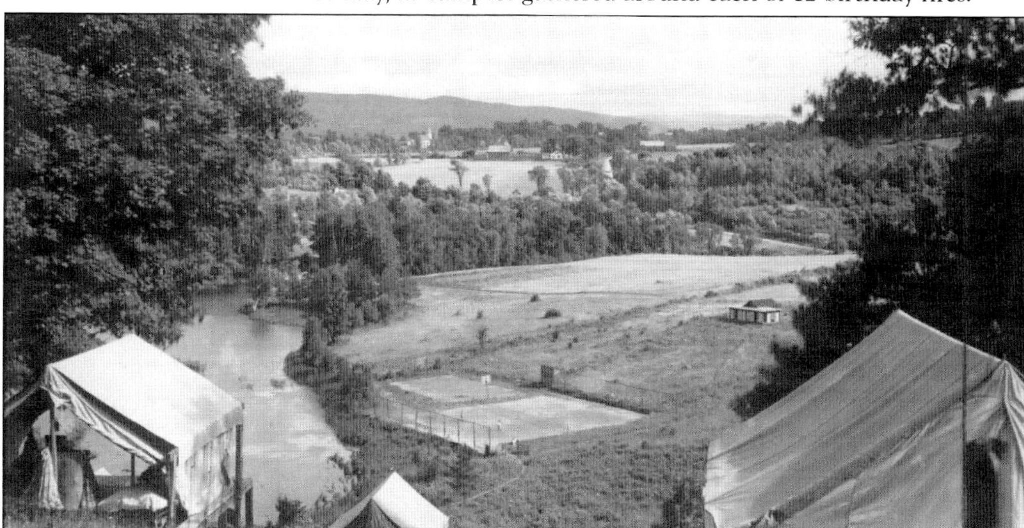

Thetford Hill lies in the middle distance beyond Lake Abenaki. When the camp outgrew its original location on Houghton Hill Road in 1916, the older girls moved onto the shores of Lake Abenaki, and the camps were connected by a mile-long trail. After Charlotte Farnsworth died in 1946, two former campers bought Camp Hanoum. It became a Girl Scouts of America camp in 1959, and was renamed Camp Farnsworth.

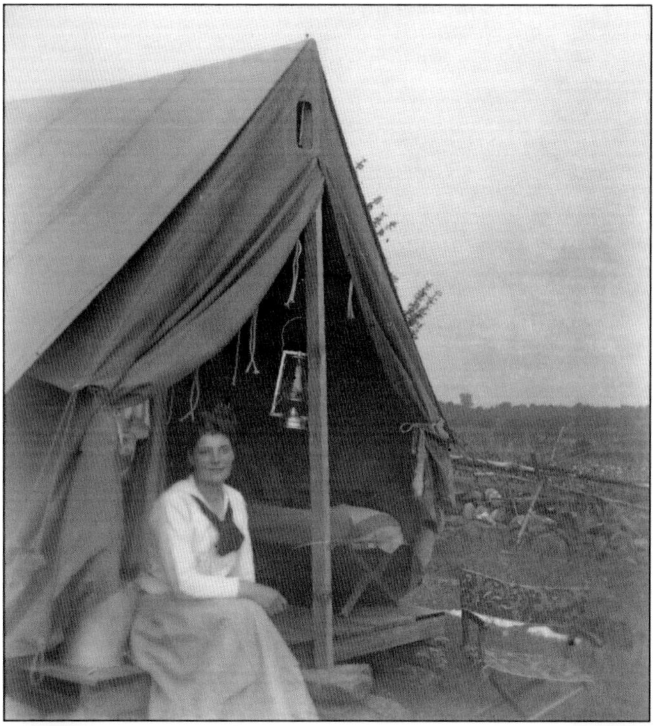

In addition to providing traditional camp activities like archery and canoeing, Camp Hanoum also offered opportunities to study music, mathematics, and foreign languages. Domestic activities were even part of the program. Hanoum means "gracious lady" in Turkish.

Girls from Camp Quinibeck in Fairlee ride their horses through Thetford Hill. Campers from the many girls' camps in the area often played, camped overnight, and held ceremonies together.

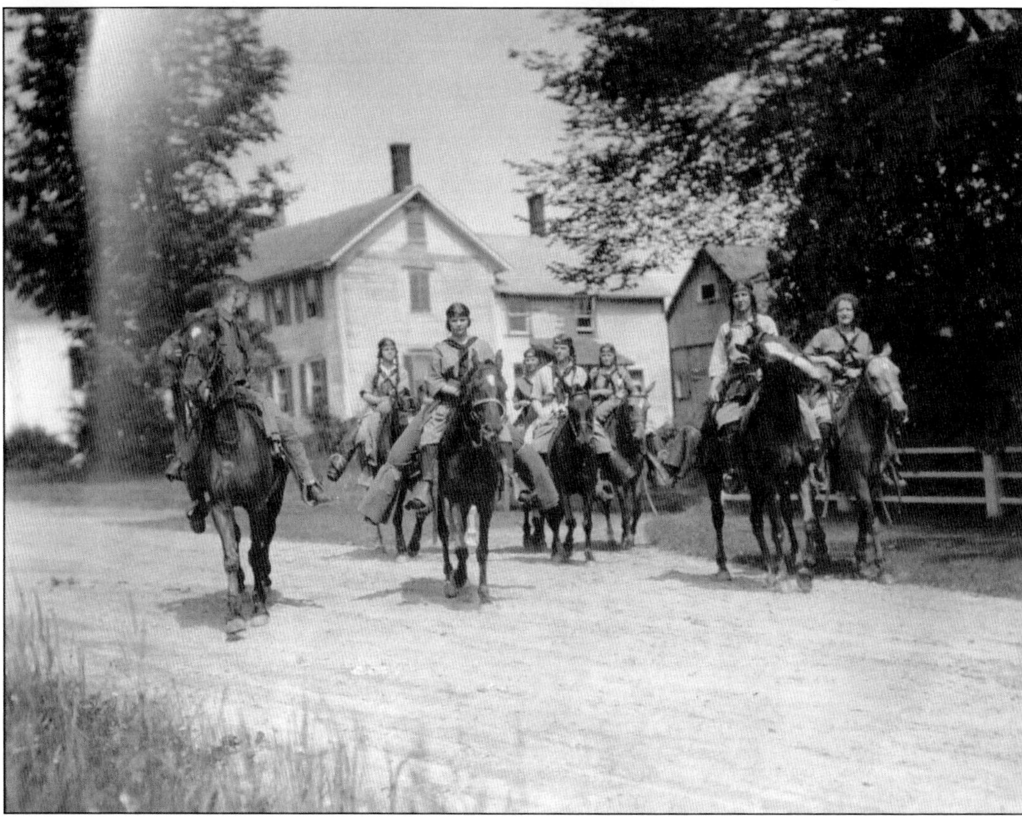

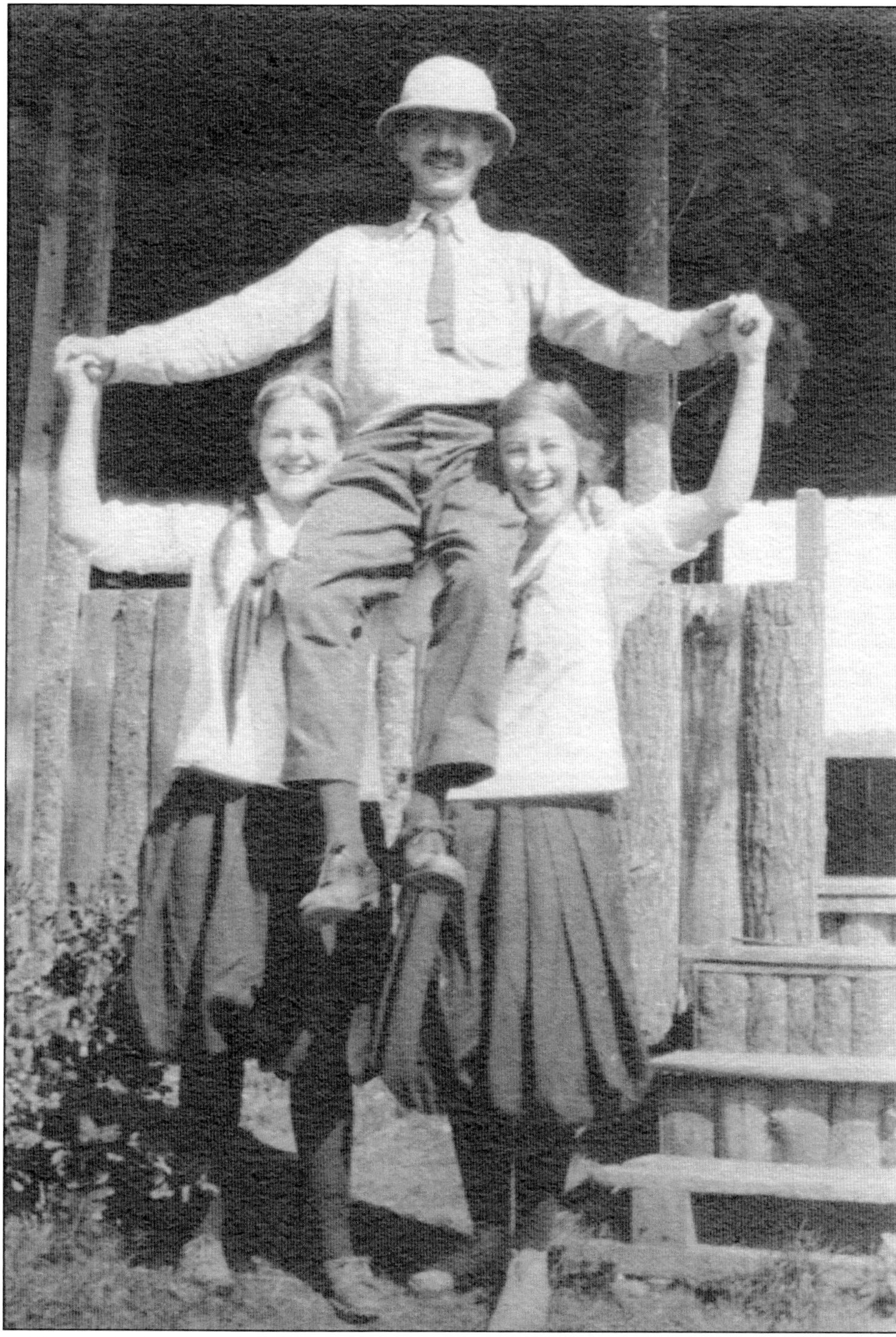

Camp Hanoum's founder, Charles Farnsworth, is held aloft by nieces Carol and Johnny. Farnsworth was a music professor, so it comes as no surprise that Camp Hanoum was known as a "singing camp," with a heavy emphasis on music. The camp got its start when about a dozen students from Columbia Teacher's College spent the summer with the Farnsworths; it evolved into an eight-week program.

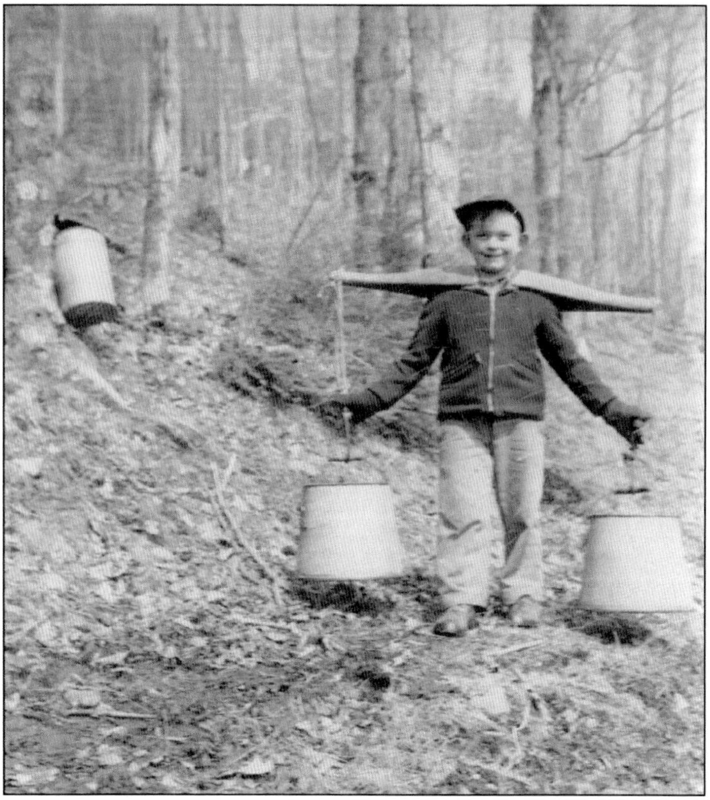

Thetford photographer Gladys Estabrook photographed Oliver Randall's maple sugaring business in the 1940s. Many farmers such as Randall turned to sugaring in spring, when the fields lay dormant. As days began to warm but nights stayed cold, sugar makers would drill holes in tree trunks and insert spouts to channel the sap. They hung covered buckets on the trees, and as the sap ran, it was collected for boiling.

Randall and helpers brought buckets to a tank mounted to a sledge. When the tank was full, it was transported to the sugarhouse.

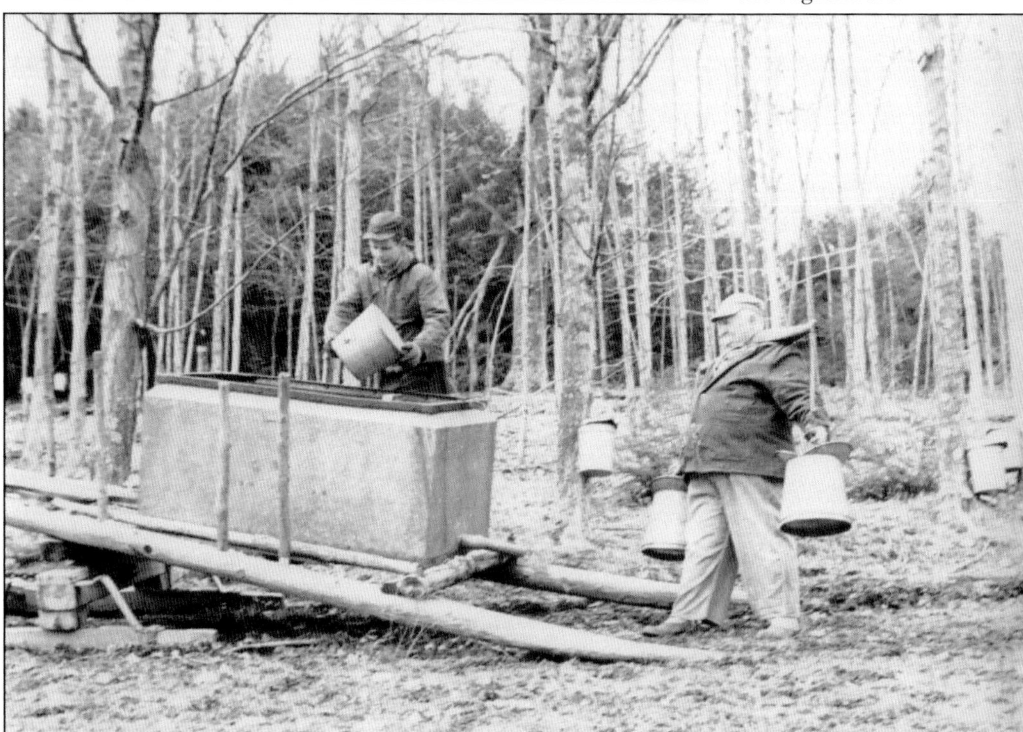

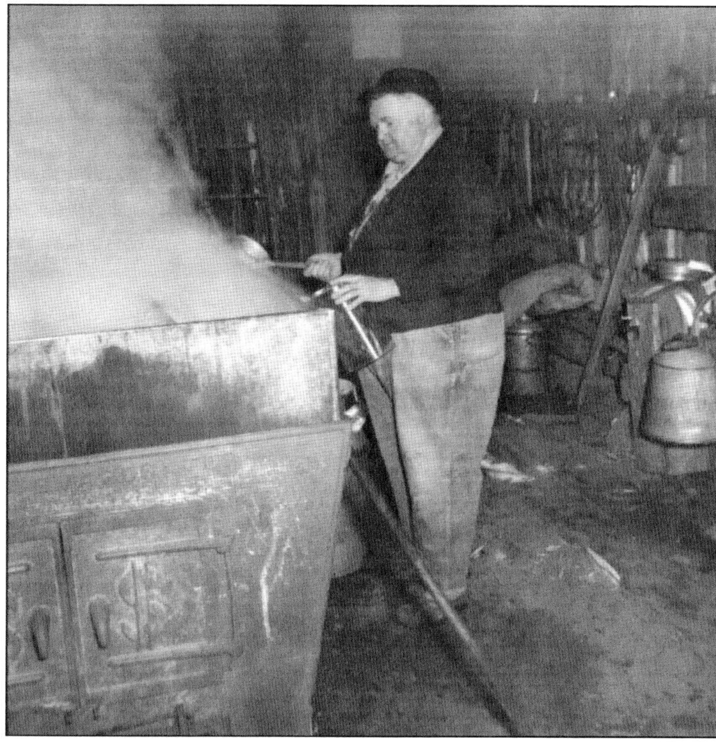

Randall boiled the sap in his evaporator, a series of pans through which the sap moved as it turned to syrup. Only a tiny percentage of sap is sugar; the rest has to be boiled away.

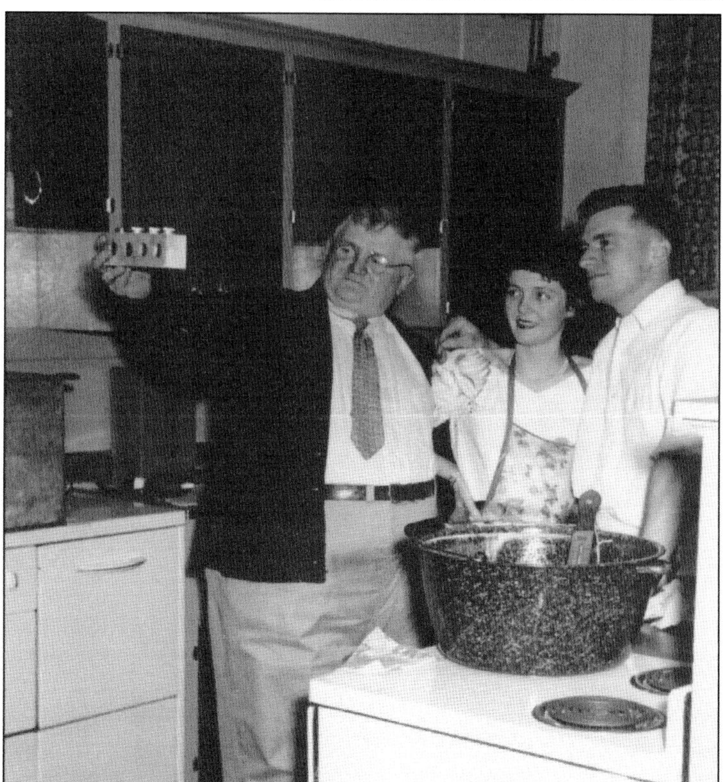

At a Thetford Academy "sugar on snow" celebration, Randall showed Charlotte Judd and a friend different grades of maple syrup, which a syrup maker used to determine the grade of his own product. This may have been the July 9, 1948, party held to raise money for new Thetford Academy facilities after a fire in 1942 destroyed the original buildings. Snow had been preserved in a freezer through the spring especially for the party; the region's maple products were to be a main feature of the celebration.

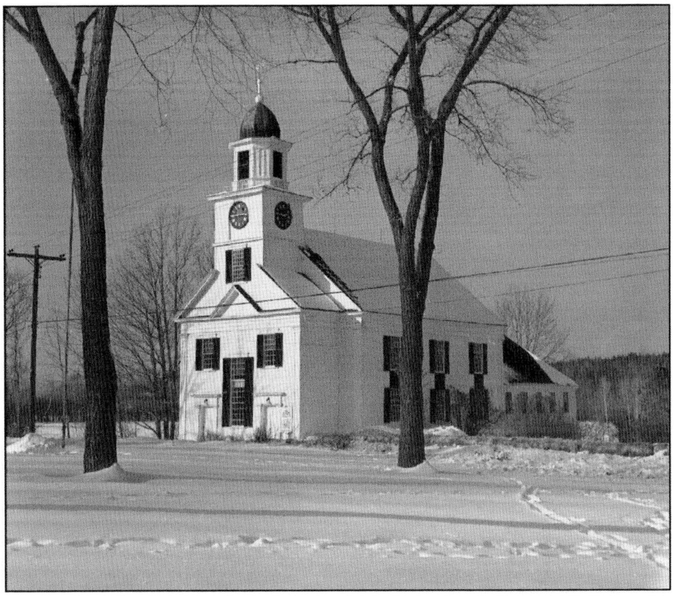

Built on the green in 1787, the First Congregational Church is the oldest meetinghouse in continuous use in Vermont. It originally served a dual purpose, being the town meetinghouse as well, but as the divide widened between church and state, it ceased to be supported by taxes. The Congregational Church bought the building in 1830, adding a bell tower after moving it off the common. A town hall was built in Thetford Center the same year. The church was expanded in 1953. (Courtesy of the Vermont State Archives and Records Administration.)

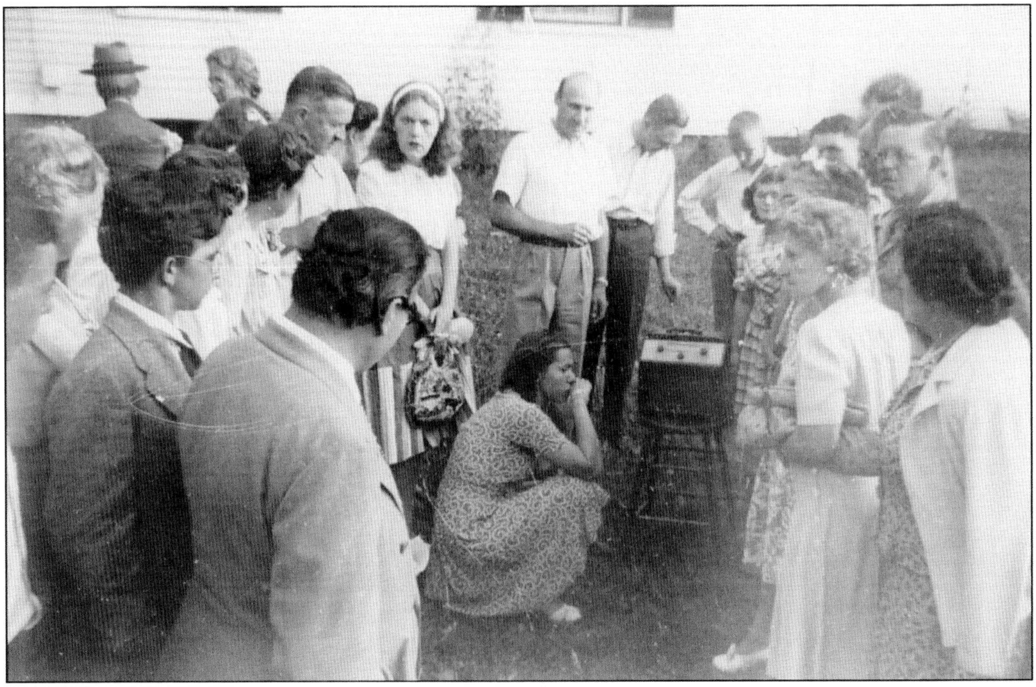

Thetford residents listen to the radio outside the First Congregational Church on V-J Day, 1945. "Thank God the war is over at last," West Fairlee resident Nellie Southworth wrote in her diary. "The news that Japan had surrendered came over the radio at 7 P.M. Horns began to blow and now at 9:30 you can hear a horn blowing. Radio is full of the celebration."

Two

Thetford Center

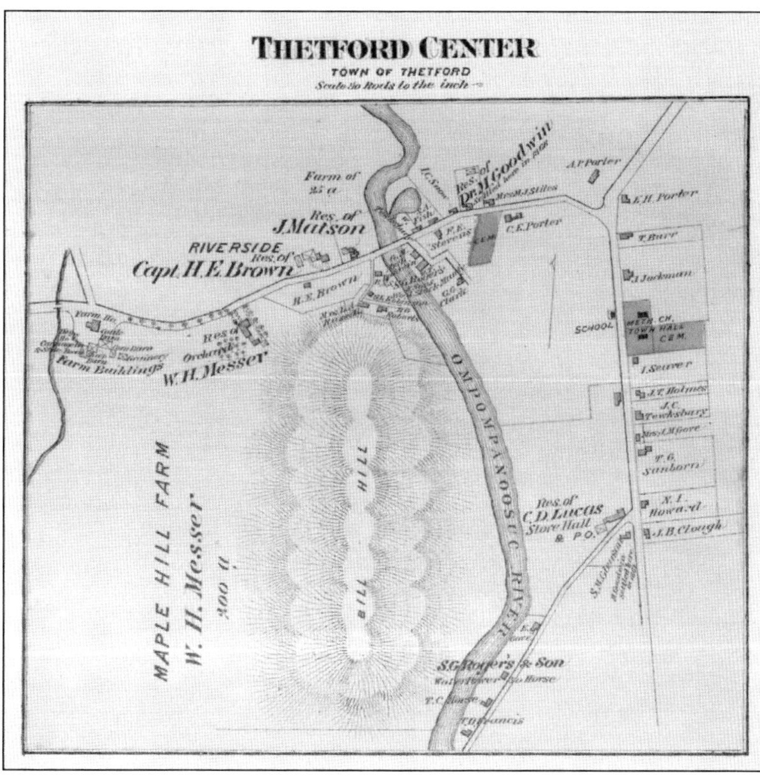

This map shows Thetford Center as it was in 1877. For most of the 19th century, Thetford Center's business district lay on the Ompompanoosuc River, where mill owners took advantage of a 45-foot drop in the river by building dams to harness its power. Most of the village's commerce took place within a knot of buildings clustered around the river's intersection with Tucker Hill Road. (Courtesy of University of Vermont Special Collections.)

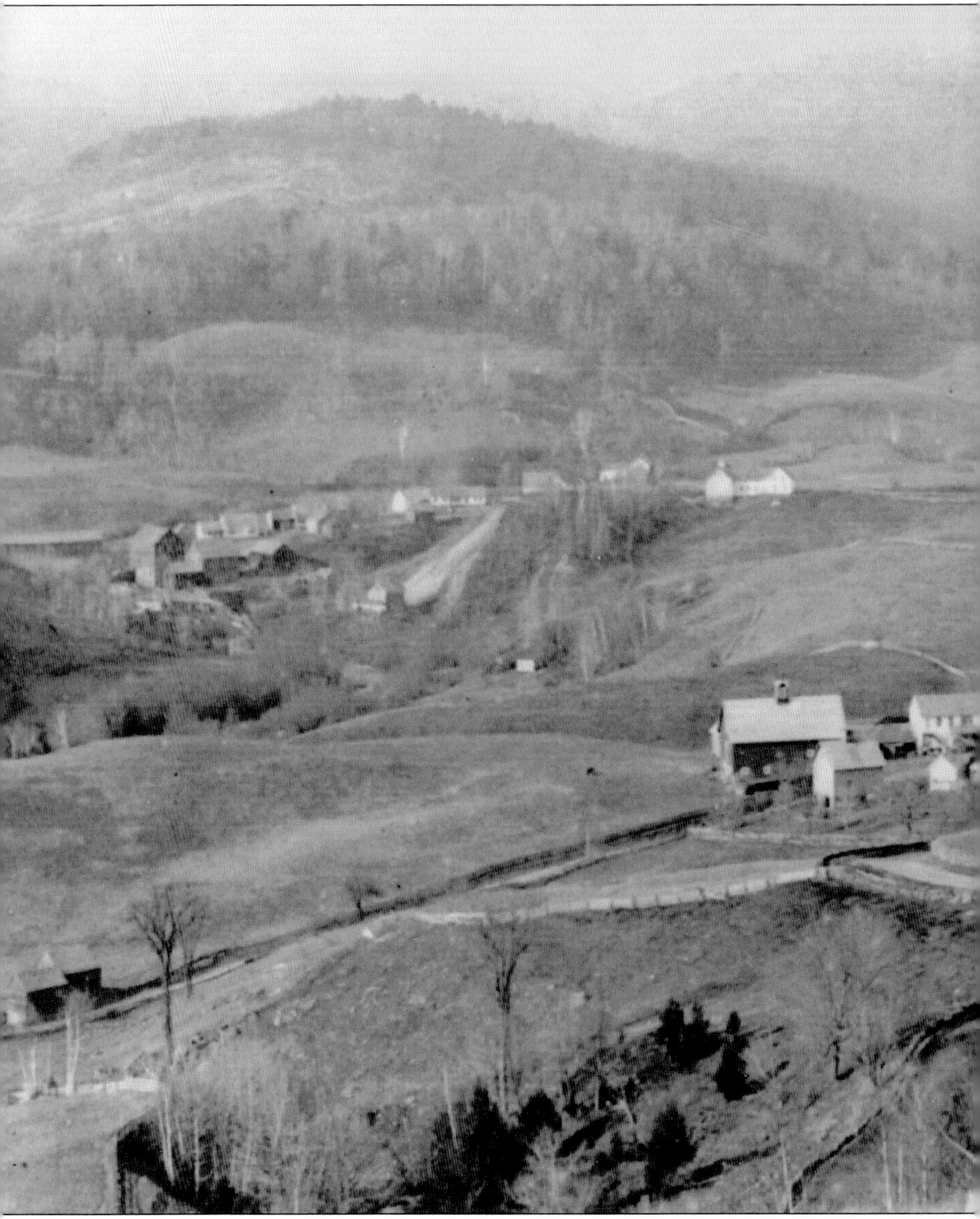

Thetford Center looked strikingly bare in this bird's-eye view photographed from a hill along Route 113. The covered bridge is at far left, and the original brick schoolhouse is visible across

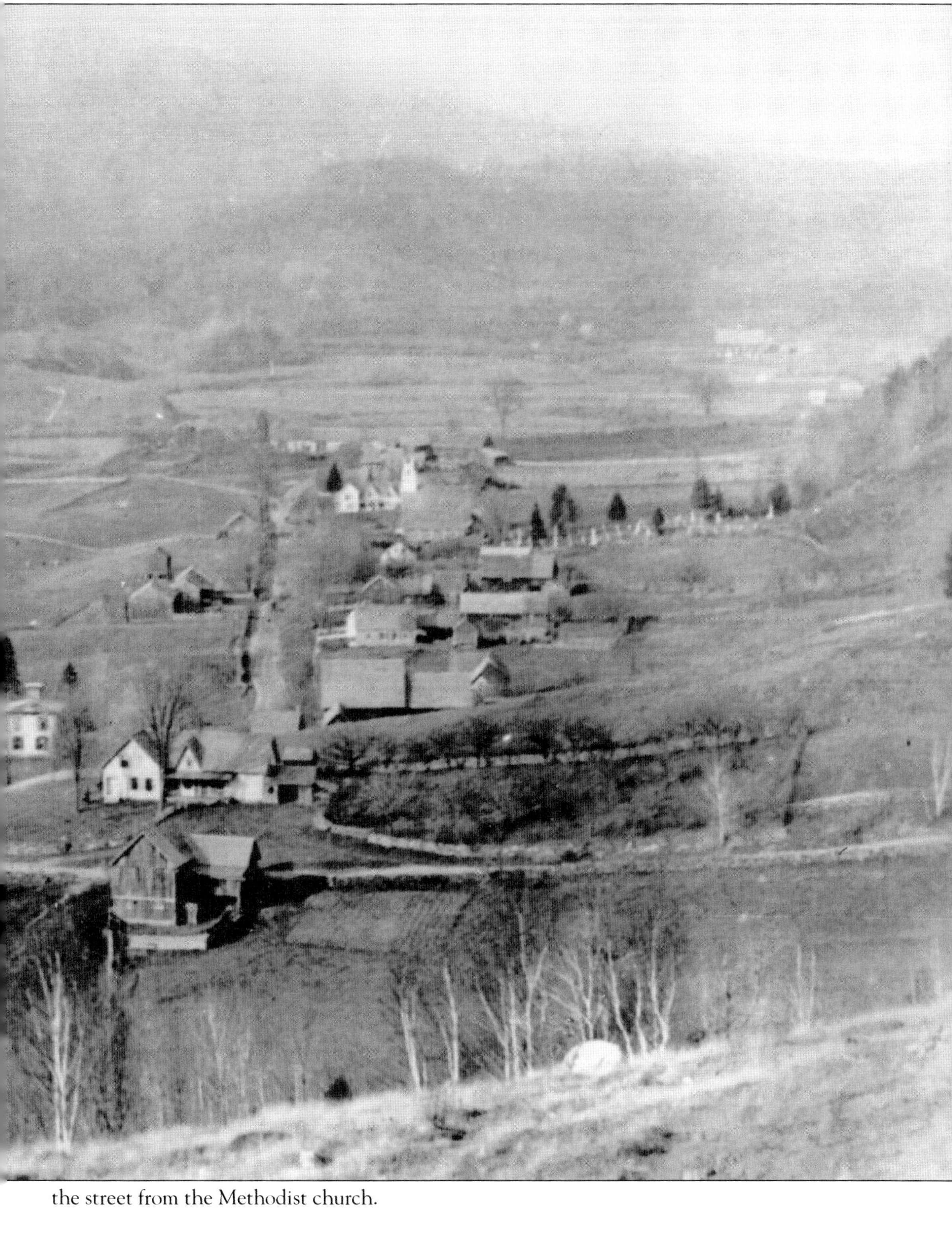

the street from the Methodist church.

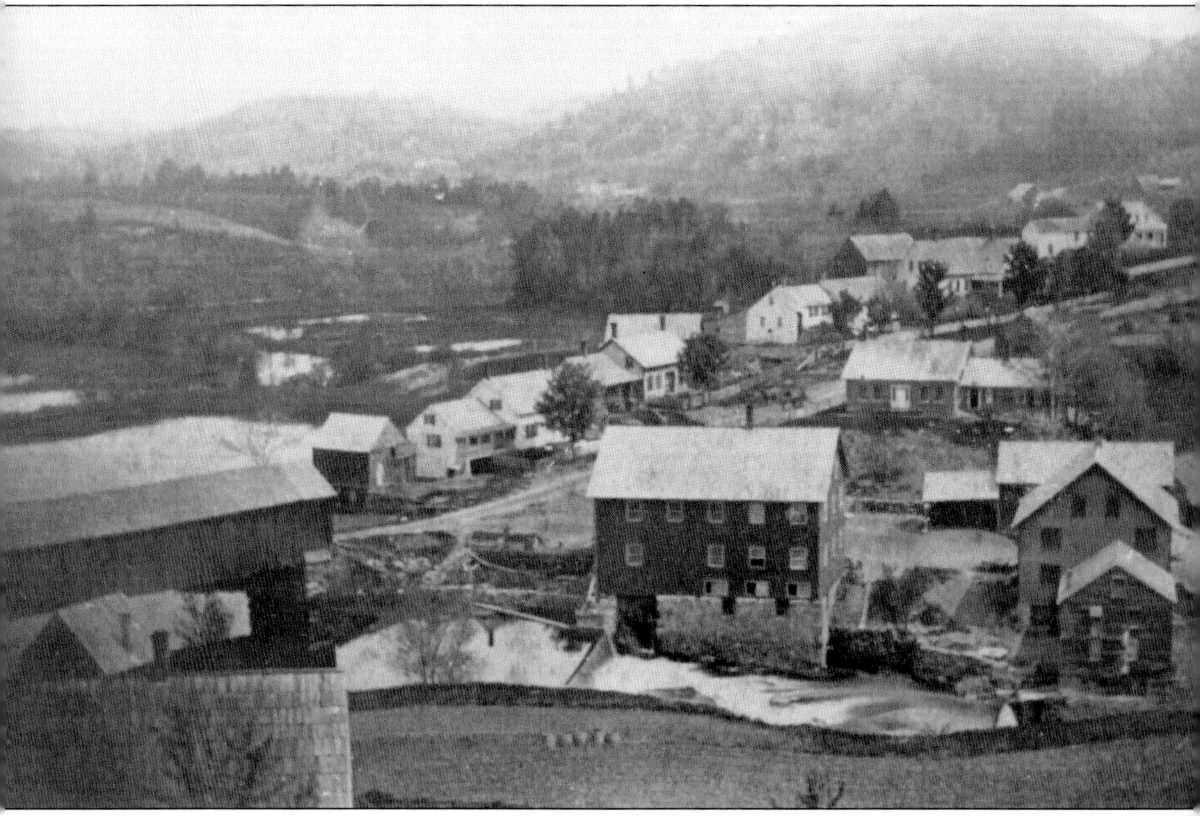

This is an 1874 view of the mill section of Thetford Center. The village was regionally known for its factories that produced cloth, shingles, starch, sash and blinds, musical instruments, shoes, and furniture, but most of this industry died out as mills burned or were swept away in floods in the late 19th century. Due to the changing climate of rural business in New England, most mill owners opted not to rebuild. Charles Vaughan adapted the last gristmill in Thetford Center as a hydropower plant, bringing electricity to Thetford.

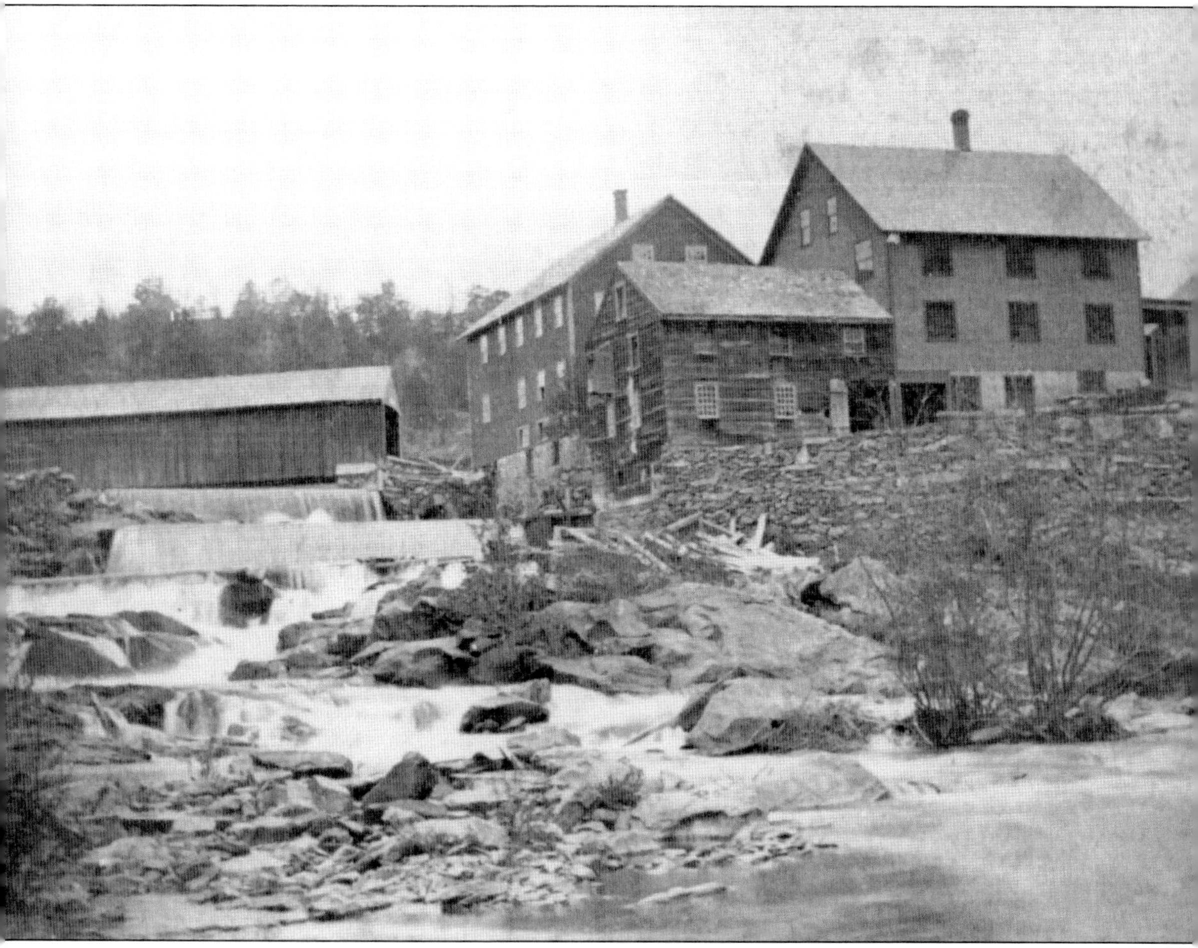

Mills were the heart of the village. A gristmill came first, then a fulling (cloth-finishing) mill, then a fiber-carding mill, then a sawmill. Hammond Porter's mill made trip hammers, used in heavy forging. Because each mill had to take the water from the mill above it, negotiating the order of water use in the dry season could be a delicate balance. In this 1874 photograph, the three dams used by the mills near the covered bridge are visible.

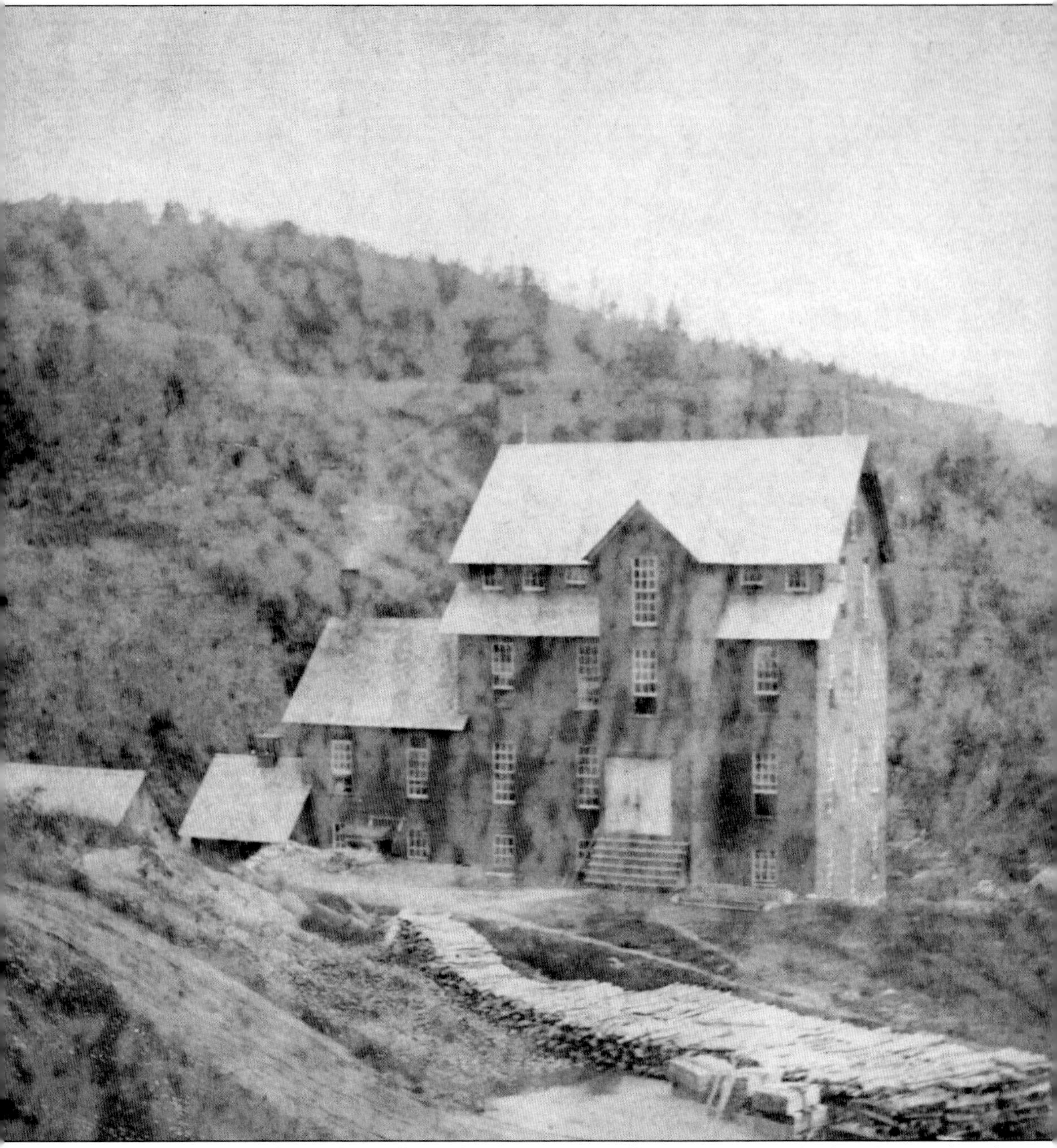

Downstream from the Tucker Hill Road mills, Rogers' Mill was a four-story facility that produced finished cloth from raw fibers. That kind of one-stop service was rare in rural New England. Weavers worked on the ground floor, carding took place on the second floor, workers dried and pressed the cloth on the third, and spinners worked on the fourth. The mill made up to 2,000 yards per week of blankets, flannel, and waxed fabric for raincoats. Built in 1865, the mill burned in the 1870s.

The Hiram Preston house and sawmill (also known as the Tewksbury furniture mill) was next to the Sawnee Bean covered bridge over Barker Brook.

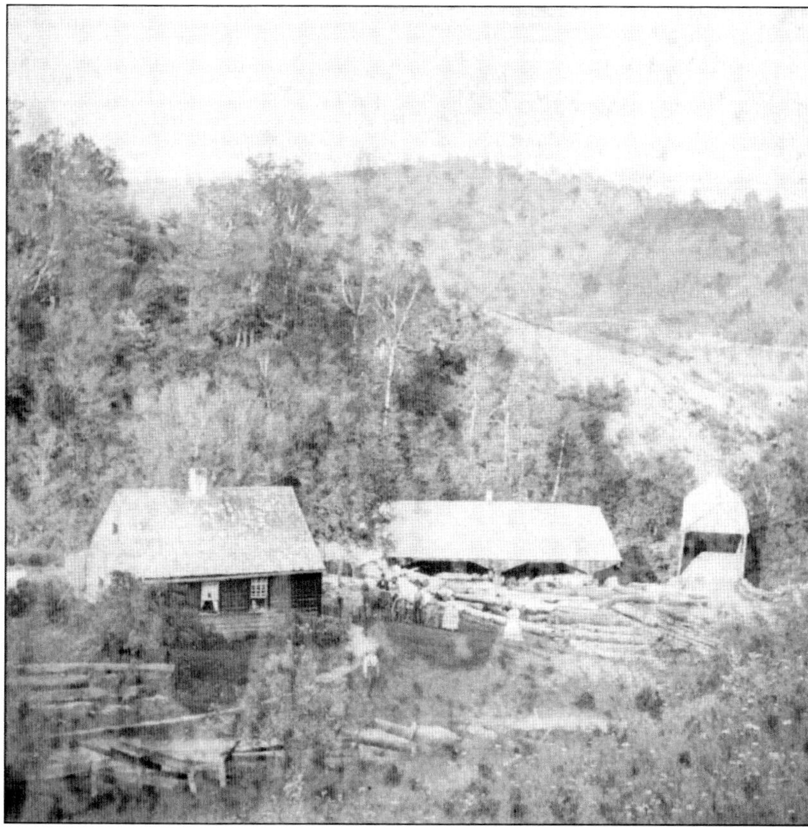

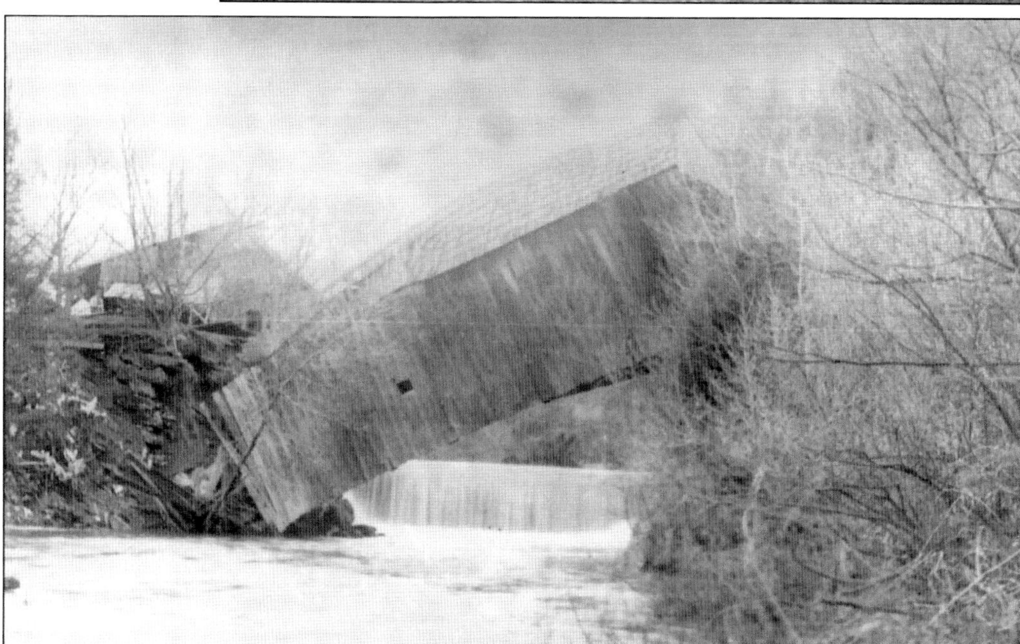

The Sawnee Bean bridge collapsed in 1916 and was replaced by an iron bridge. Behind the bridge is the Preston milldam and the Tewksbury mill.

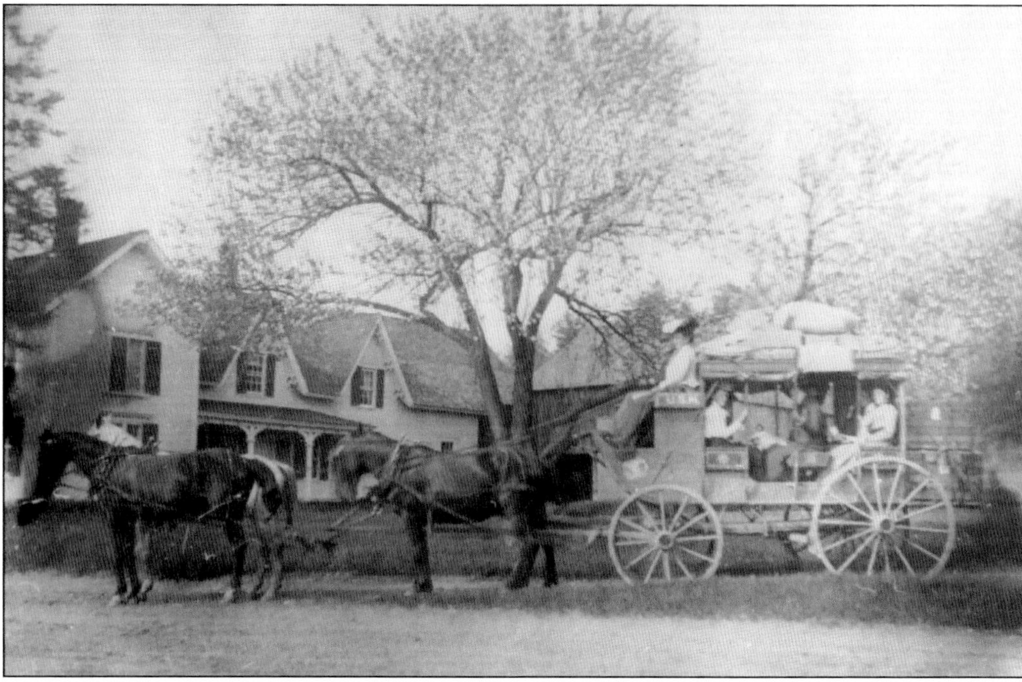

The Thetford-Hanover stagecoach waits in Thetford Center. Privately owned stagecoaches were the primary form of long-distance transportation in New England before the railroad arrived. Henry Barstow recalls that his grandfather, a "star route" stagecoach driver, was required to come up with a bond of $400 to secure a route in the 1890s. His circuit ran 23 miles and more than five hours from Chelsea to the depot in East Thetford, making stops along the way. After 1845, the US Postal Service contracted with these drivers to carry the mail. It would award routes to the lowest bidder who could provide "celerity, certainty and security" of transporting the mail. The phrase was shortened to three asterisks, hence the nickname "star routes."

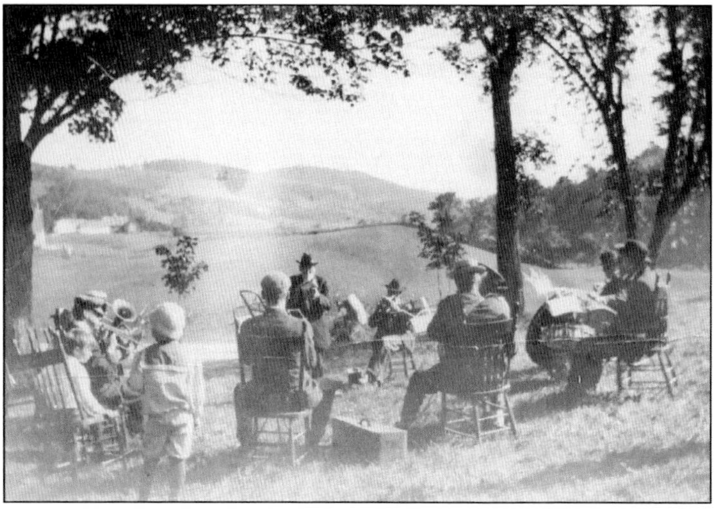

The Thetford Center Cornet Band practices on Nelson A. Porter's lawn on Tucker Hill Road. At far left in the distance are the 1900 schoolhouse and Sayre's store at the corner of Buzzell Bridge Road. Before the phonograph or radio, town bands were a popular form of entertainment in the Victorian era. Many communities had at least one band.

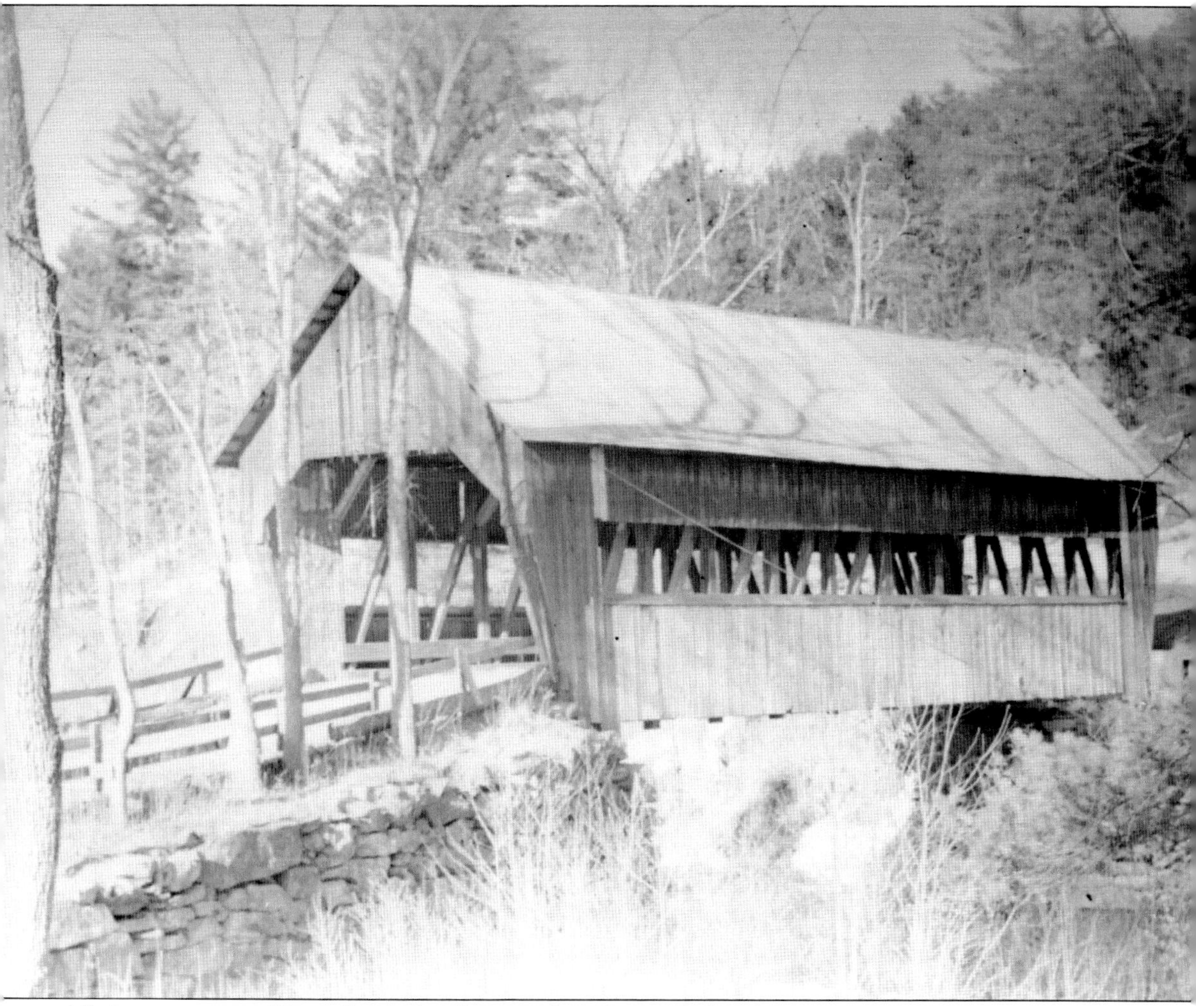

All that remains of Buzzell's Bridge (pictured) is the road that bears its name. It was removed for the Union Village Dam project, along with Cook's Bridge and Clark's Bridge in Union Village, as well as several houses and farms. At one time, there were six covered bridges over the Ompompanoosuc River.

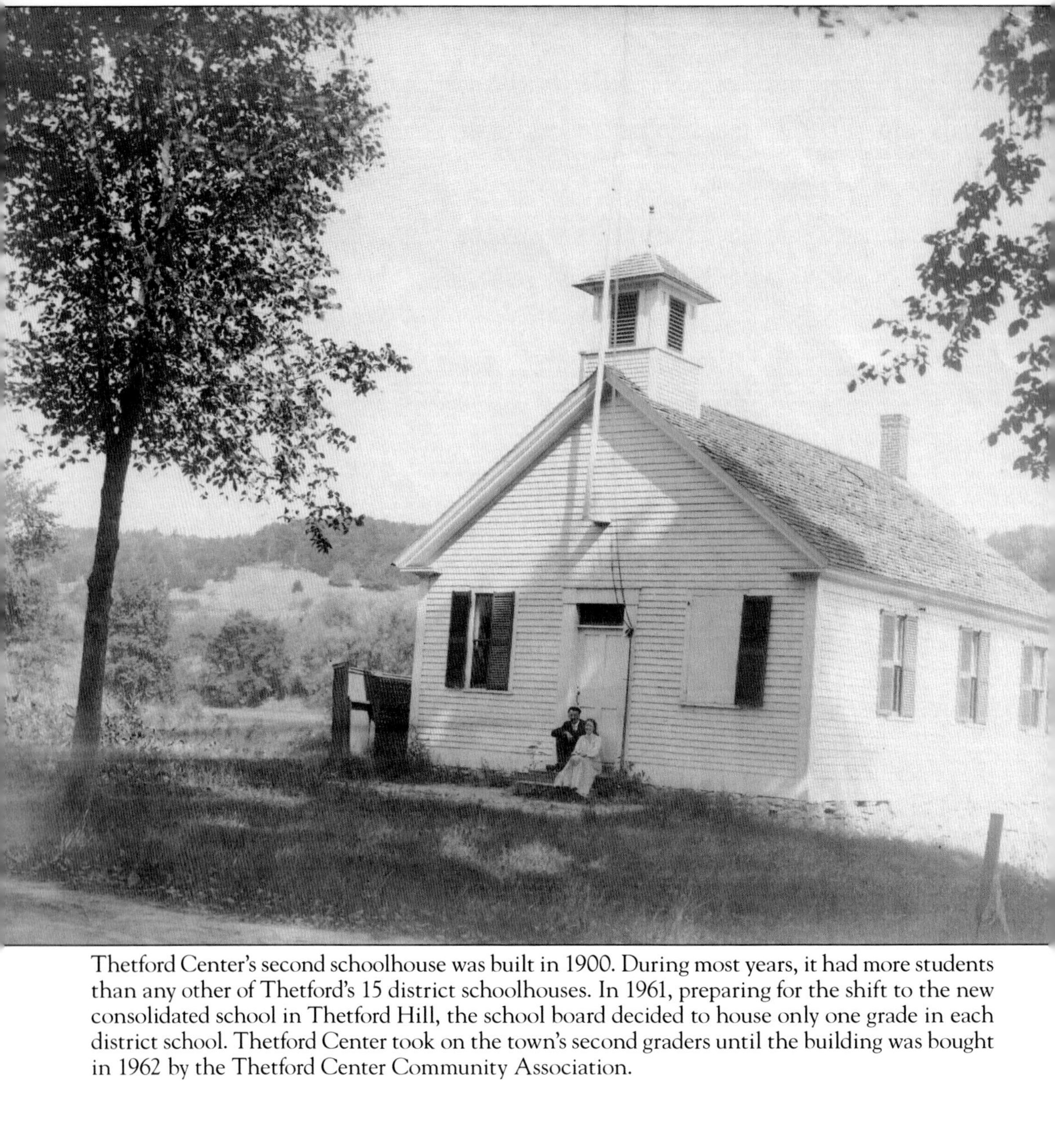

Thetford Center's second schoolhouse was built in 1900. During most years, it had more students than any other of Thetford's 15 district schoolhouses. In 1961, preparing for the shift to the new consolidated school in Thetford Hill, the school board decided to house only one grade in each district school. Thetford Center took on the town's second graders until the building was bought in 1962 by the Thetford Center Community Association.

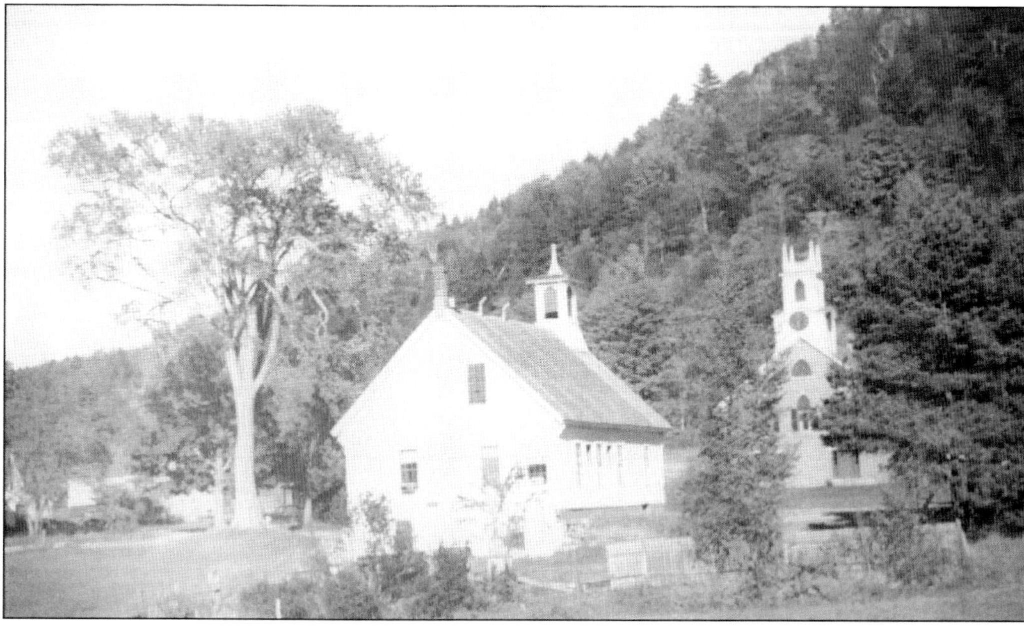

The elm tree that grew across the street from the Village Store is visible in many old photographs of Thetford Center. It was cut down on September 15, 1955.

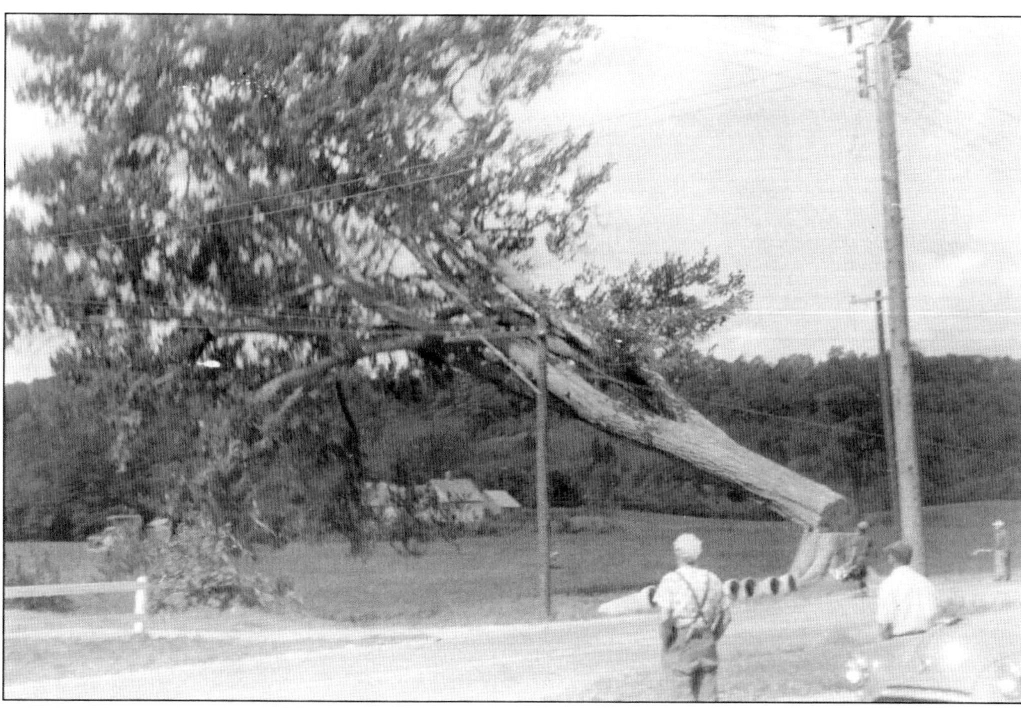

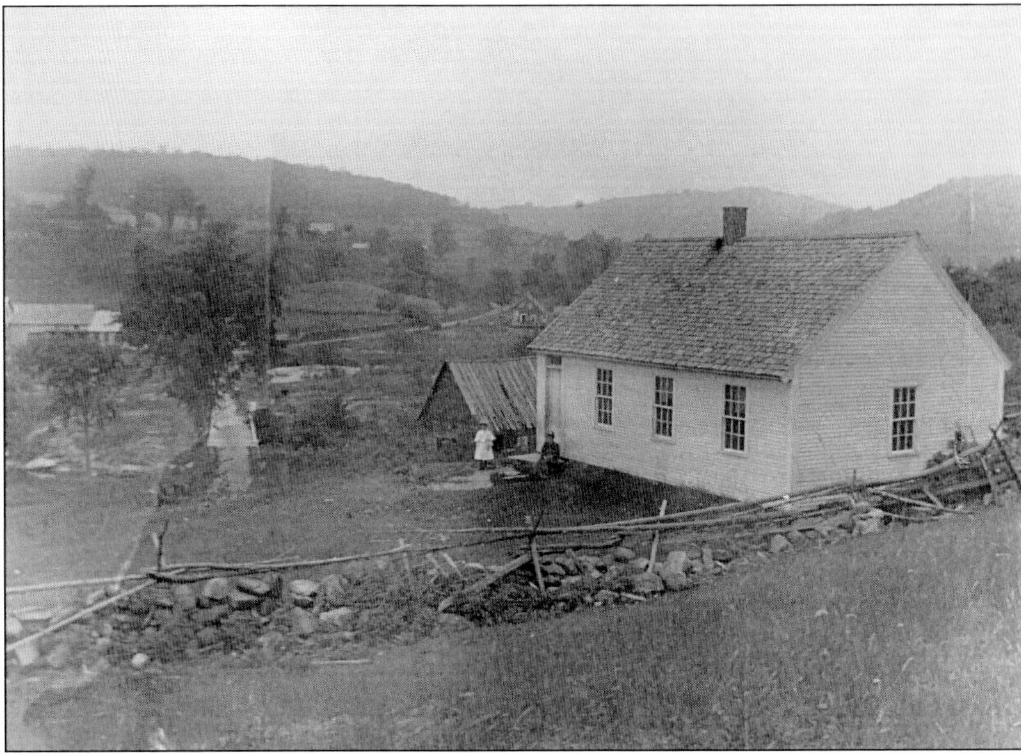

Rice's Mills had two schoolhouses. In 1900, the school superintendent claimed that the first was "not a fit place for cattle, and it is not as good a building as many barns. It is cold, unhomelike and barren." But it was not until 1930 that they addressed the issue. When the town attempted to move the first one in order to bring it up to state standards in 1931, it collapsed. The current building is now a community center.

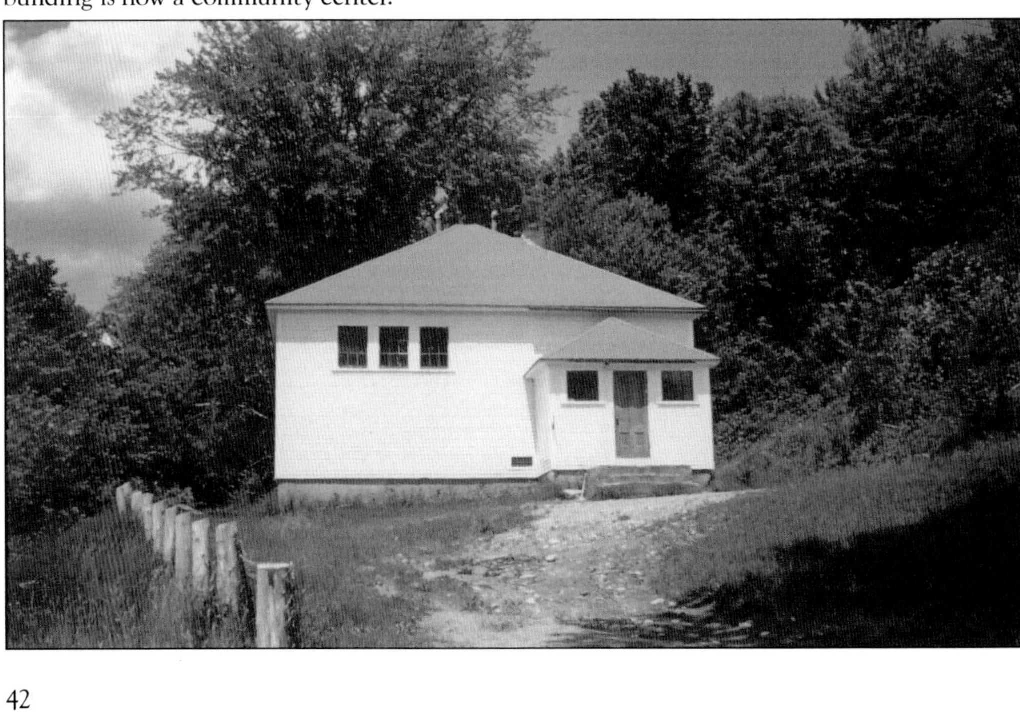

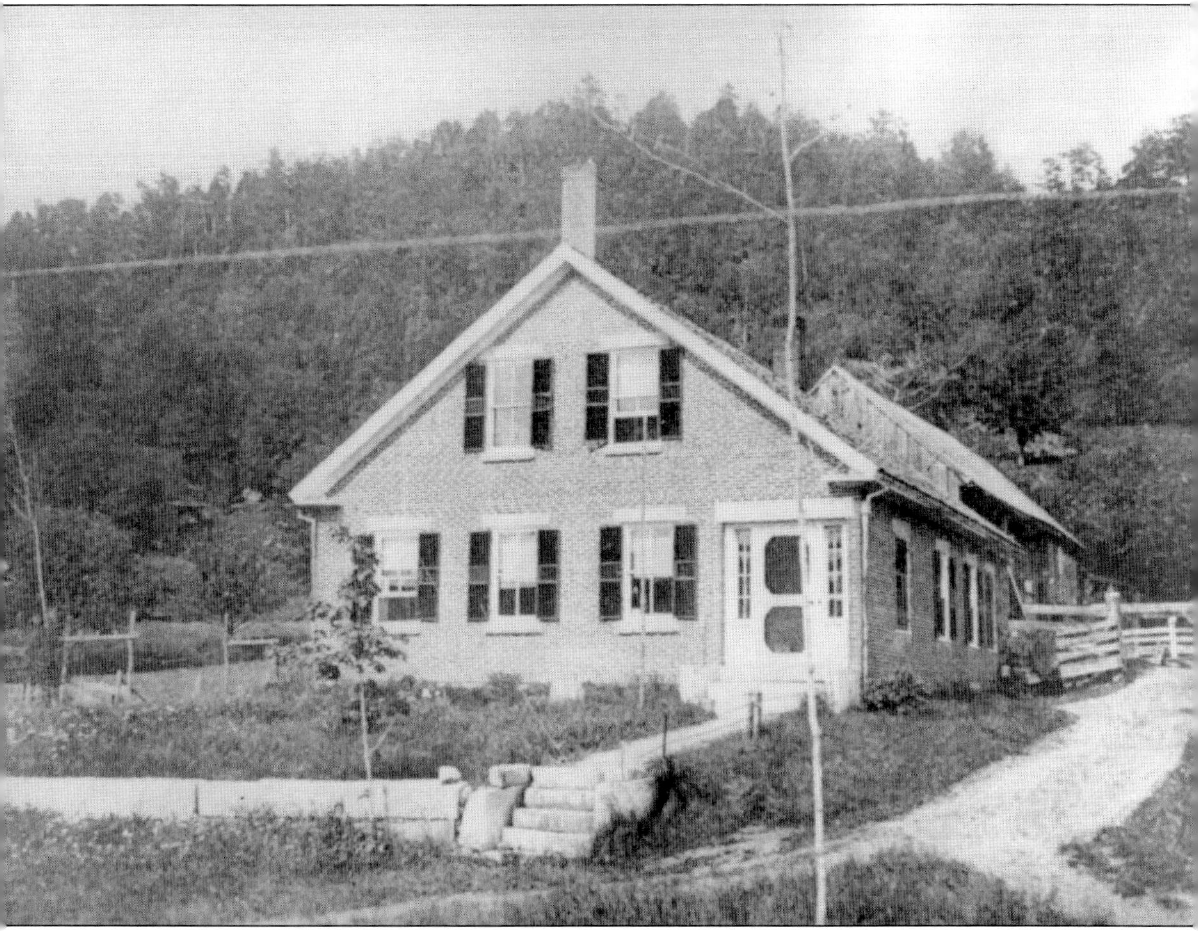

The Thomas Sanborn house was a stop on the Underground Railroad. Dr. Ezra Worcester transported escaped slaves from his house in Thetford Hill to the Sanborn house, where they would hide in an underground room between the house and the barn. From there, they went to Samuel Saville's house in Post Mills. Sanborn's Civil War connections ran deeper still; his son Alanson, an officer in charge of the 1st US Colored Volunteers, was murdered by a secessionist while drilling his troops in Norfolk, Virginia, one week after the battle of Gettysburg. Alanson is buried in the Evergreen Rest cemetery in Thetford Center.

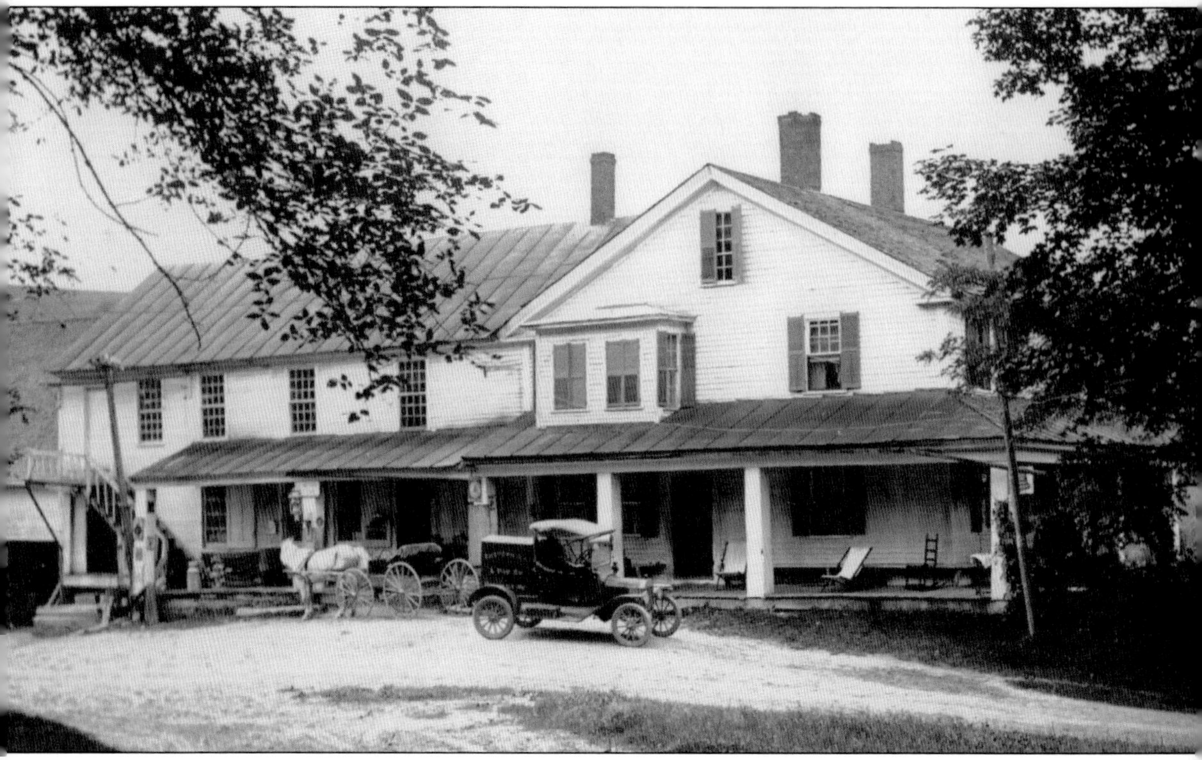

At the junction of Buzzell Bridge Road and Route 113 is possibly the oldest building in Thetford Center. Thayer's Store and Tavern (built around 1780) became a stagecoach stop and store in the early 19th century. It became a hotel and store after that, changing ownership again and becoming a store and post office. For some years, one could spend an evening upstairs at the El Dorado Dance Hall.

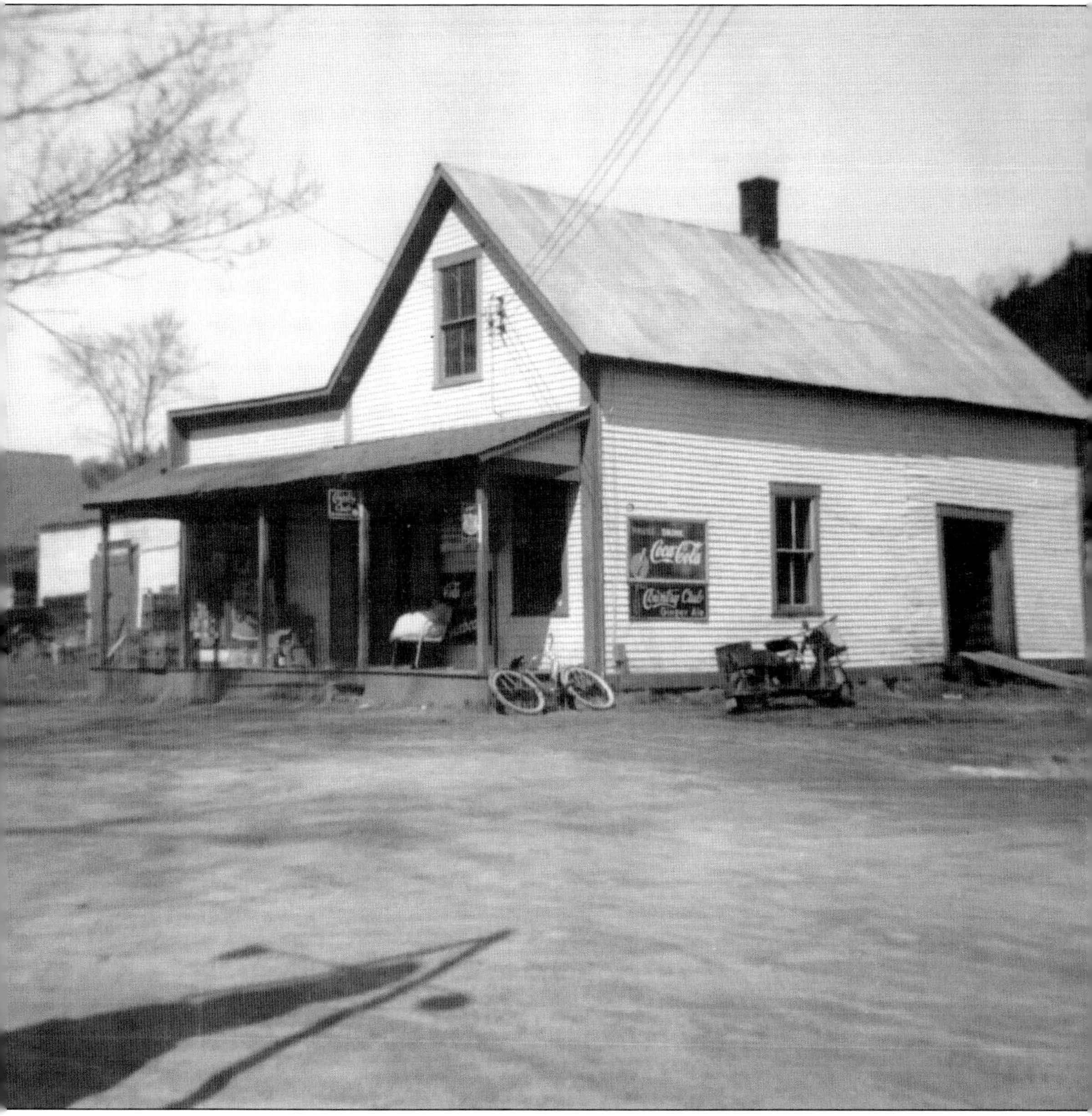

The Village Store has not changed much over the years, although it was once a corncrib at C.F. Porter's farm on Tucker Hill Road. It was then moved across the road and expanded by George Fifield in 1895.

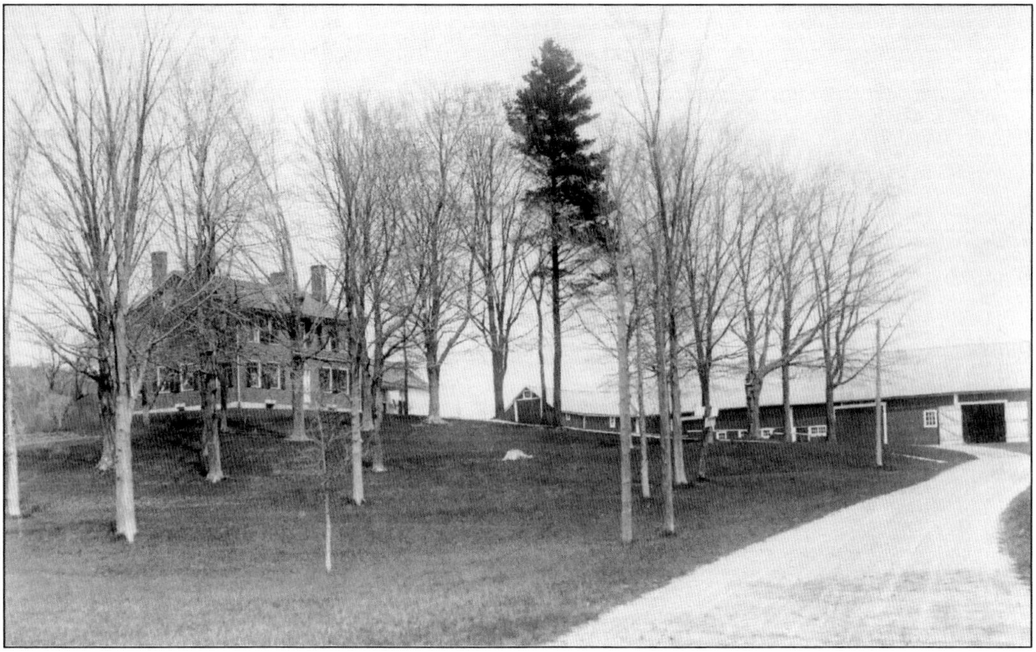

Hezekiah Porter's house, built in 1817, sits above Thetford Center. Bricks were produced on site for the house, as well as for the Methodist church and town hall across the street. Porter came to Thetford in 1806 from Hebron, Connecticut. (Most of Thetford's earliest landowners hailed from Hebron.) Porter was one of the few from that town who actually settled in Thetford; his fellow landowners, for the most part, promptly sold their parcels soon after buying them. Porter partnered with Samuel Farnsworth to rebuild nearby gristmills and sawmills and later built carding and fulling mills of his own. At one point, the house was a tavern.

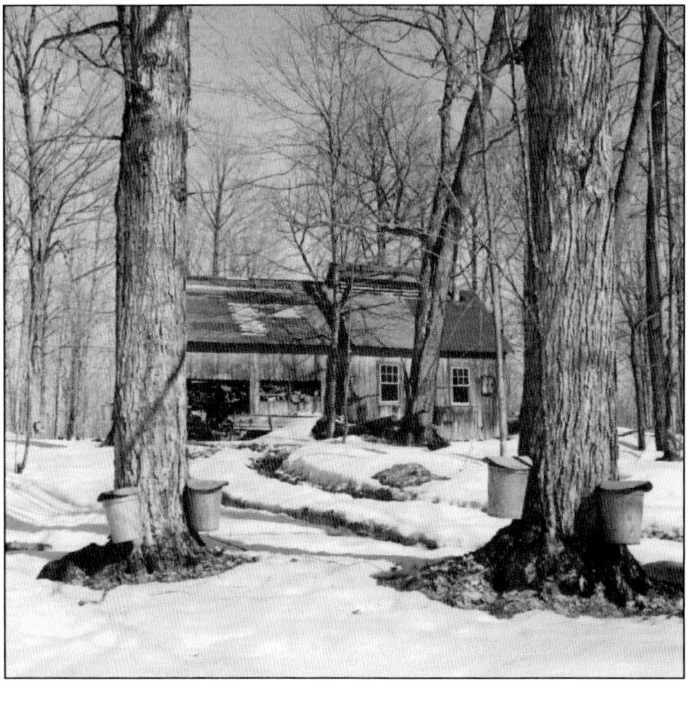

Late author Noel Perrin's sugarhouse on Bill Hill was a replica of Henry David Thoreau's cabin at Walden Pond. Perrin sought to carry on Vermont's long tradition of maple sugaring at home, which he described in his 1972 book *Amateur Sugar Maker*. (Courtesy of the Vermont State Archives and Records Administration.)

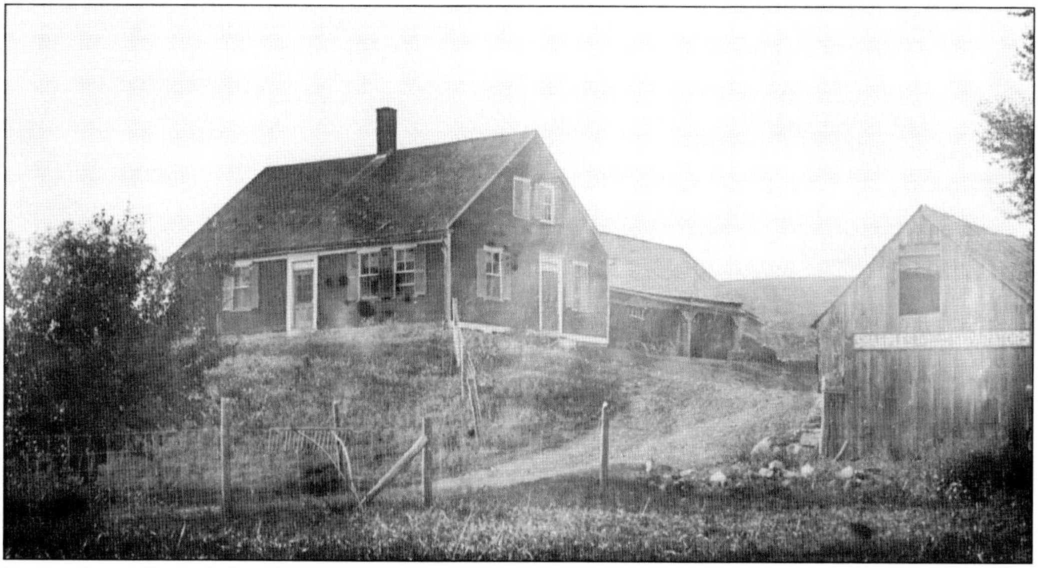

Richard and Bathsheba Wallace lived on what is now Bathsheba Lane. Richard was famous for swimming across Lake Champlain during the Revolutionary War to bring messages to Gen. Benjamin Lincoln. While he was away, Bathsheba worked the farm by herself. She was a respected midwife who delivered 1,666 babies and never lost a mother. The home burned in 1933.

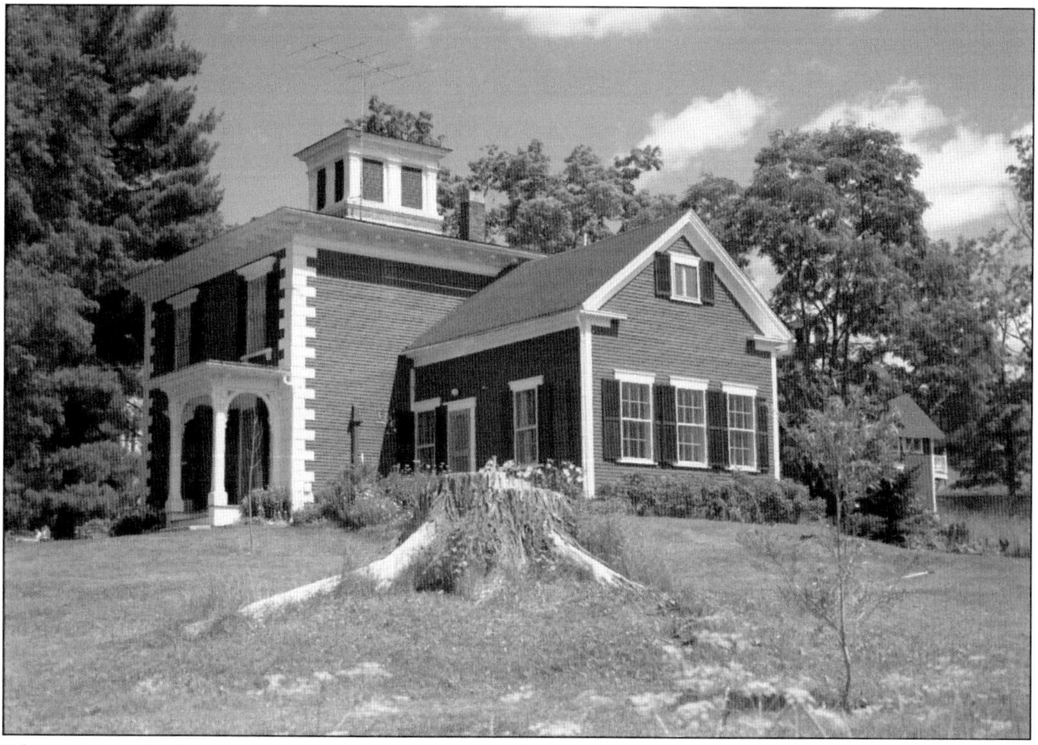

This unusual Italianate-style house was built in 1861. Its most prominent owner was Judge Samuel M. Gleason, a co-owner of the nearby Noosuc Mill, which manufactured strawboard (used as insulation behind clapboards), brown wrapping paper, and board for book covers. (Courtesy of the Norwich Historical Society.)

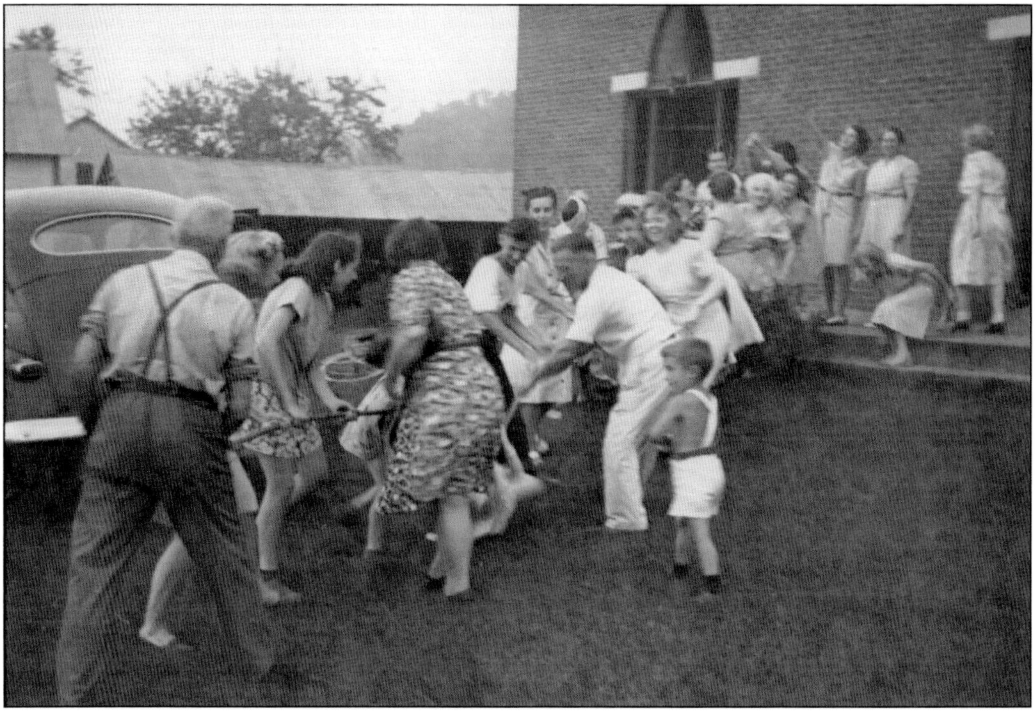

Residents ring the bell of the Thetford Center Methodist Episcopal Church on V-J Day in 1945. Among Thetford's war dead was the church's former minister, Rev. George Fox. Fox was one of the "Four Chaplains" who died when the USAT *Dorchester* was torpedoed by a German submarine in February 1943. They helped evacuate the ship, then gave up their own lifejackets when supplies ran out. They joined hands, prayed, and sang hymns as the ship sank.

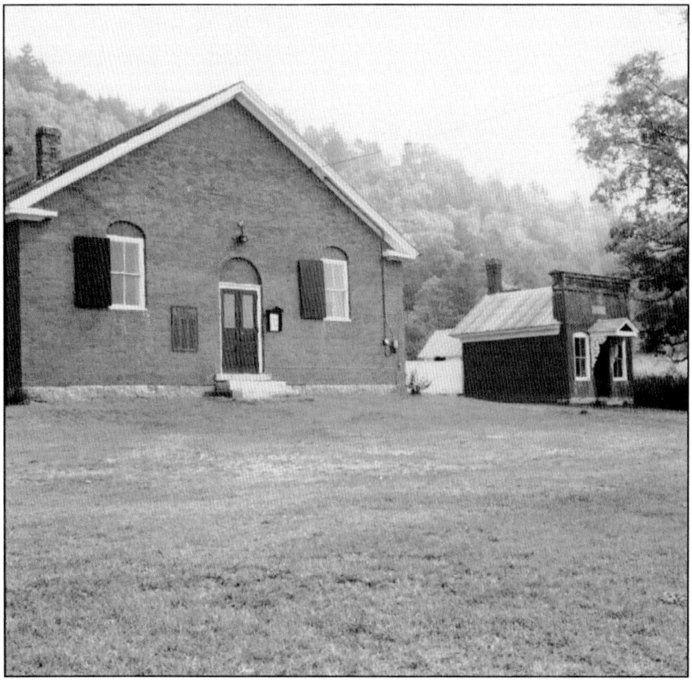

Town hall used to be in the First Congregational Church in Thetford Hill, but as church and state separated, it became necessary to relocate, and town business shifted in 1830 to Thetford Center. The Wallace Vault was built in 1910 to house town records. Although it had a heavy door and thick walls, it was also built with two glass windows in front. (Courtesy of the Vermont State Archives and Records Administration.)

Three

Post Mills

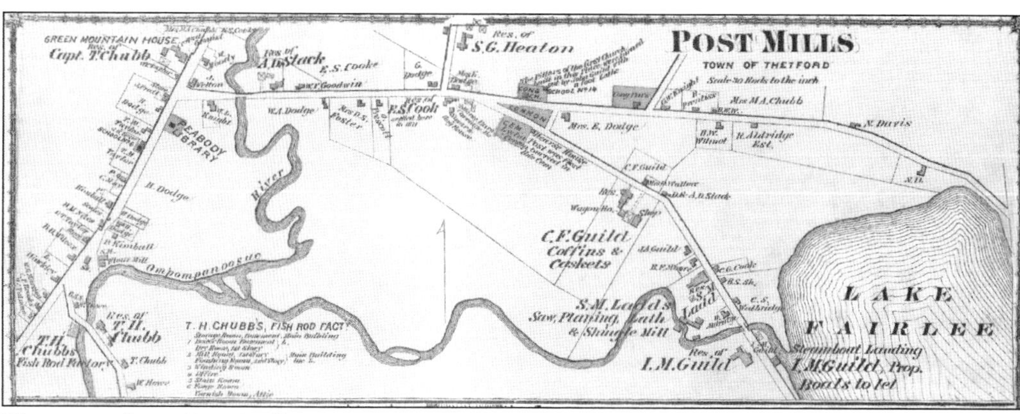

This map shows Post Mills as it was in 1877. Thetford's founders offered land to anyone who would build a sawmill in town, as lumber was badly needed. Eldad Post and his sons built sawmills and gristmills near Lake Fairlee in the late 1700s. Later, Joseph Hinckley ran a linseed oil mill farther down the river. After the substantial dam for the oil mill was built, businesses sprang up downstream to take advantage of the newly available waterpower. (Courtesy of University of Vermont Special Collections.)

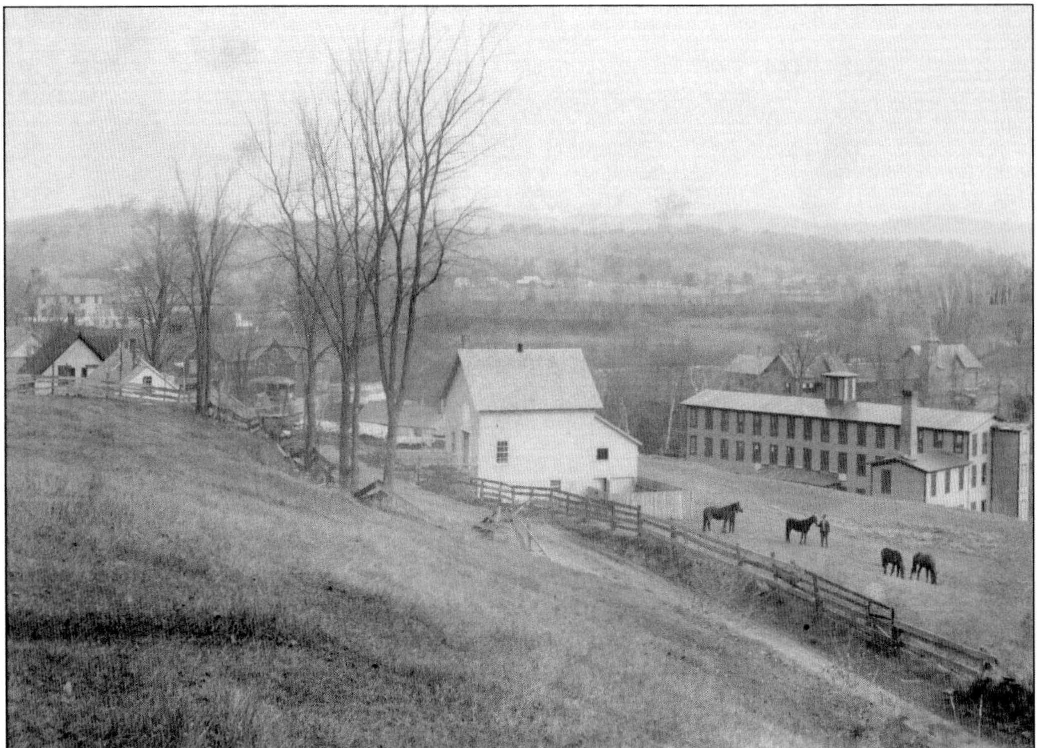

T.H. Chubb's house is visible behind the Chubb factory in this view of Post Mills from Barker Hill in 1902. At the turn of the 20th century, due to competition from the Midwest and southern New England, industry was declining in Thetford's other villages. But the factory (by then owned by the Montague Rod & Reel Company) continued to thrive, providing much-needed jobs for dozens of Thetford residents for many years to come.

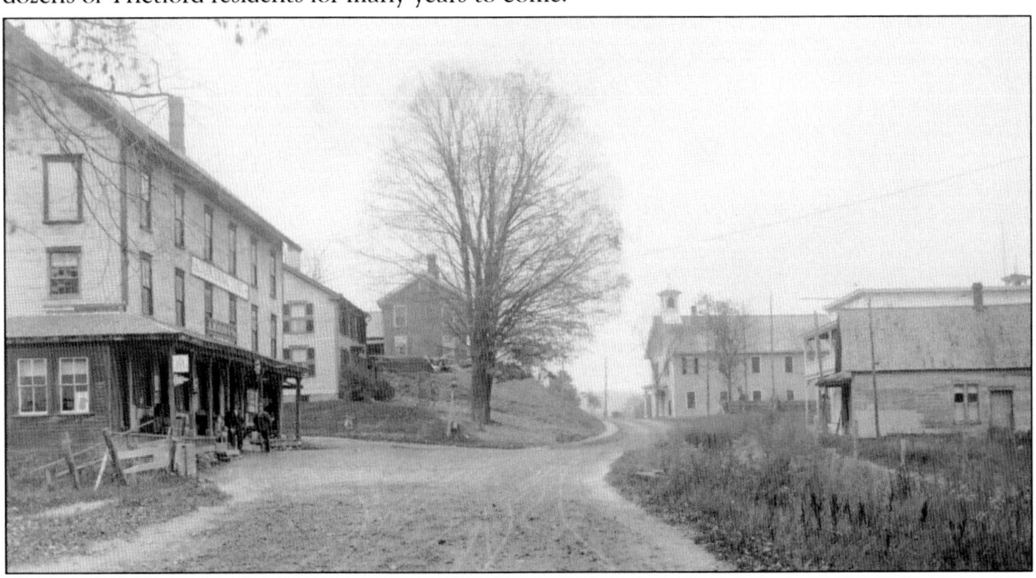

In this image of Post Mills's main street, the general store is at left and the Odd Fellows Hall is in the background at right center. The belfry of the school is at right.

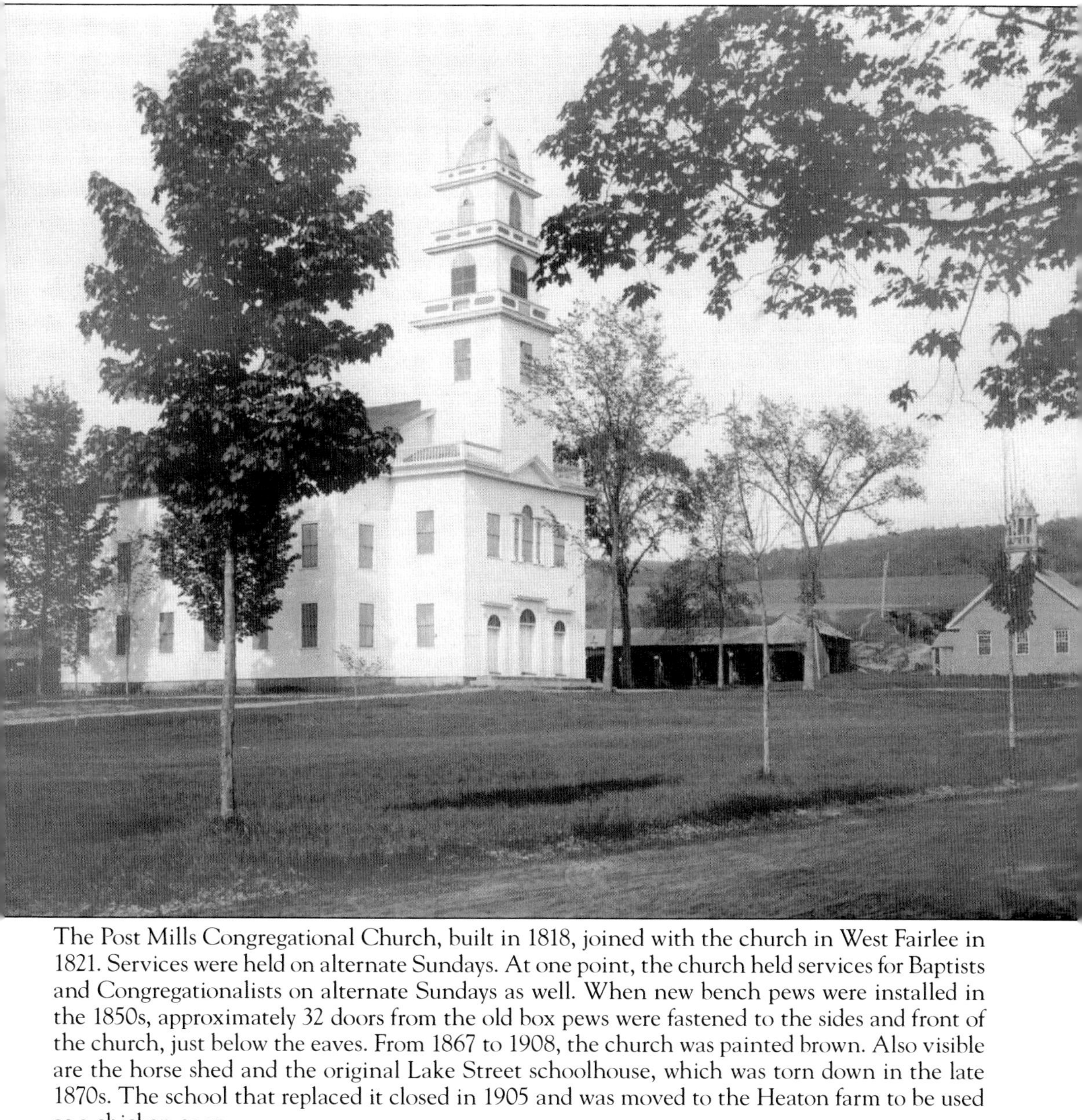

The Post Mills Congregational Church, built in 1818, joined with the church in West Fairlee in 1821. Services were held on alternate Sundays. At one point, the church held services for Baptists and Congregationalists on alternate Sundays as well. When new bench pews were installed in the 1850s, approximately 32 doors from the old box pews were fastened to the sides and front of the church, just below the eaves. From 1867 to 1908, the church was painted brown. Also visible are the horse shed and the original Lake Street schoolhouse, which was torn down in the late 1870s. The school that replaced it closed in 1905 and was moved to the Heaton farm to be used as a chicken coop.

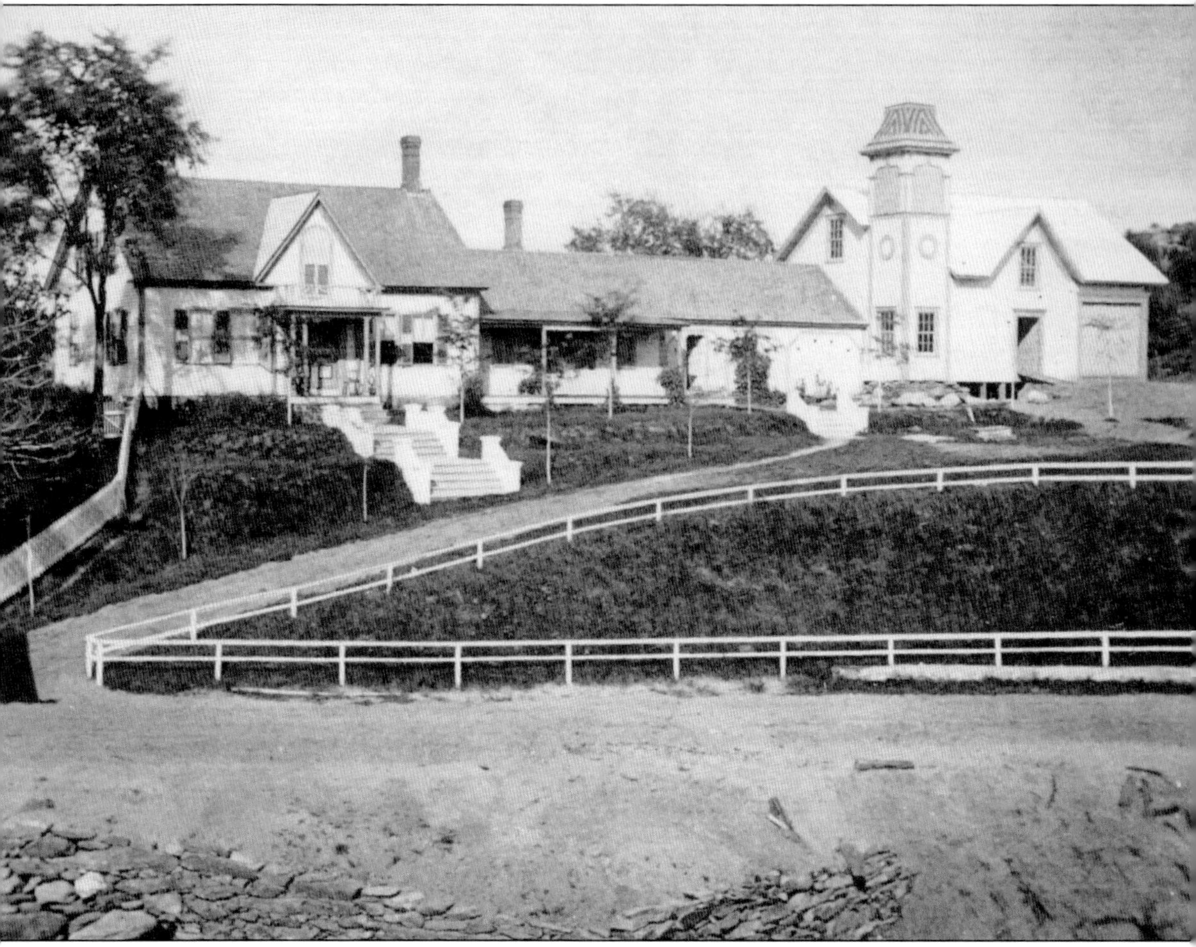

When T.H. Chubb came to the area after the Civil War from Galveston, Texas, he was refused lodging in West Fairlee because he was a southerner. Finding a friendlier reception in Post Mills, he bought the former linseed oil mill and began making rake handles. It was not a success, and he switched to making fishing rods. He lived in this house across the street from the mill. At one time, there was a mineral spring next to the house.

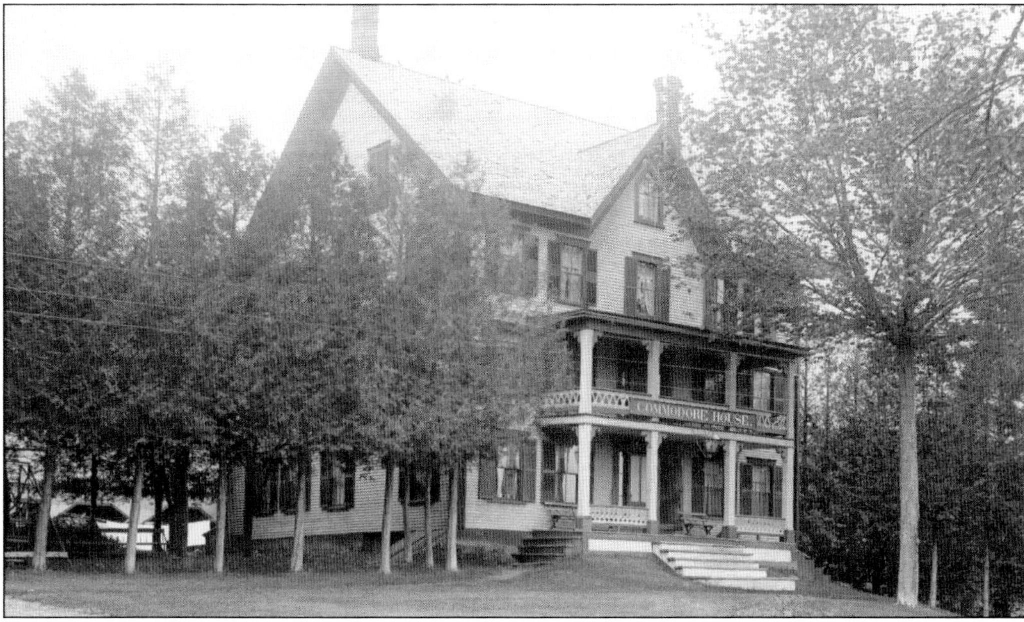

Chubb's father, Thomas B. Chubb, also settled in Post Mills and opened Thetford's first summer hotel, the Commodore House. It is understandable why the Chubbs' arrival in this abolitionist town caused a stir: the junior Chubb had served in the Confederate navy. His father, an admiral in the Texas navy and a friend of Sam Houston, had bought and sold slaves as a young man. (Courtesy of University of Vermont Special Collections.)

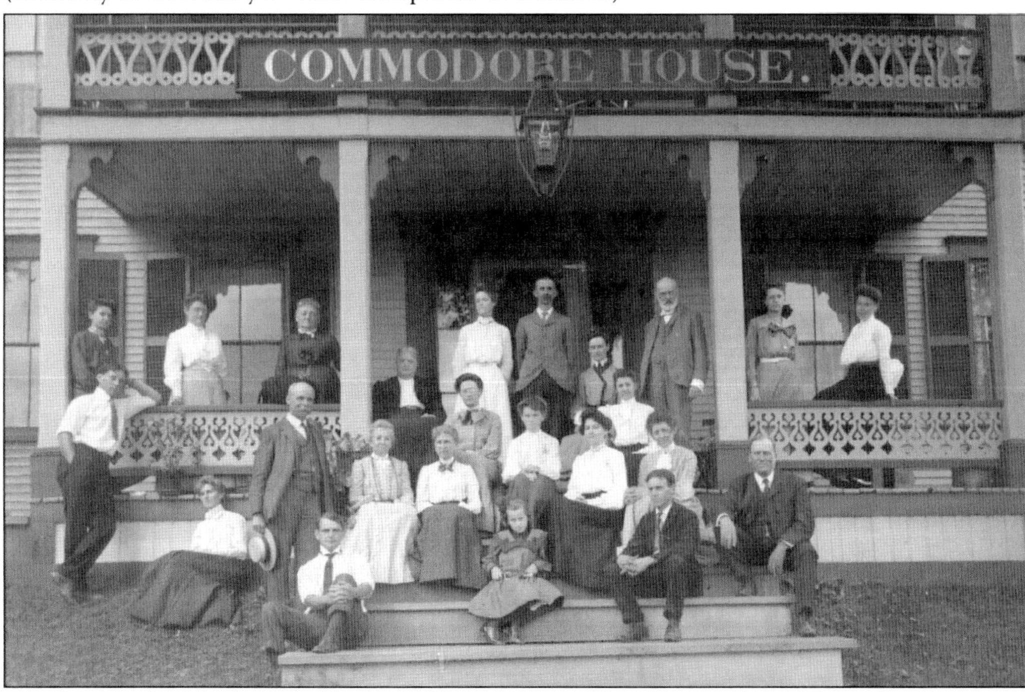

Boarders at the Commodore House relax on the porch. The inn, formerly at the junction of Routes 244 and 113, catered particularly to those seeking to escape the heat of the South. The Commodore House burned in 1910.

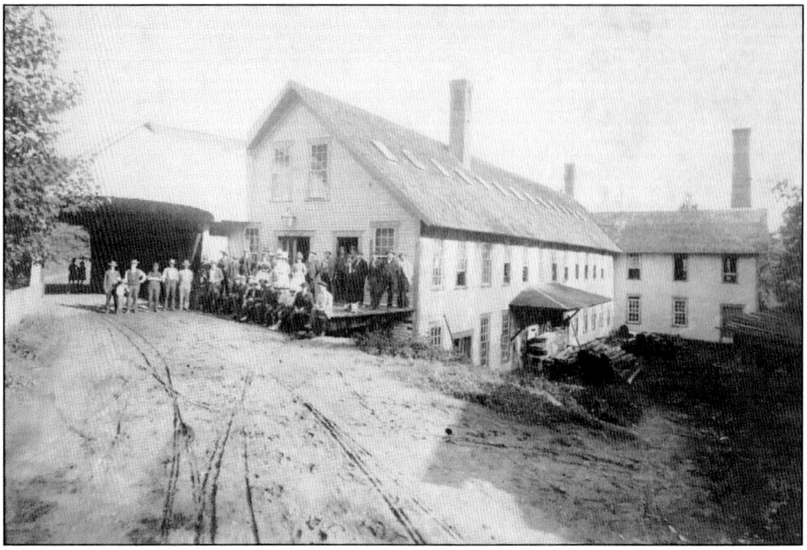

Employees gather in front of the Chubb fishing rod factory. The building was destroyed three times: by a flood in 1869 and by fire in 1875 and 1891. Chubb rebuilt each time.

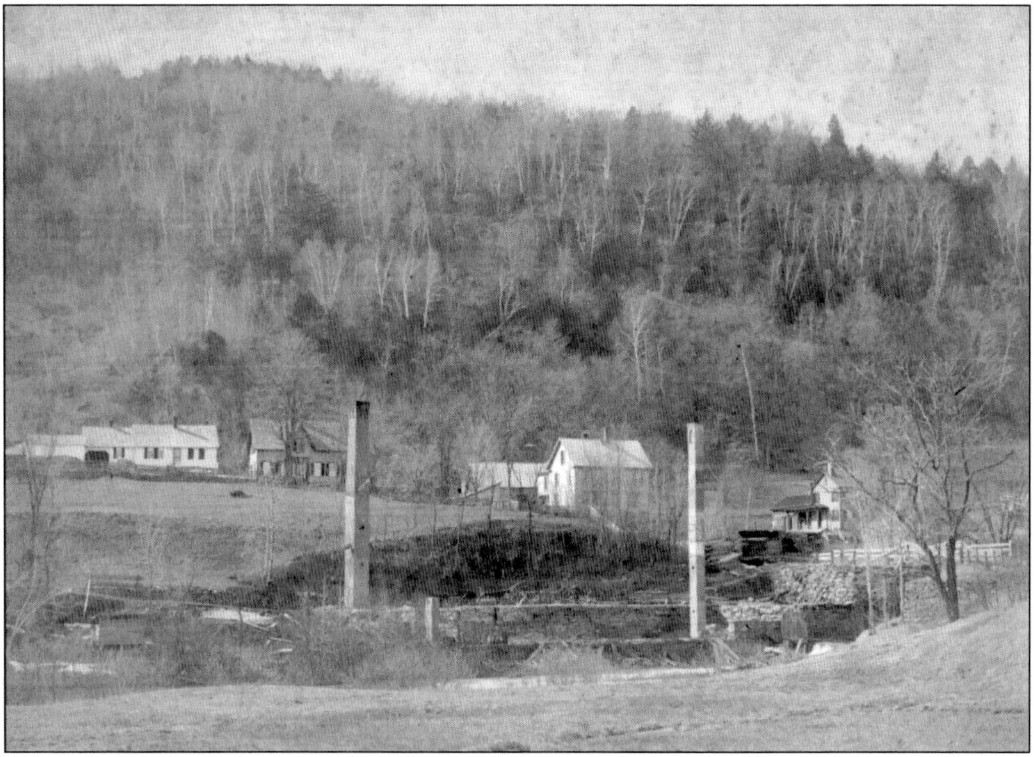

Smokestacks were all that remained of the factory after the 1891 fire. The factory whistle got stuck during the fire and blew continuously as the building burned; Helen Paige recalled that because that memory lingered in people's minds, the rebuilt factory seldom used its new whistle. Chubb could not recover from this third disaster and sold the business to the Montague Rod & Reel Company, which continued to produce Chubb fishing rods.

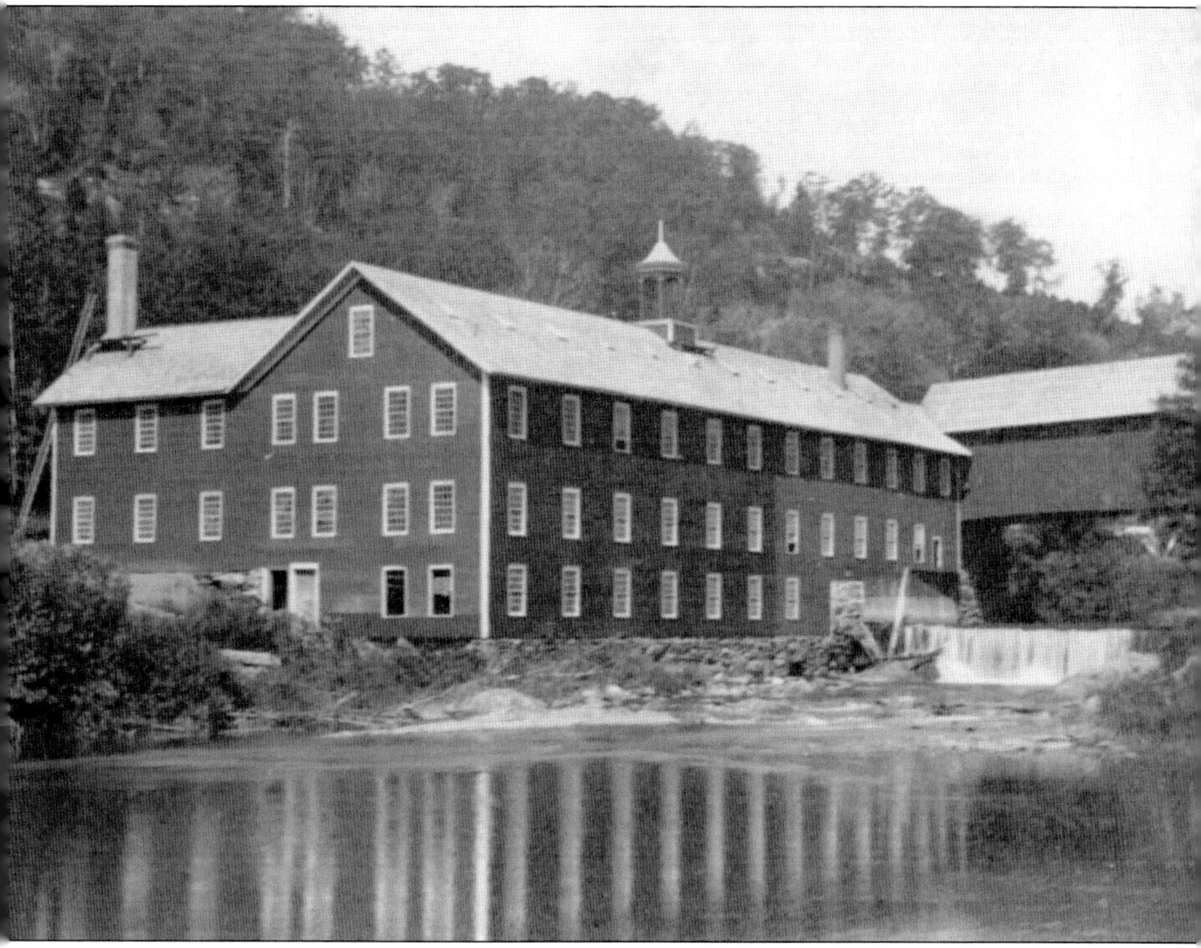

The rebuilt factory closed in the 1930s. In 1938, the Malmquist Wood Products Company took over the building. It first made bobbins for mills around New England, but as demand for bobbins decreased after World War II, it shifted to making concrete forms and furniture. The Union Village Dam project was one of its customers. It closed in the 1990s and the building was demolished in 2010.

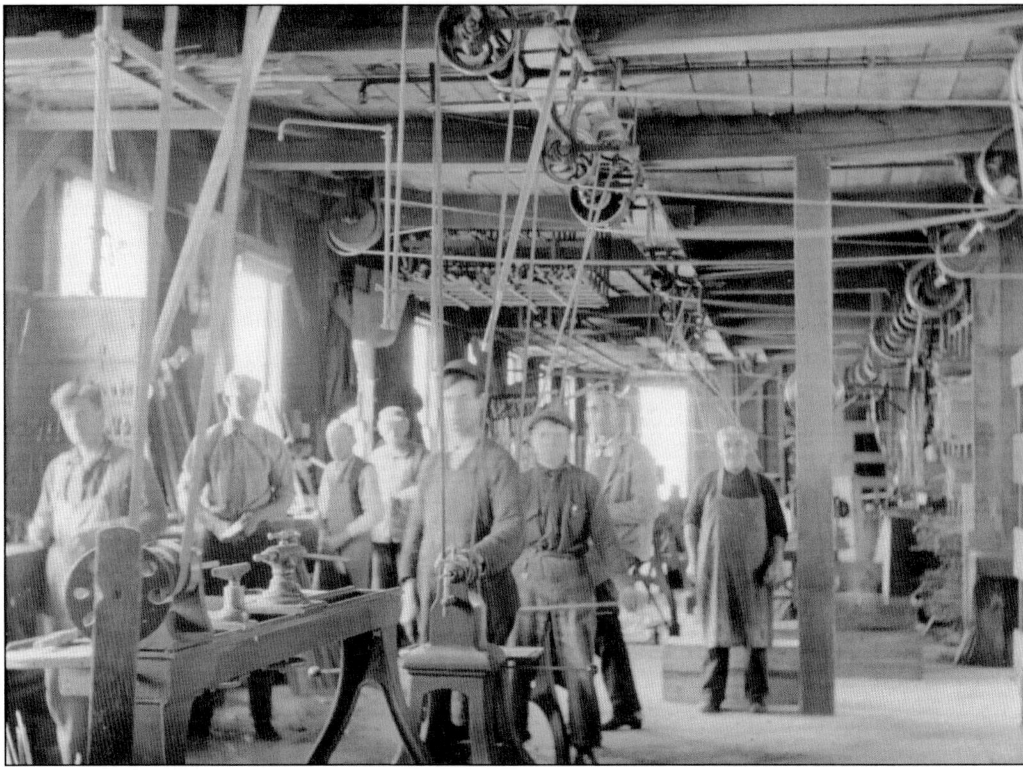

There was a significant market for outdoor sports after the Civil War. T.H. Chubb made a range of fishing rods, using bamboo from Calcutta and silver from Germany. Everything else was made on site. He was known for his split-cane bamboo fly rod. Unusual for the times, he advertised directly to consumers in newspapers and magazines.

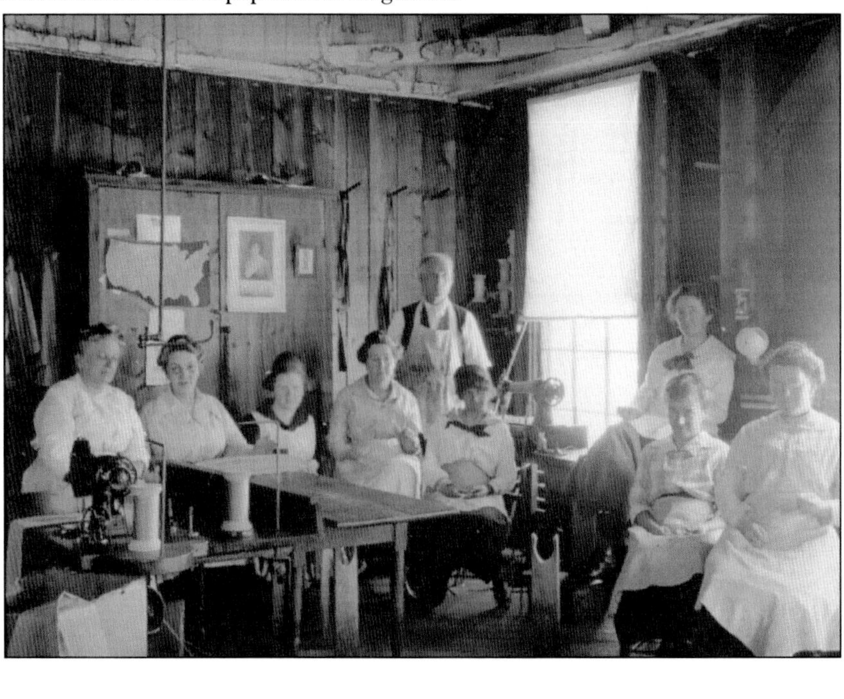

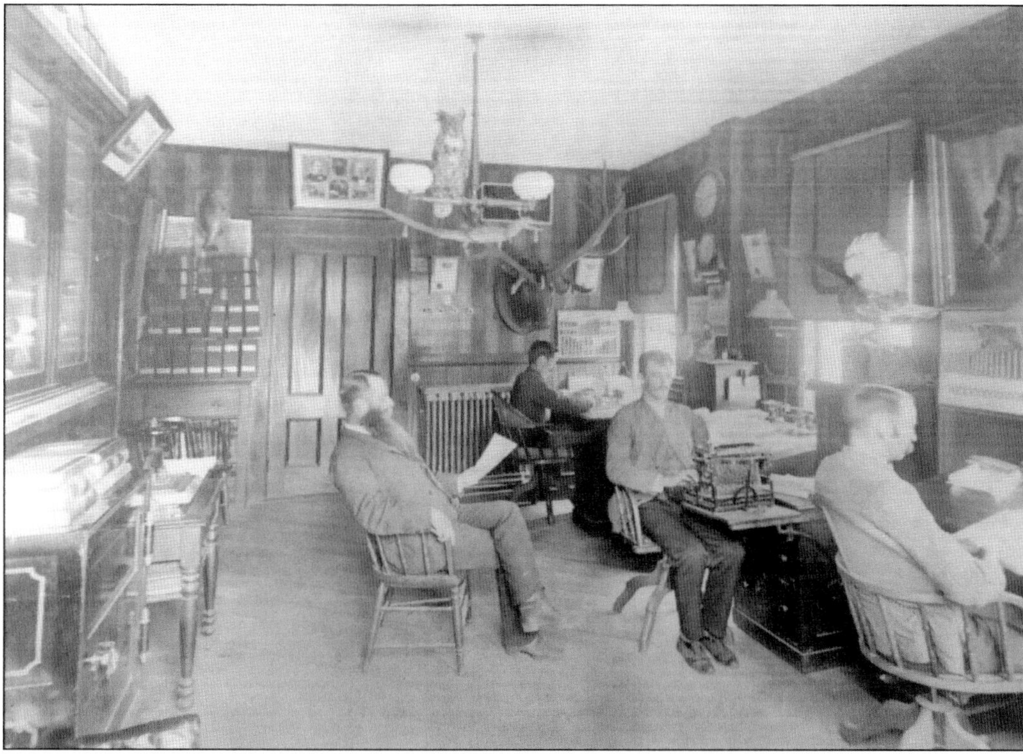

At its height, the Chubb Rod Company was the largest fishing rod business in the country. The factory saw success just as Thetford's population began its decline. After a number of fires and floods, many of Thetford's mills were not rebuilt, but the factory employed up to 50 local workers through the 1920s. T.H. Chubb is pictured above and below working in his office.

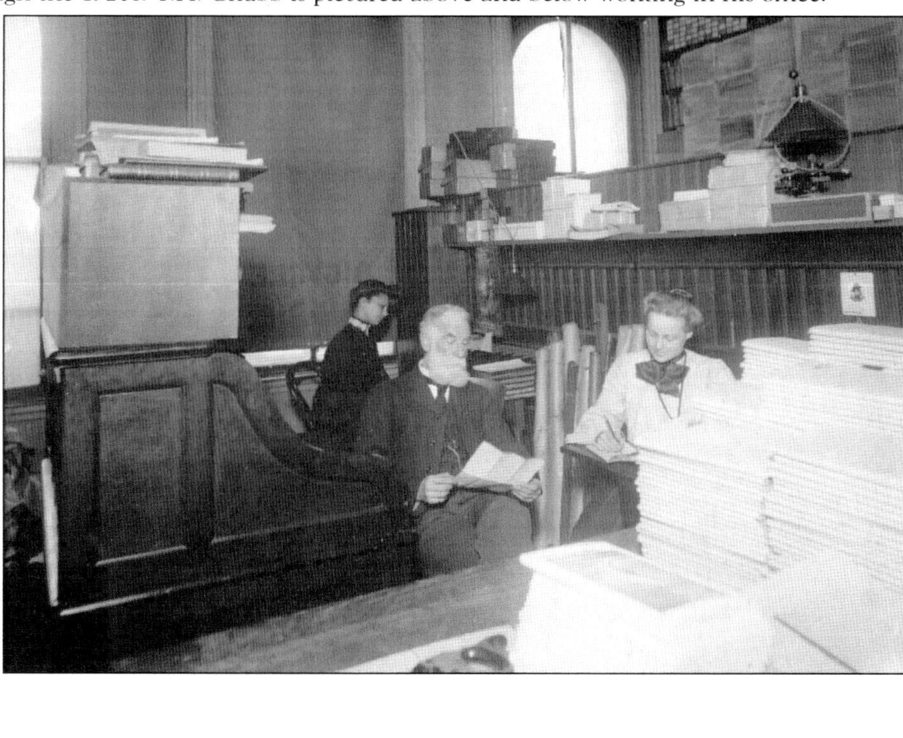

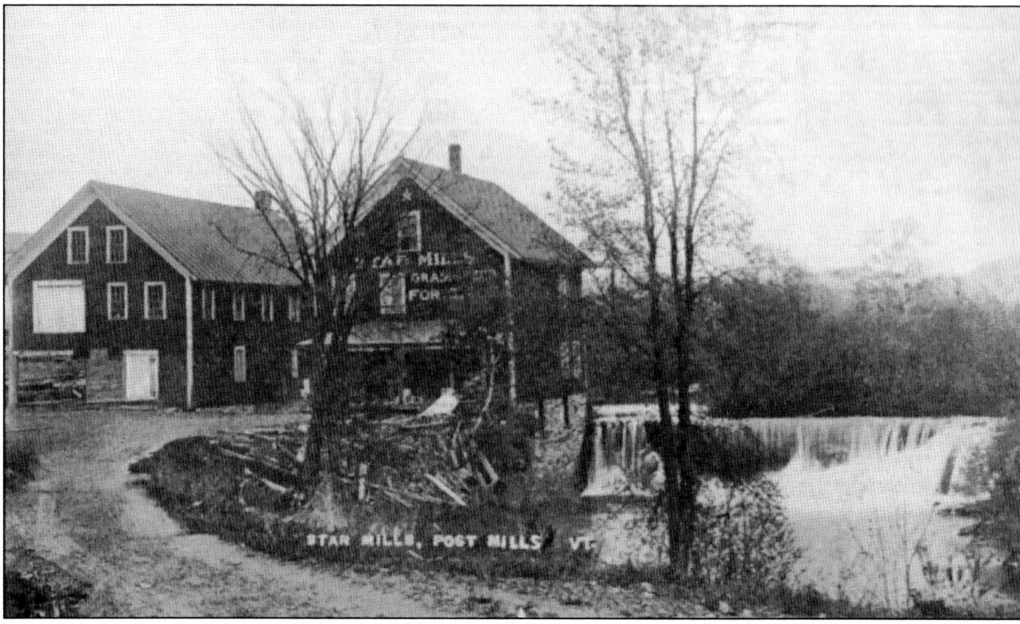

The flood of 1869 destroyed every mill on the Ompompanoosuc River. Many mills never recovered; a few, like the Star Mills, were built later. Star was a gristmill and sawmill that operated upstream from the Chubb factory. When the Star Mills burned in 1914, the fire was large enough that the roof of the Odd Fellows Lodge and the schoolhouse belfry briefly caught fire.

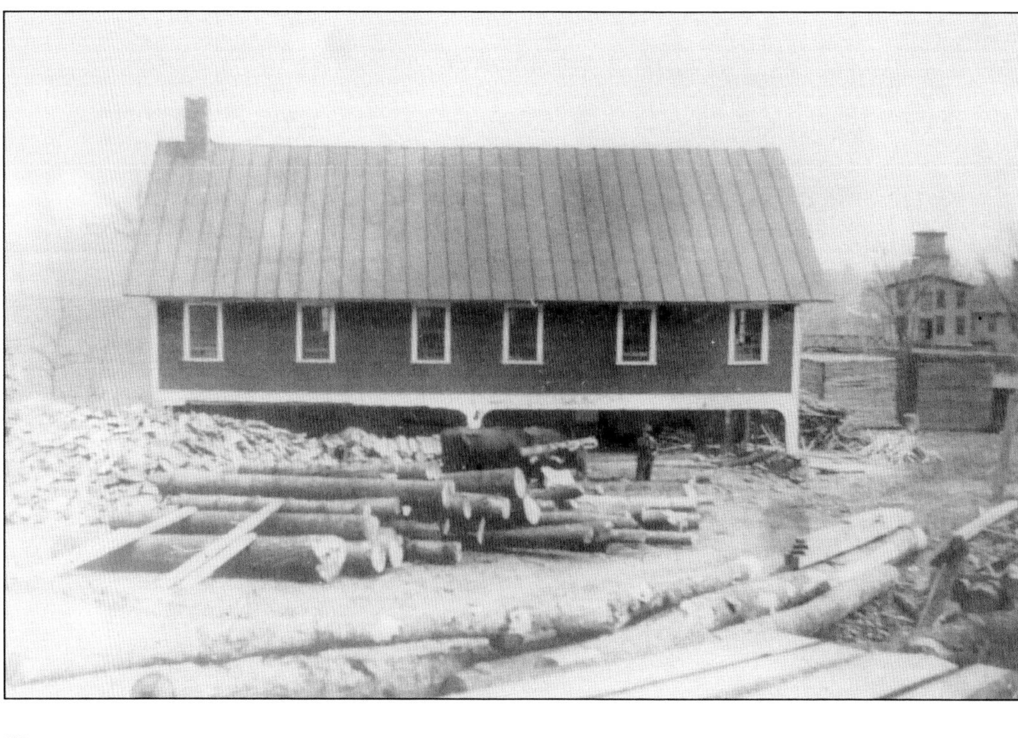

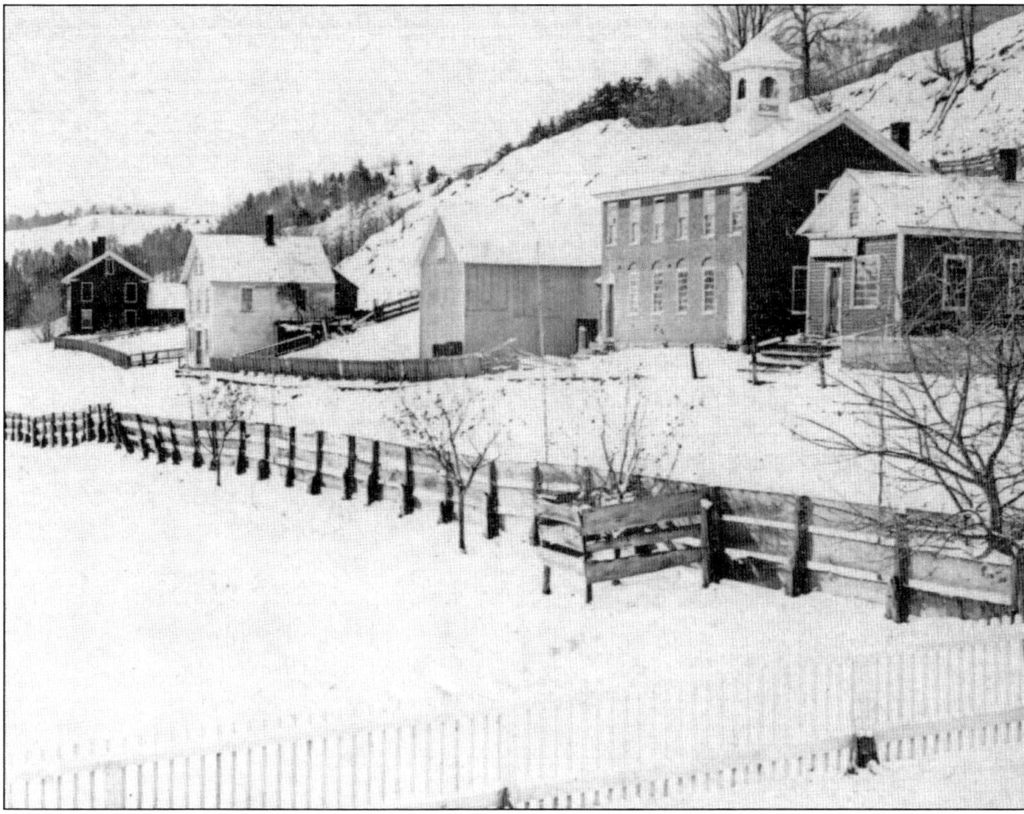

Above, on Route 113, south of the intersection with Route 244, from left to right, are the Kimball house, Rollin Hatch's general store and post office, the Taylor barn, schoolhouse no. 6, and Isaiah Colburn's harness shop. The second floor of the schoolhouse also originally accommodated the Odd Fellows, a singing school, and an apartment, though not all at once. Built in 1814, it was demolished (as pictured below) in 1885.

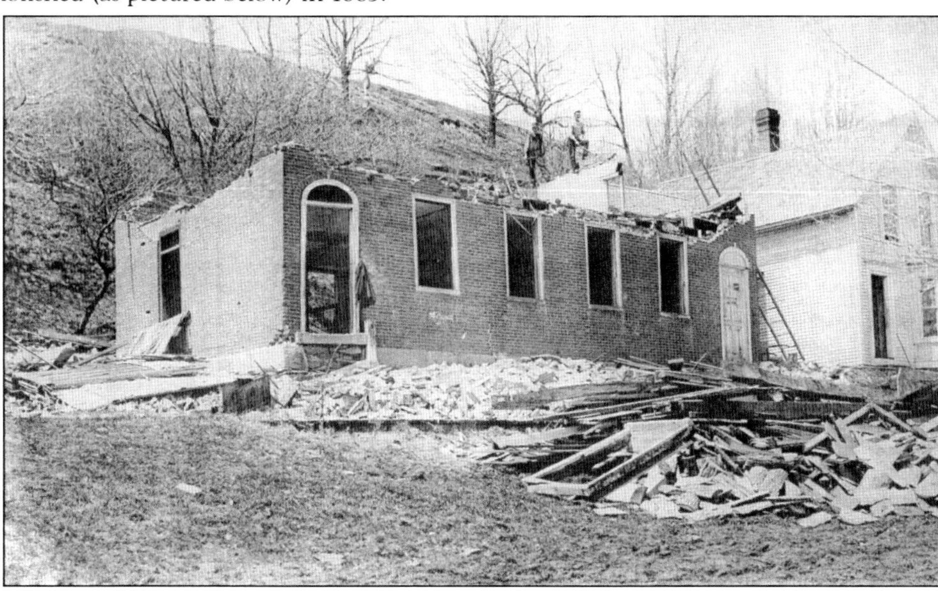

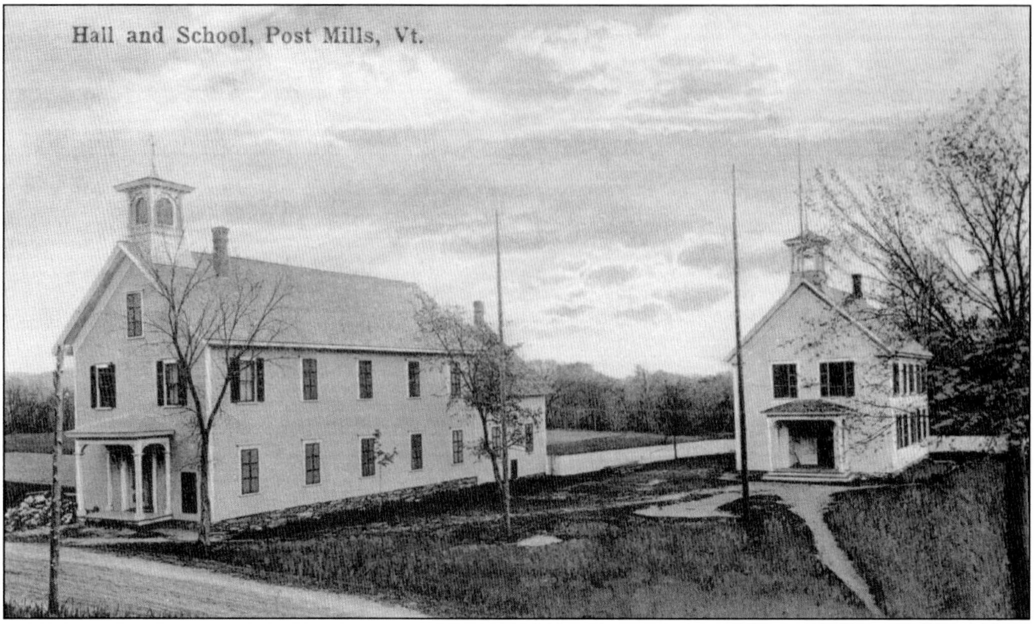

The Independent Order of Odd Fellows hall was built in the 1870s. The Odd Fellows and their sister lodge, the Rebekahs, met upstairs; a hall and stage were on the first floor. Next door was Post Mills's second schoolhouse. A larger schoolhouse replaced this one in 1941, which was closed in 1962 when the school district was consolidated.

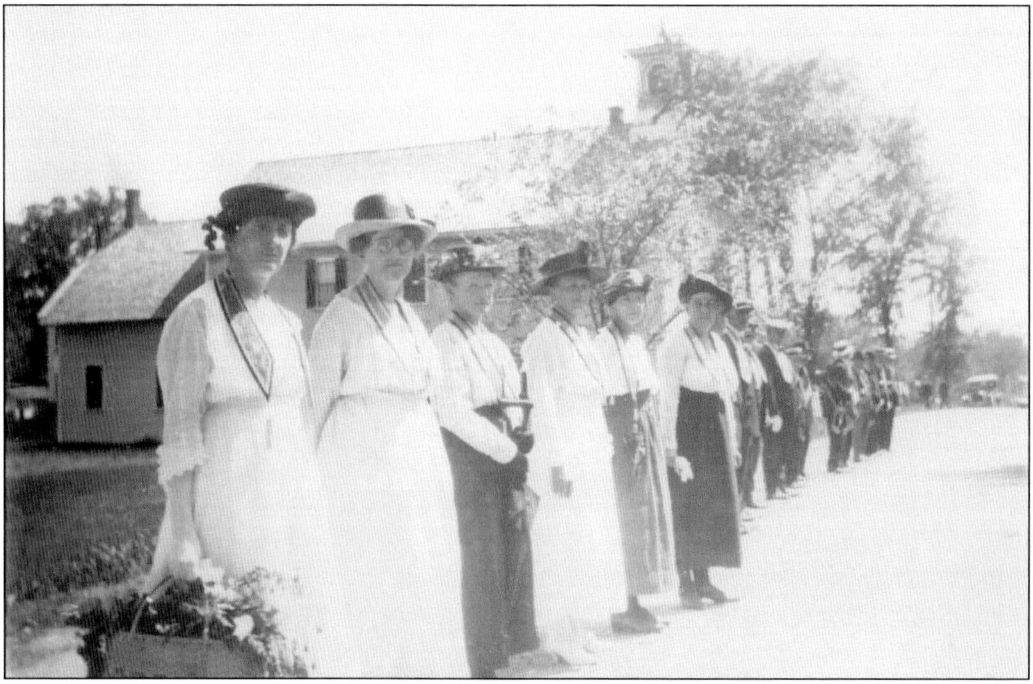

From left to right, Mary Johnson, Gladys Ward Buggee, Nettie Waterman, Florence Kent, Arlene Andrews, and Grace Stellman from the Rebekah Lodge line up at the Post Mills Fair around 1915. In the 19th century, the fair was held at the racetrack on Route 244, featuring a Ferris wheel and a merry-go-round.

Born around 1775, Prince Saunders was raised in Thetford by lawyer George Oramel Hinckley. Sponsored by Hinckley, Saunders attended the Indian Charity School at Dartmouth College and went from there to work at Boston's African School. Saunders became secretary for the African Masonic Lodge and founded the Belle Lettres Society, an integrated literary group. He negotiated for grants to support the creation of four more schools for black children. He supported the emigration of African Americans back to Africa, speaking across America and Europe for his cause. Saunders became the official courier to the emperor of Haiti, later publishing the *Haytian Papers*, the first translation of, and commentary on, Haiti's laws. He brought English teachers and vaccinations to Haiti, now convinced that Haiti, not Africa, was the best destination for free African Americans. Before his dream could be realized, there was a revolution in Haiti and the emperor committed suicide. Saunders lived in Haiti for the rest of his life, dying in 1839. (Public domain.)

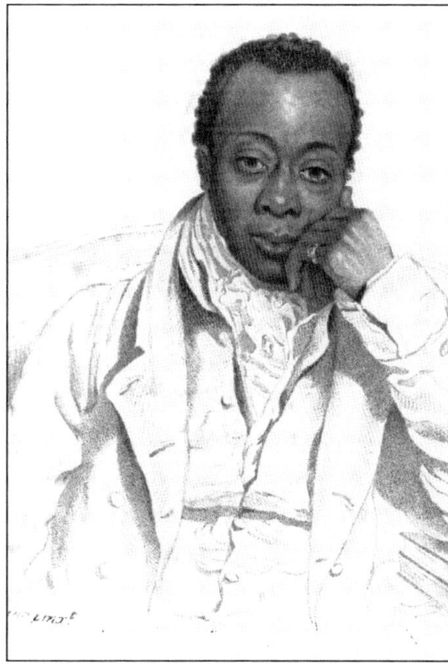

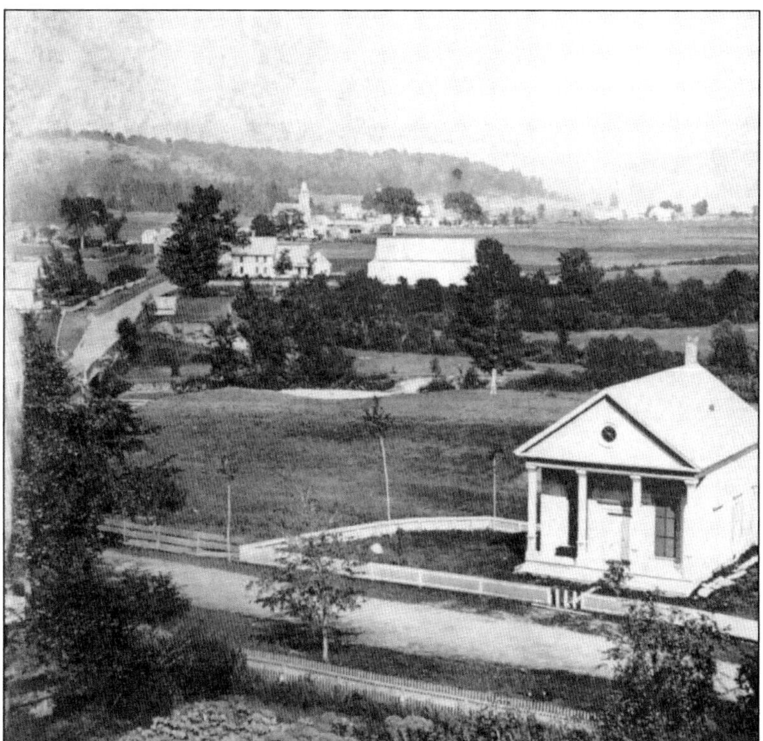

The 1866 Peabody Library is the oldest library building in Vermont. Philanthropist George Peabody, who funded its construction, spent some time as a boy in Post Mills with his relatives in the Dodge family before growing up to found the company that would become J.P. Morgan. He also funded Peabody Museums in Boston and Salem, Massachusetts.

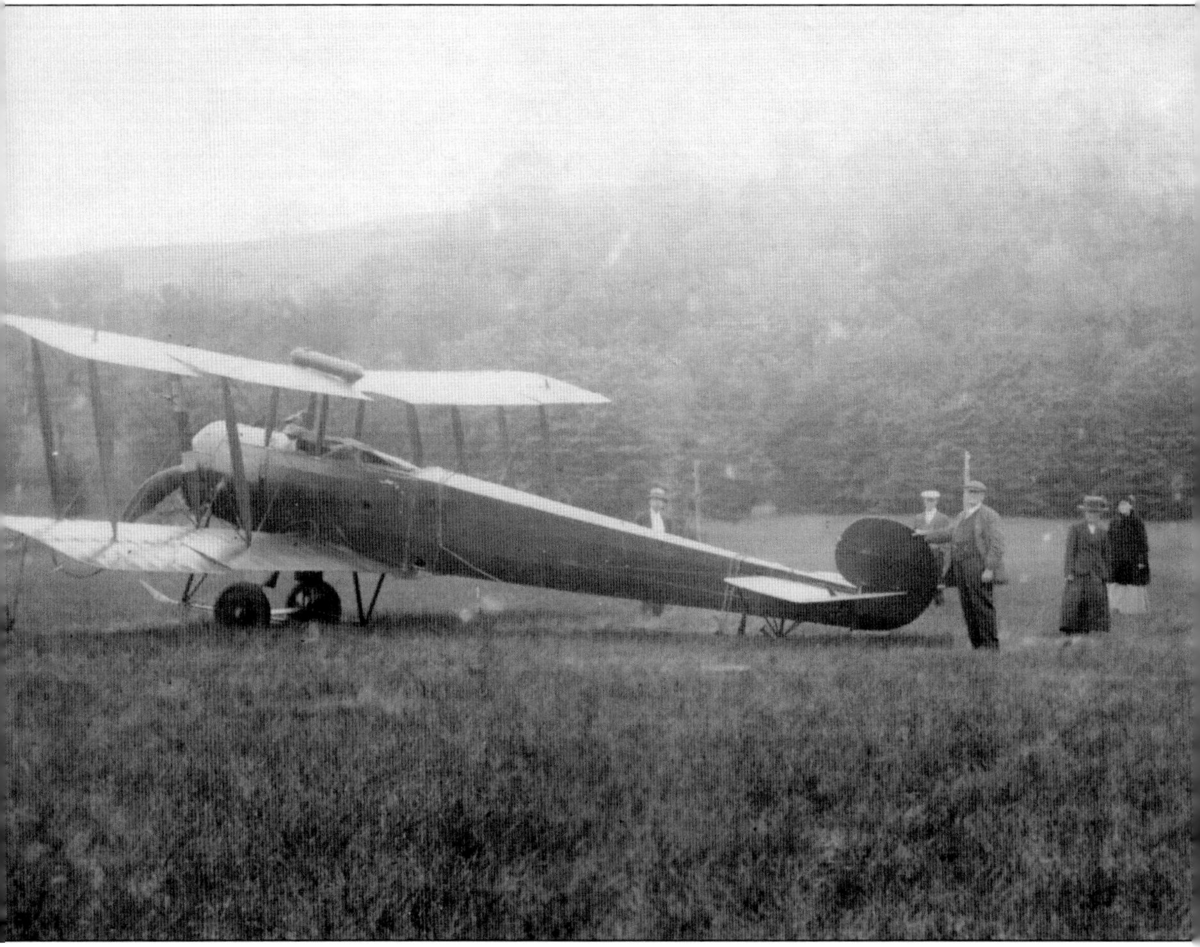

Aviation's long history in Post Mills might have started with an emergency landing by an Avro biplane in Florence Miller's field around 1920. Airports were scarce in those days, so even non-emergency landings in the nearest available field were common occurrences.

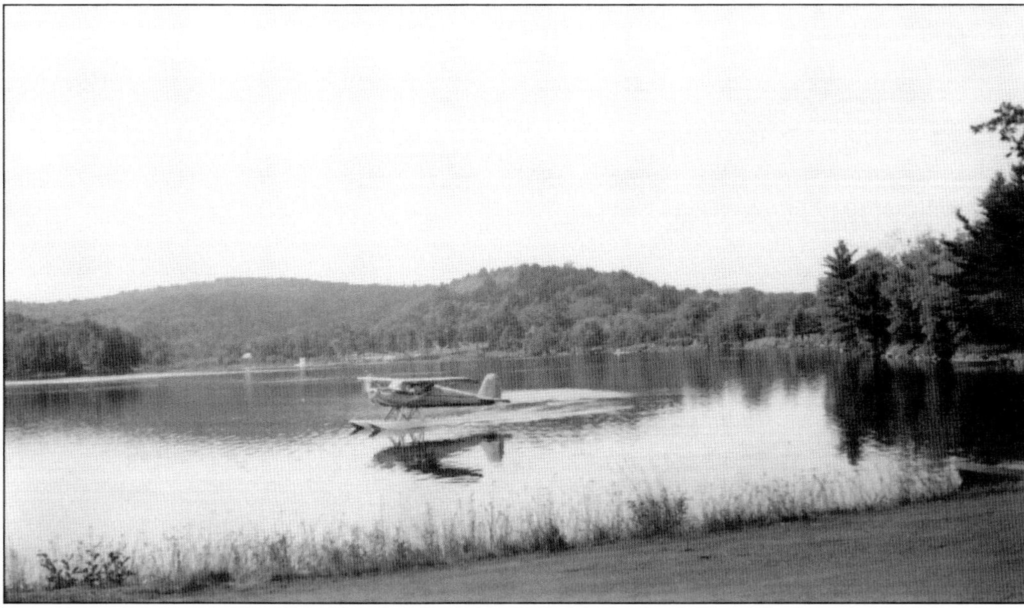

Post Mills is the only village in Thetford to boast an airport, as well as seaplane access on Lake Fairlee. The airport got its start in 1945 when Len Hoyt, a chicken farmer, took flying lessons in White River Junction and decided to open an airport in Post Mills. He and his friend Chuck Stoddard, a flight instructor, bought a Piper Cub and leased land on the MacFarlane farm for the runway. The first gliders appeared in the 1950s. After David and Babs Nutt bought the airport in 1978, Post Mills became famous for its soaring—not least because Babs herself held the world altitude record for sailplanes.

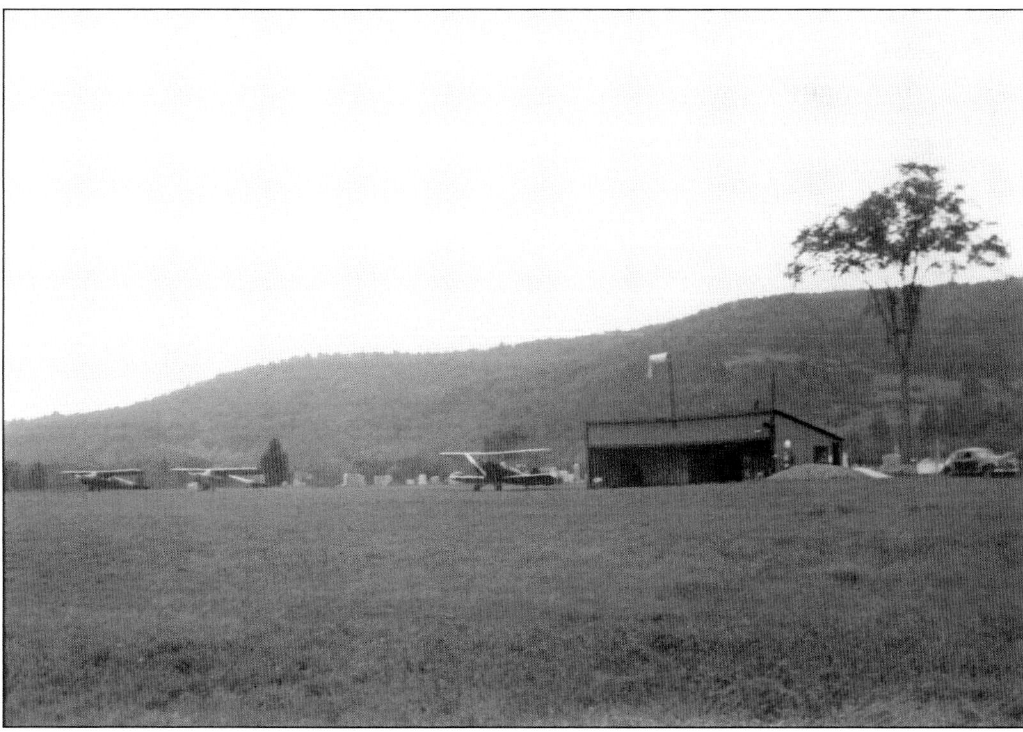

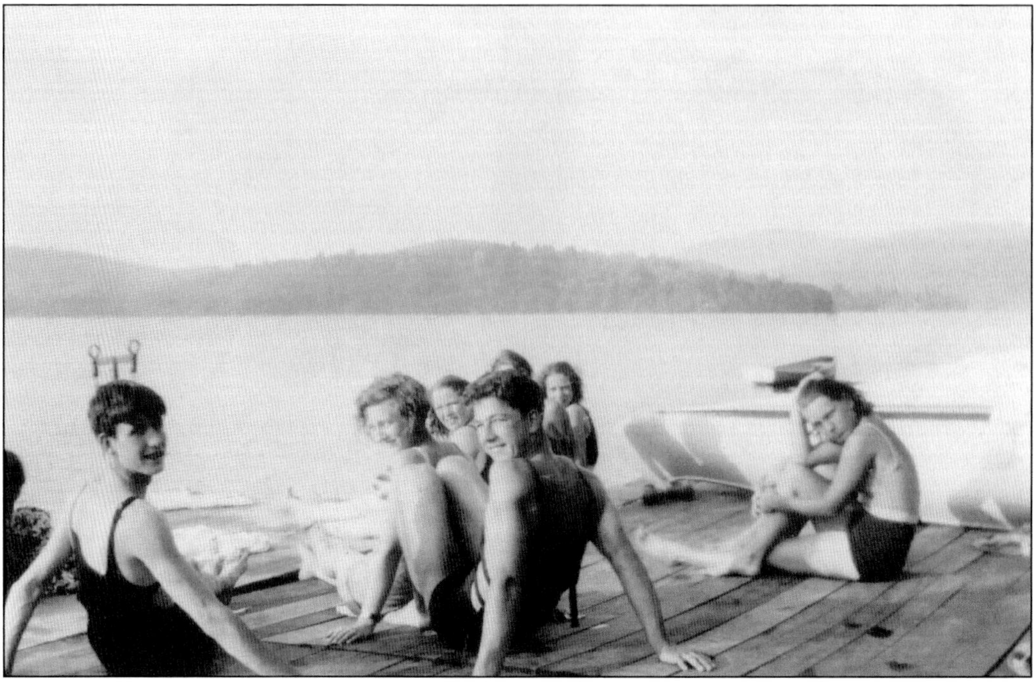

Campers lounge by Lake Fairlee in 1932. About half of the lake lies within Thetford's boundaries. Its shores were crammed with boys' and girls' camps in the camping craze of the early 1900s; some of those camps exist to this day, such as Lochearn and the Aloha camps. (Courtesy of the Aloha Foundation.)

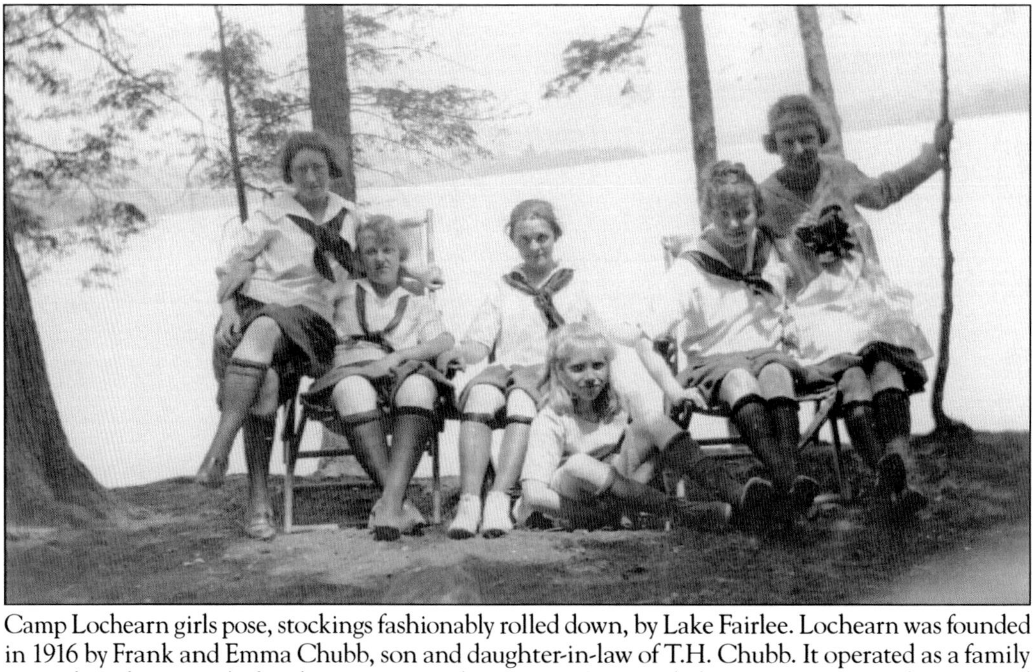

Camp Lochearn girls pose, stockings fashionably rolled down, by Lake Fairlee. Lochearn was founded in 1916 by Frank and Emma Chubb, son and daughter-in-law of T.H. Chubb. It operated as a family camp for a few years before becoming a girls' camp at Emma's behest. Campers' uniforms—and camp traditions—had a decidedly Scottish flavor. (Courtesy of the Aloha Foundation.)

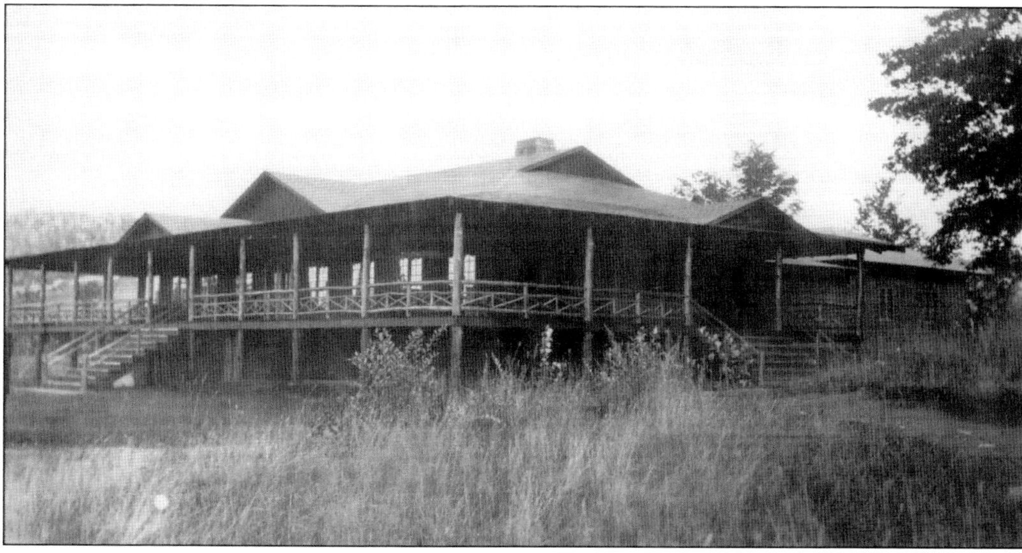

Shanty Shane, later Camp Ohana, opened in 1911 for the families of those at nearby camps. Below, campers ride in Shanty Shane's famous oxcart (Courtesy of the West Fairlee Historical Society.)

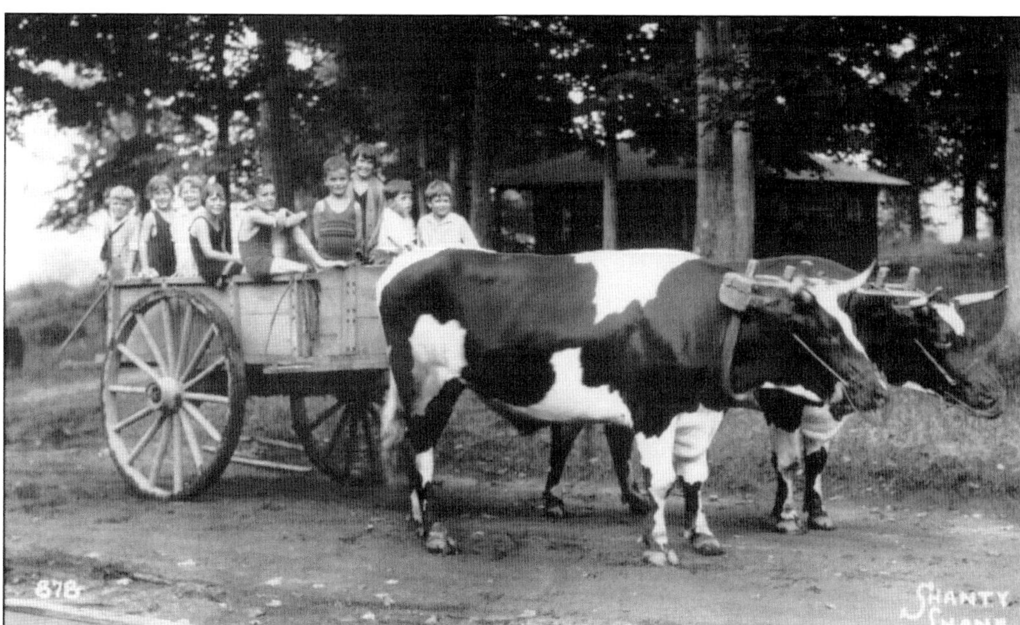

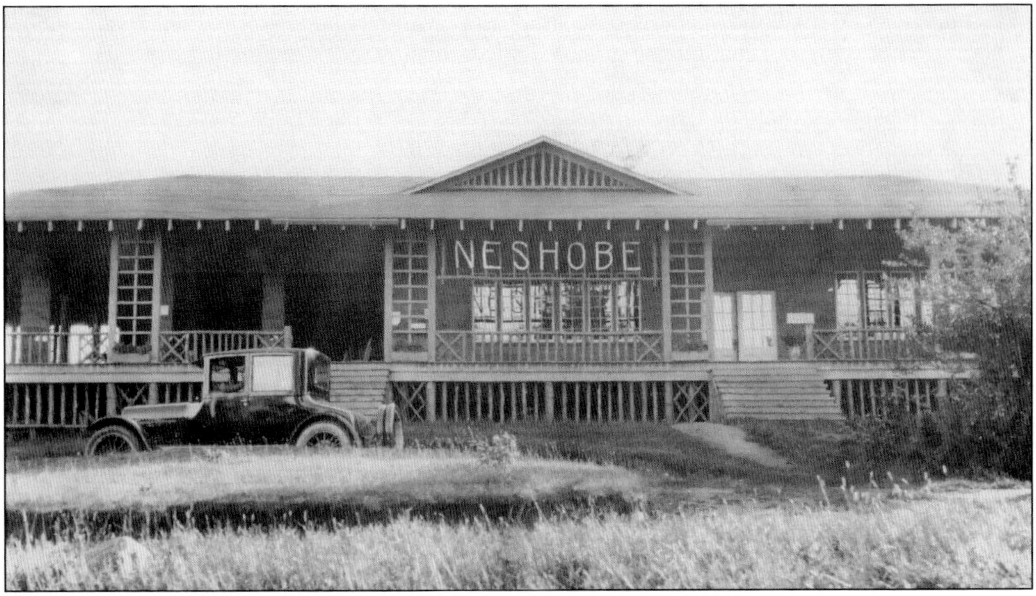

Camp Neshobe was established in 1921 by Mr. and Mrs. Edward G. Osgood. At first, it was open exclusively to girls; it later became Camp Norway for boys. (Courtesy of the West Fairlee Historical Society.)

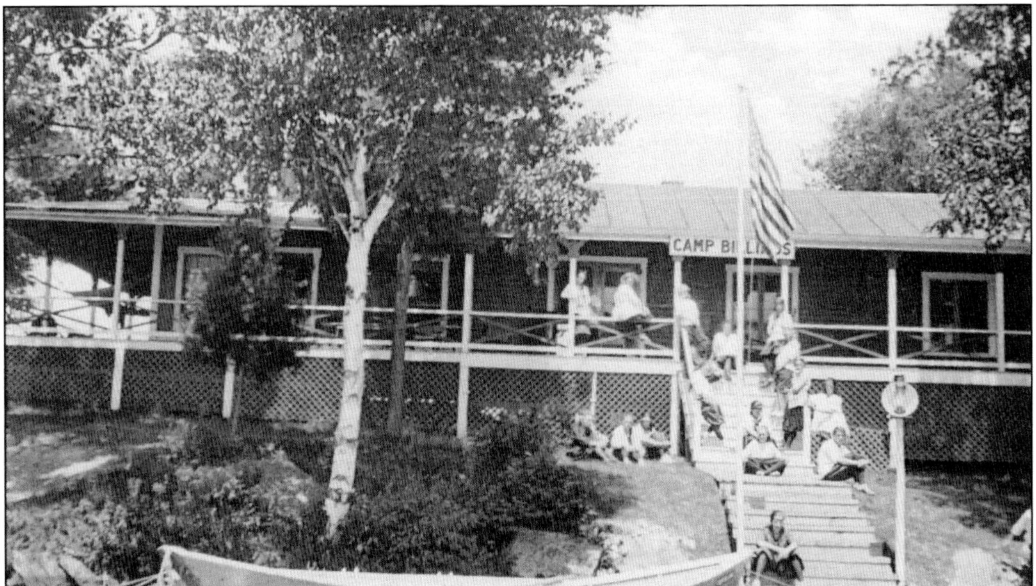

Camp Billings started as a YMCA camp in 1906 for Windsor County residents. The land was a gift from the Billings family of Woodstock. In 1915, the camp split its season: one half for boys, the other for girls. The camp expanded in 1916, and the distinctive clock tower was added in 1921. (Courtesy of University of Vermont Special Collections.)

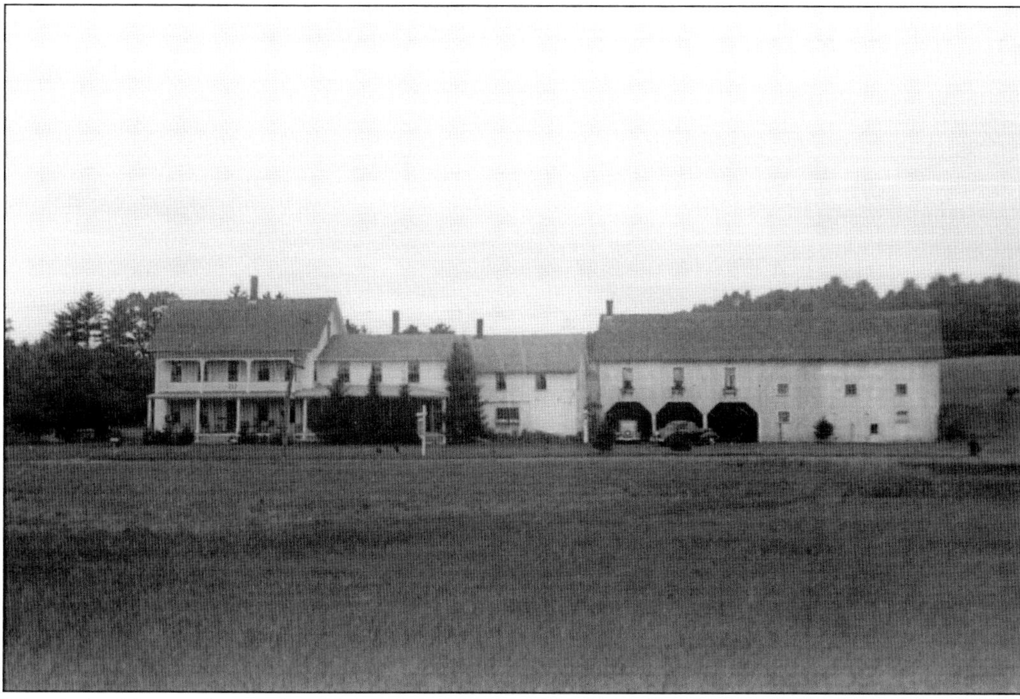

The Lake House, located at the corner of Route 244 and Lakeshore Road, was originally a summer hotel. One of its more famous guests was the Massachusetts artist and art teacher William Bartholomew, who came often to Post Mills to paint.

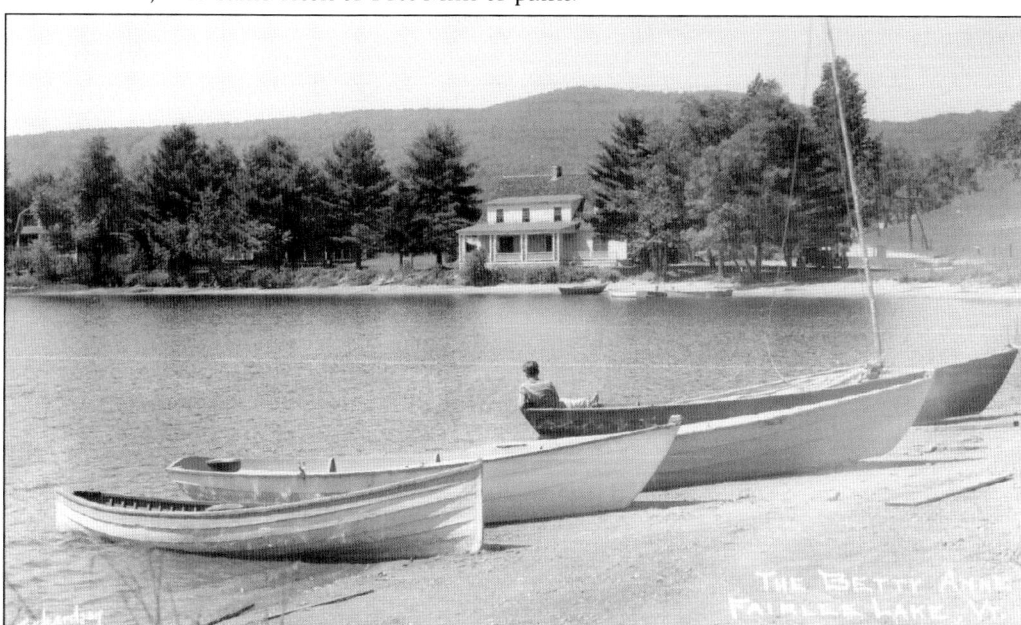

In the early days of the Betty Anne tearoom and inn (later the Cross Roads), situated at the corner of Route 244 and Lakeshore Road, visitors could take steamboat rides around Lake Fairlee on Howard Tibbetts's *Gypsy*. The Betty Anne was a haven for lake campers—and after hours, their counselors—until it closed in 1942.

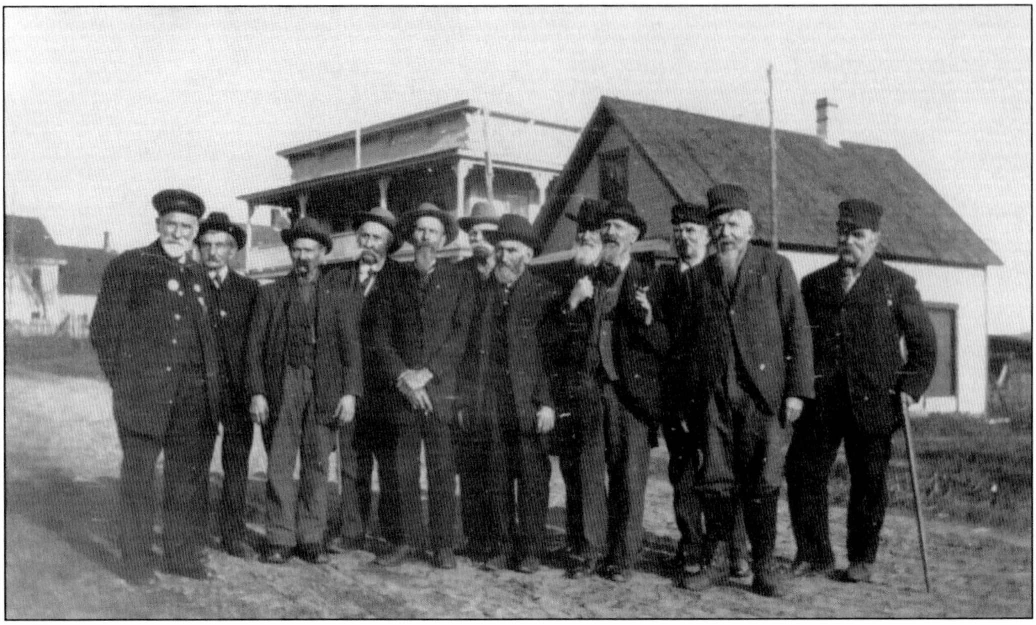

Civil War veterans gather in Post Mills. Perhaps Thetford's most famous Civil War veteran was Gustavus Loomis, one of the oldest soldiers to serve in the war. Loomis retired with the rank of brevet brigadier general. Fellow veteran and Thetford Academy graduate Thomas Chester was the only African American journalist to write about the war for a major daily newspaper.

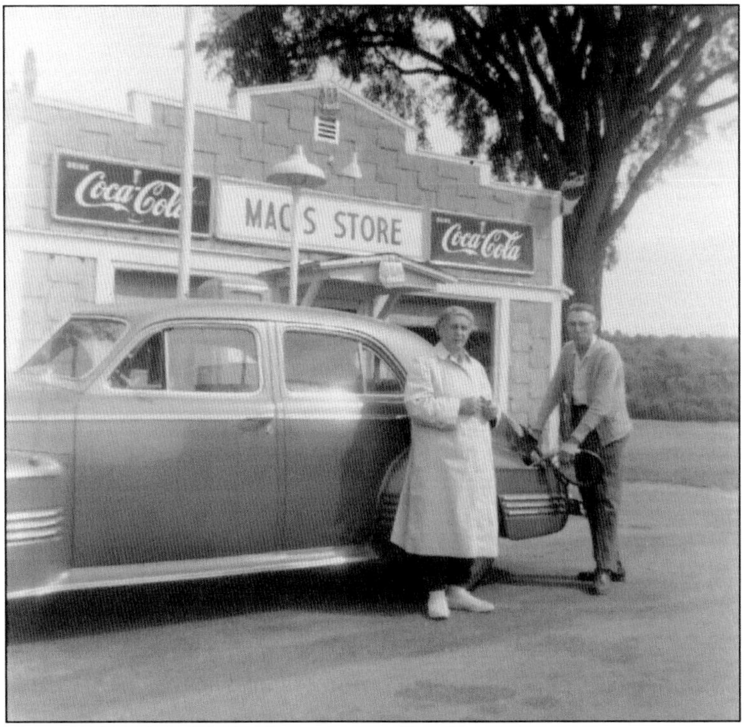

A woman gets a fill-up in 1961 at Pearly MacFarlane's store, a small store and gas station next to the Post Mills Congregational Church. A longtime resident of Post Mills, MacFarlane had been a farmer most of his life until changing careers.

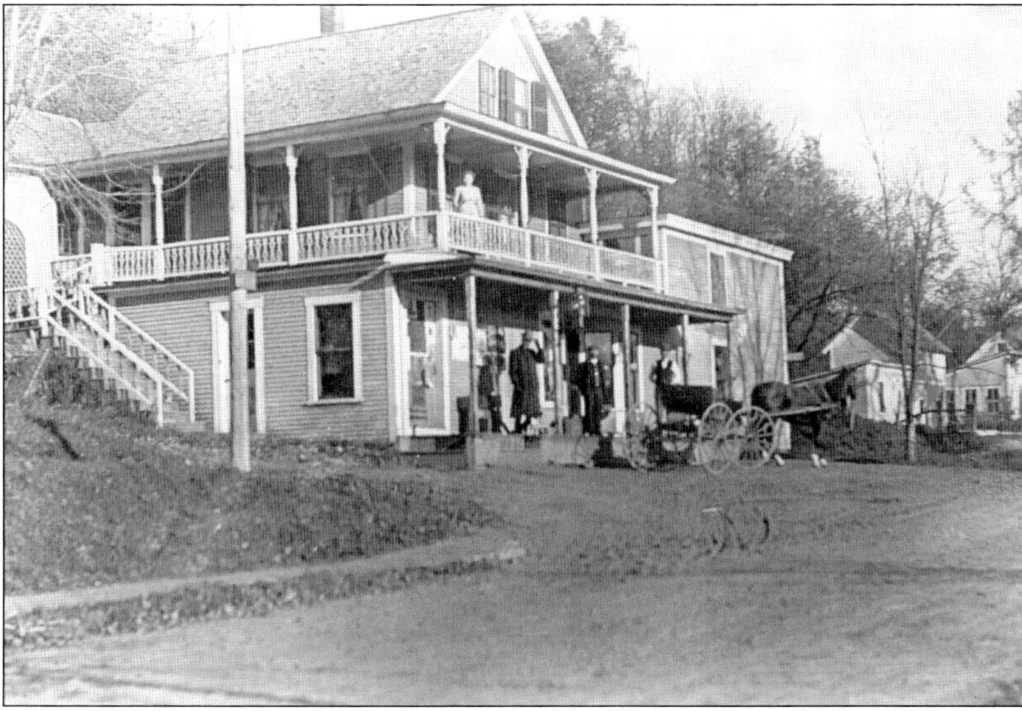

Rollin Hatch's general store is pictured above; below is the Burr & Campbell Store and post office on Route 113.

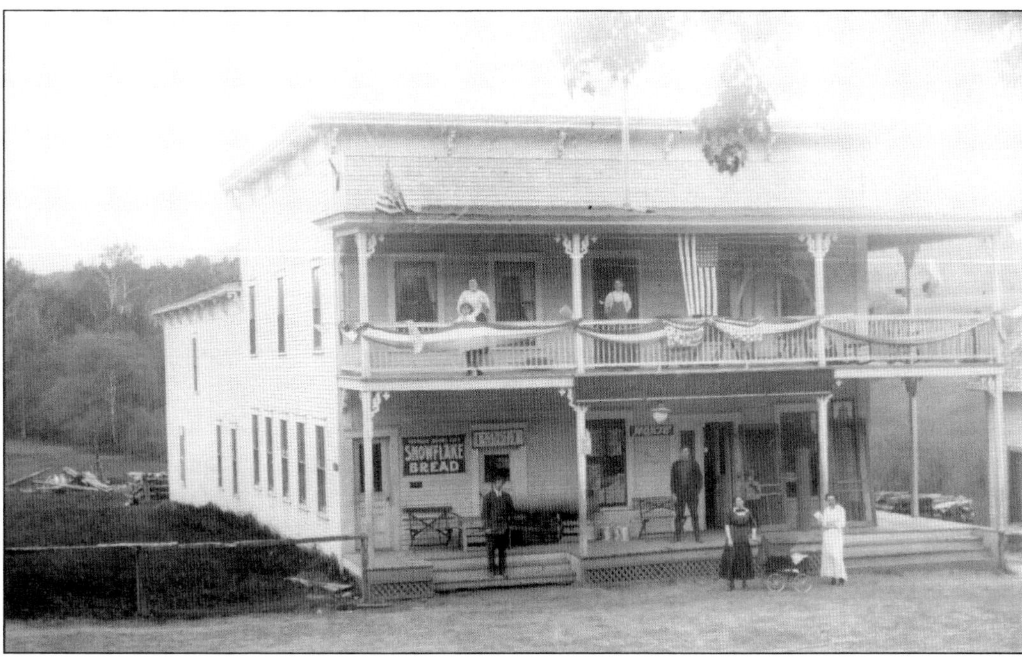

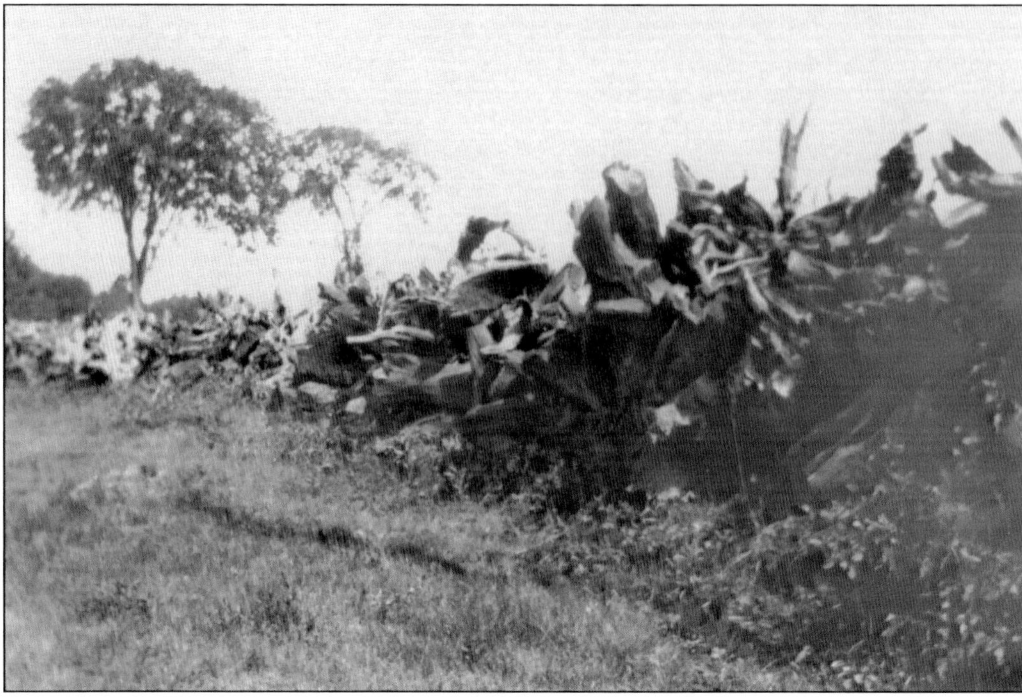

Just as stone walls were created by the necessity of removing rocks from fields, stump fences were once a common sight in Thetford because farmers needed a place to put the thousands of stumps they wrested from the land. They were particularly prevalent on the early Post Mills plain, which had few rocks but lots of trees.

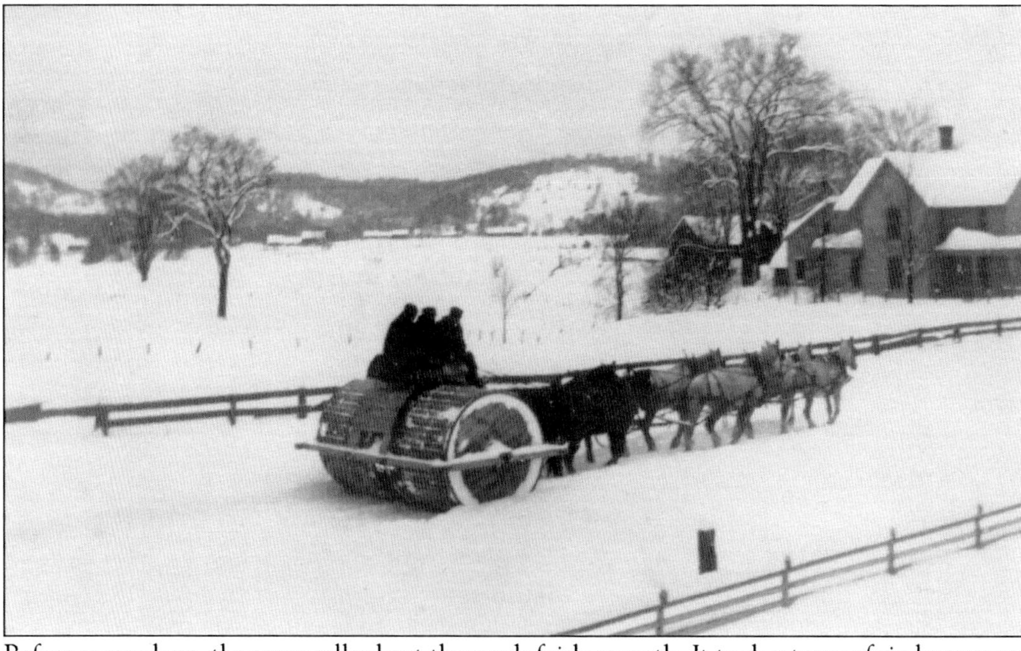

Before snow plows, the snow roller kept the roads fairly smooth. It took a team of six horses and had a tendency to slide into ditches. Covered bridges were another matter: to allow sleighs to travel through them, snow had to be added to make the surface passable.

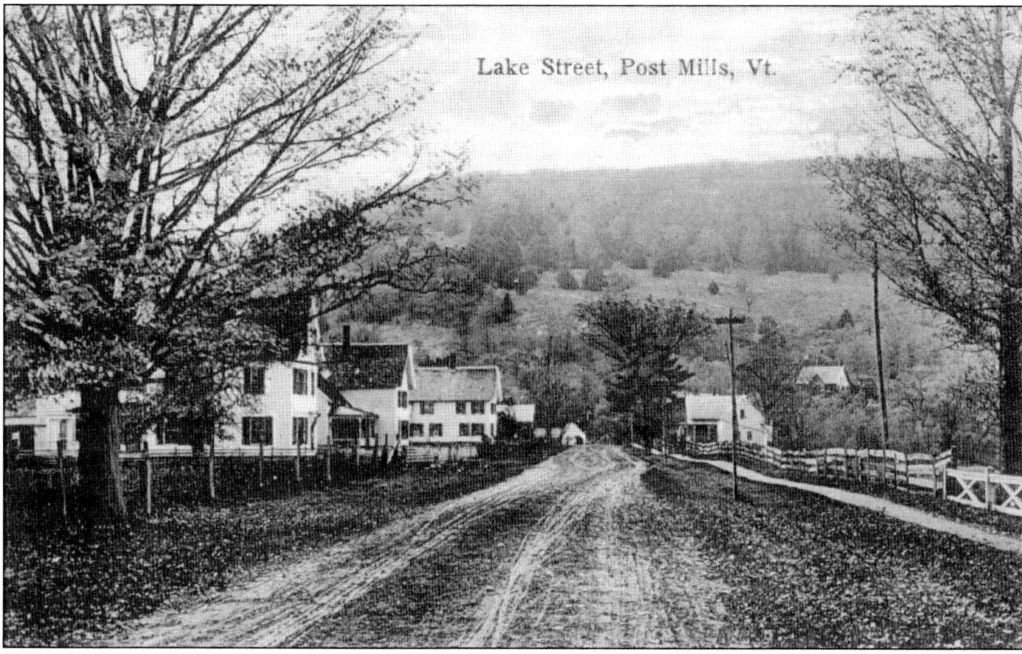

The view down Lake Street in Post Mills has not changed much over the years. (Courtesy of Frank J. Barrett Jr.)

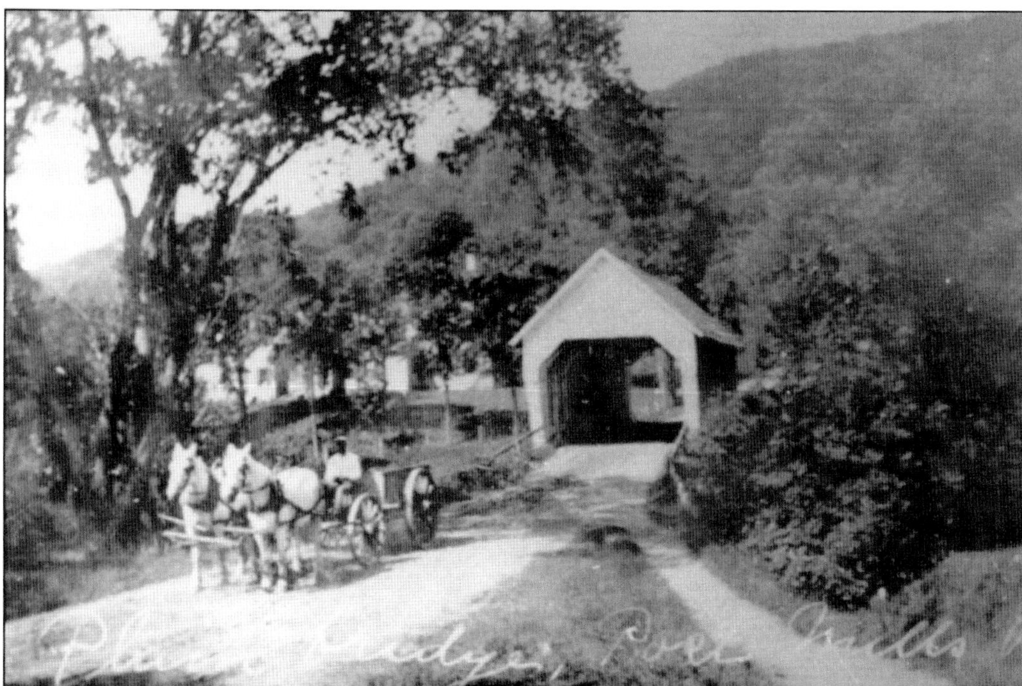

There was once a covered bridge, built in 1878, near the junction of Routes 113 and 244 in Post Mills.

Christmas Entertainment

AND

TREE!

POST MILLS, VERMONT,

MONDAY EVENING, DECEMBER 26TH, 1881.

PROGRAMME

POST MILLS CORNET BAND,	"Iona Quick Step."
SINGING,	"Merrily Coming," by Sabbath School Children.
REMARKS,	By Rev. Mr. McColom.
RECITATION,	Miss Myrtie Lyon.
POST MILLS CORNET BAND,	Waltz, Birthday.
DIALOGUE,	By Eight little Girls, "Blessed are the Peace Makers."
SINGING,	"Angel Voices."
RECITATION,	By Master Edward Dodge.
DIALOGUE,	By Seven Boys, "True Manliness."
POST MILLS CORNET BAND,	Quick Step, "When you and I were young, Maggie."
RECITATION,	By Sunday School Children.
"SINGING 'ROUND THE CHRISTMAS TREE,"	By Sunday School Children.
DIALOGUE,	"Ten Little Lazy Boys."
DIALOGUE,	By Eight Young Ladies, "Goddess of Liberty."
POST MILLS CORNET BAND,	"Forest Polka."
SINGING,	"Little Reapers," by Children,
BROOM DRILL,	

DISTRIBUTION OF PRESENTS.

An 1881 Christmas concert in Post Mills culminated in a broom drill, a performance popular in post–Civil War America in which young women conducted military drill maneuvers with brooms.

Four

ELY

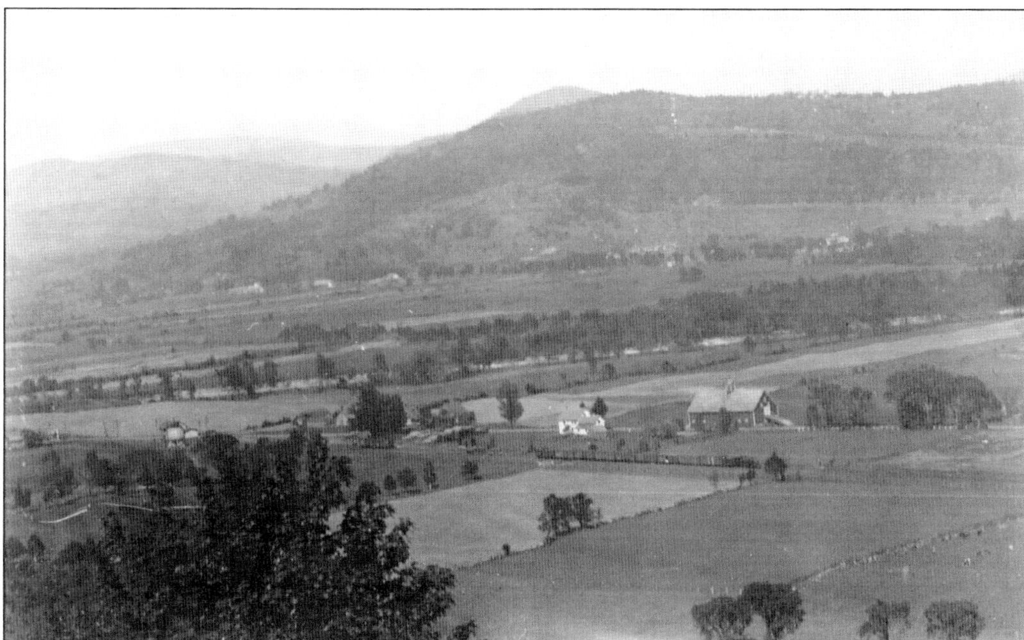

The Fairlee/Thetford town line runs through the middle of Ely, once a bustling depot village. It was originally known as both South Fairlee and Ware's Crossing, named after a prosperous landowner in the early days of the railroad. When Smith Ely bought the copper mine in Vershire (itself briefly renamed Ely) and began shipping from the village, the railroad began to refer to the village as Ely Station, although the post office stubbornly clung to South Fairlee. Smith Ely's mining operation failed, though the village did eventually change its name to Ely in 1927. In this photograph, the Ely Station water tower is visible toward the left, and the George farm is to the right. (Courtesy of Frank J. Barrett Jr.)

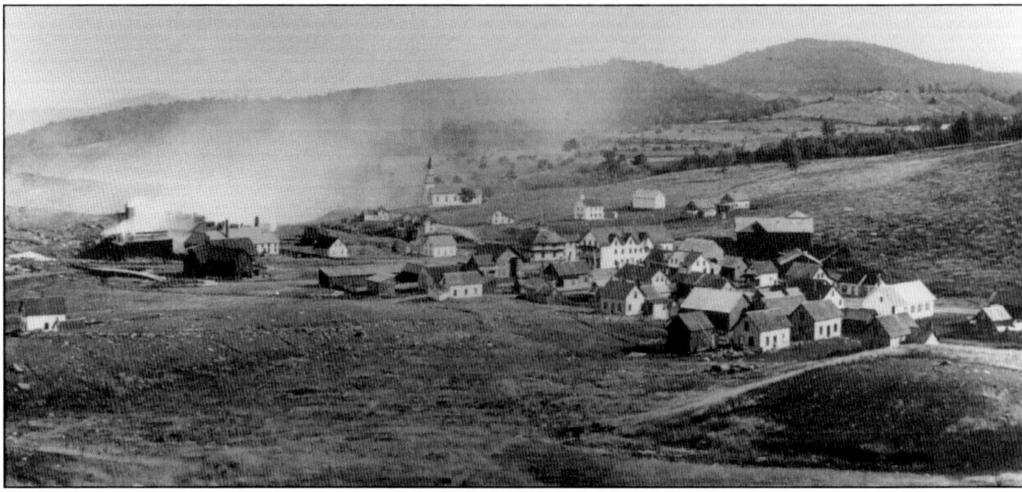

Once surrounded by a bustling mining town called Copperfield, Vershire's mine operated from 1854 to 1883. An important but little-known turning point for the mine stands as a significant moment in Vermont labor relations history. In June 1883, after working for two months without pay and under poor working conditions, the miners went on strike against the Vermont Copper Mining Company and its owner, Smith Ely. Gov. John L. Barstow called in 184 soldiers from the National Guard, who found not an angry mob but a quiet village full of unhappy miners. When the soldiers heard the miners' stories, they gave them their food and got back on the train. In the end, the company went bankrupt, and the Environmental Protection Agency later designated the mine a Superfund site. (Courtesy of University of Vermont Special Collections.)

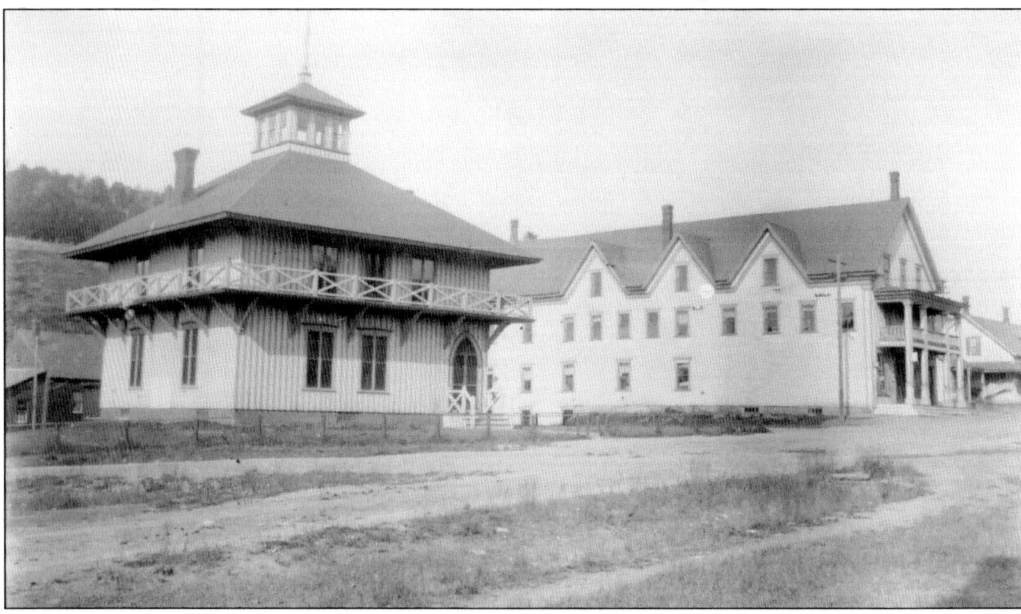

Smith Ely's grandson, Ely Goddard, owned a mansion in Copperfield called Elysium. He held elegant parties at his home and enjoyed a private theater and the music of an imported orchestra. After the mining company collapsed and the town folded, the house was moved. Many of Copperfield's buildings were moved; some went to West Fairlee to help it rebuild after downtown fires, and some, like Elysium, dotted the shores of Lake Fairlee. (Courtesy of University of Vermont Special Collections.)

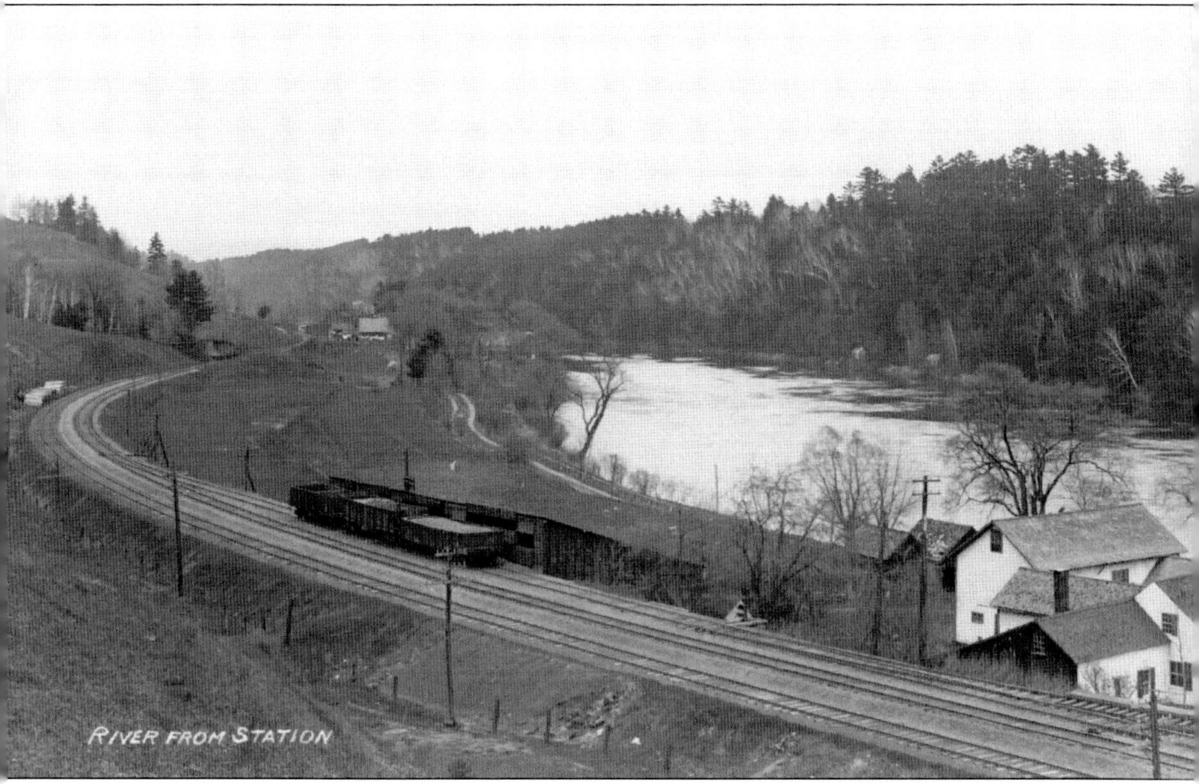

Copper from Vershire was hauled down to Ely Station and loaded into cars like these at the Pompanoosuc station in Norwich, where ore was loaded from the Elizabeth Mine in Strafford. (Courtesy of University of Vermont Special Collections.)

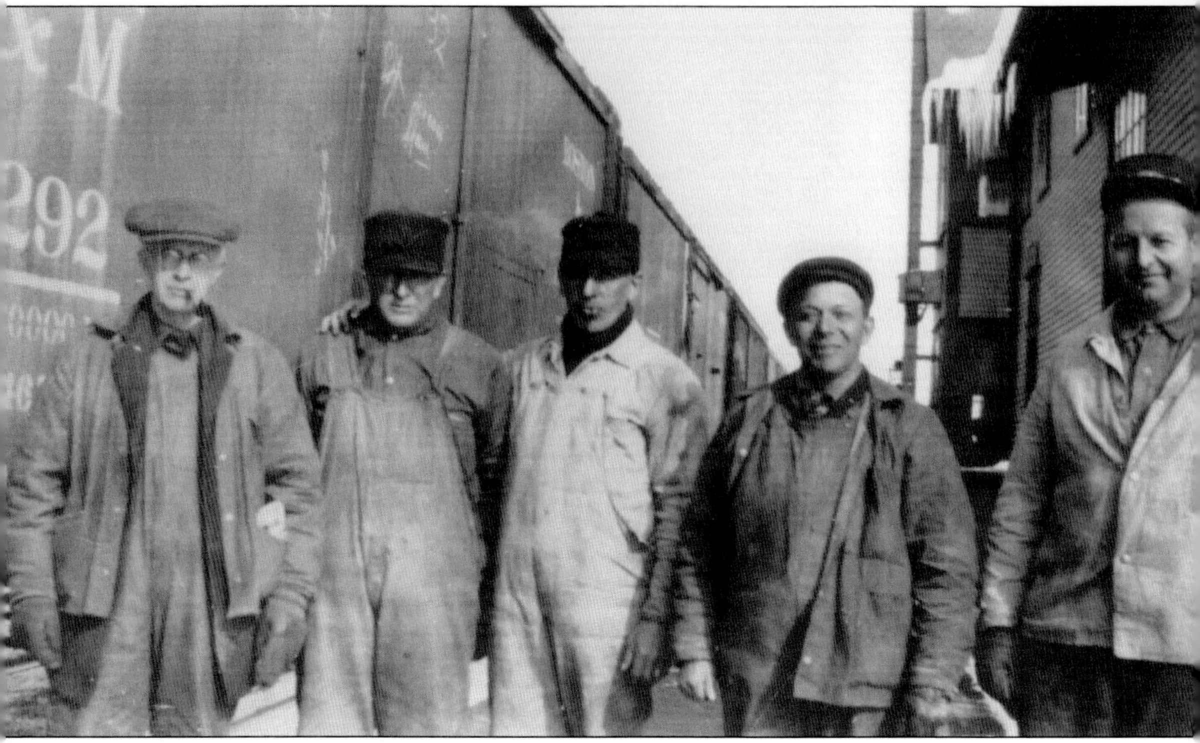

Ely station agent Banks Winslow (at right) poses with a Boston & Maine Railroad freight train crew at Ely Station. (Courtesy of Frank J. Barrett Jr.)

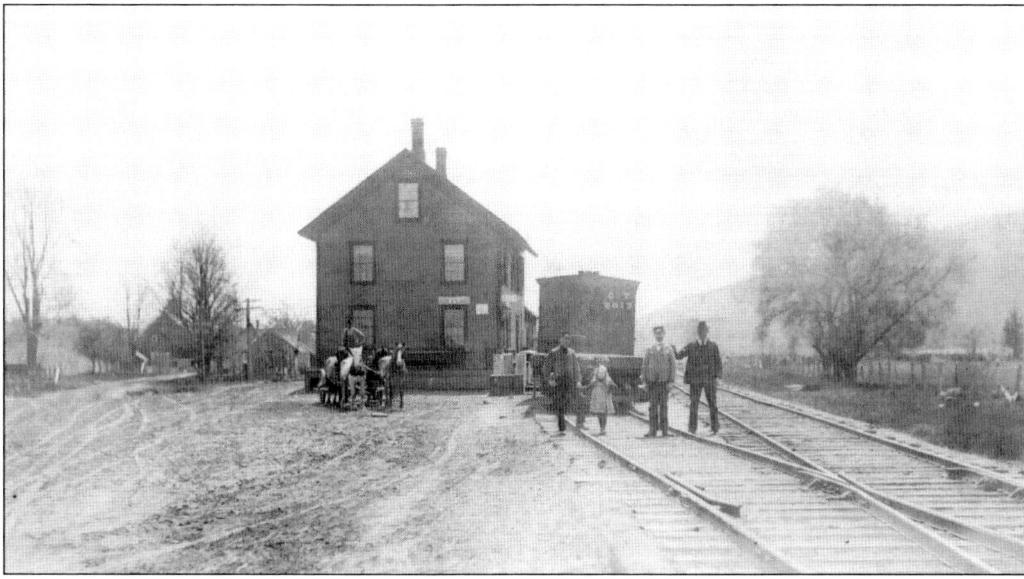

The original Ely depot stood on the site of an 1830 schoolhouse, which stood until 1871, when the schoolhouse was sold to the railroad to make way for this building. In a town meeting, Ely's thrifty residents made sure that in the sale, the town would be allowed to keep the schoolhouse's bricks and granite. At far left is Selah George's barn. Between the barn and depot are sheds used to store coke for the Ely copper mines. The depot burned in 1901. (Courtesy of Frank J. Barrett Jr.)

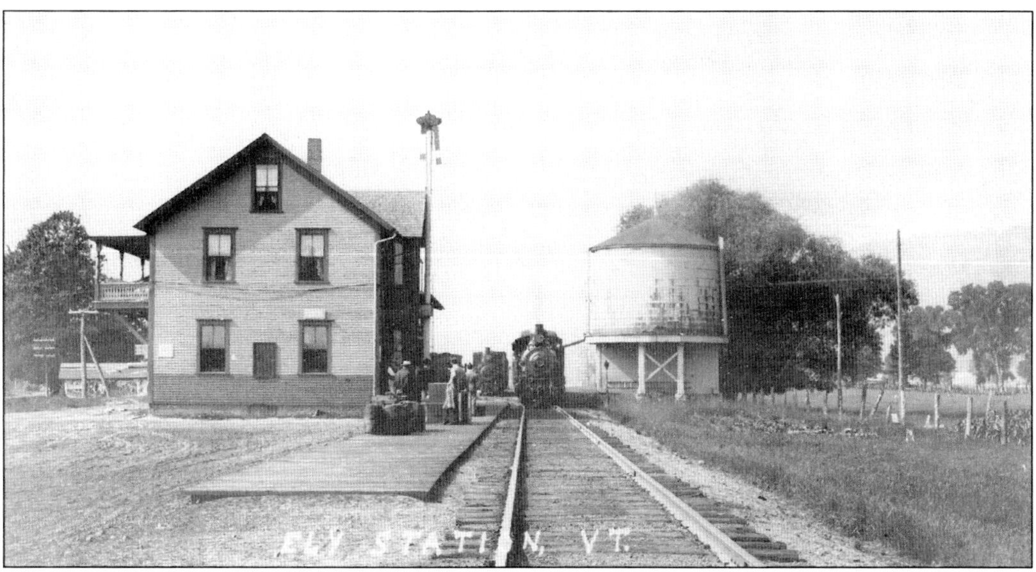

This is a 1919 photograph of the second Ely Station. It operated until 1958, when due to declining business, the Boston & Maine Railroad Corporation closed the depot. (Courtesy of Frank J. Barrett Jr.)

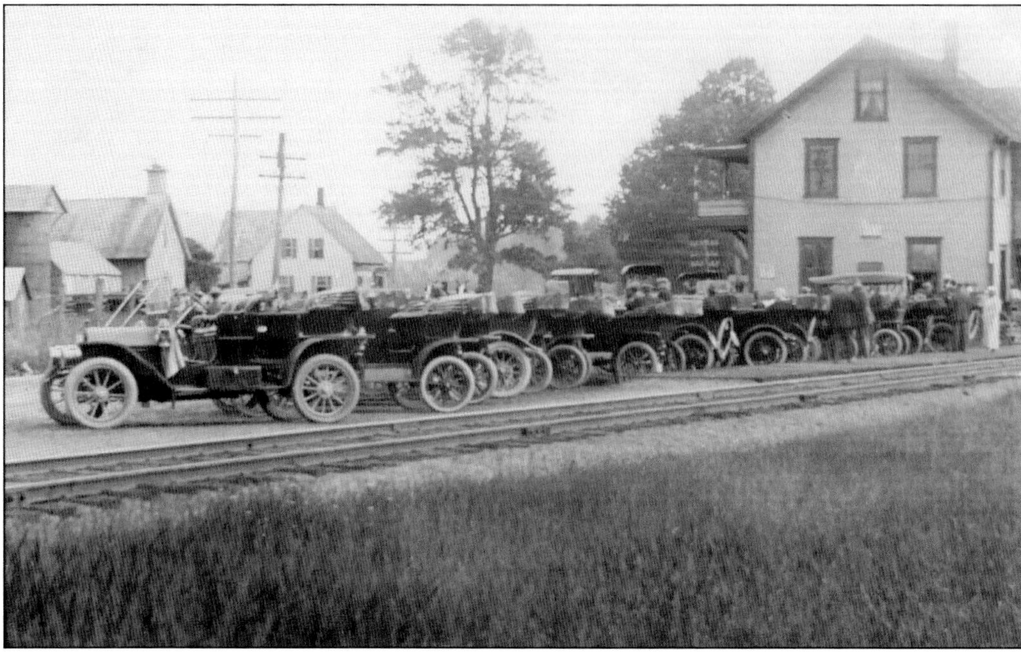

Cars line up at Ely Station, waiting to take campers to their destinations on Lake Fairlee on July 1, 1914. Enough young people thronged Thetford's summer camps that special trains were enlisted to bring them in from New England's population centers. If a nearby resident had a car, he could make good money ferrying campers to and from the train station or to church on Sundays.

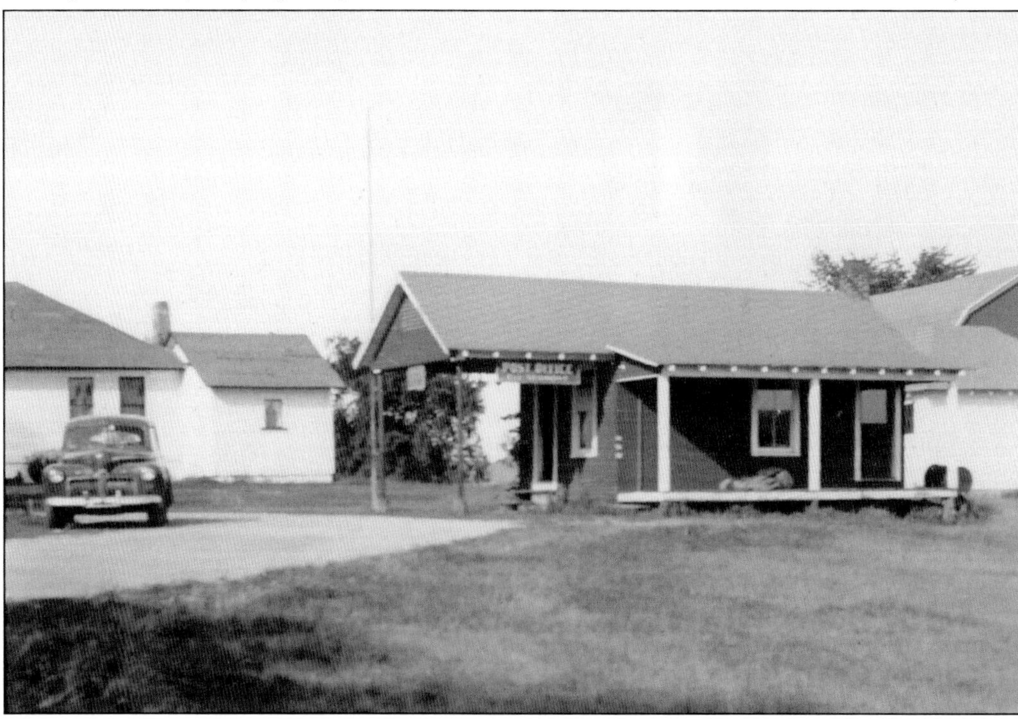

The Ely post office was once located across the street from the railroad station, next to Ely's grain store.

Five

North Thetford

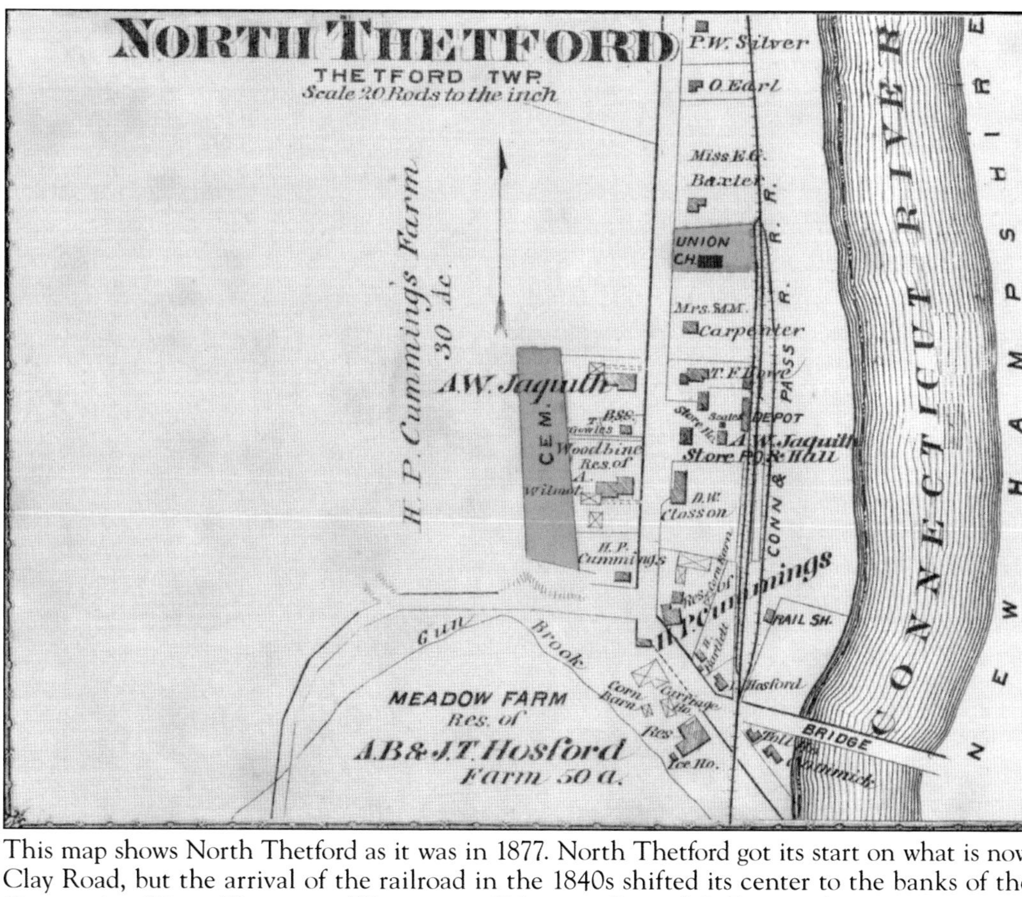

This map shows North Thetford as it was in 1877. North Thetford got its start on what is now Clay Road, but the arrival of the railroad in the 1840s shifted its center to the banks of the Connecticut River. (Courtesy of University of Vermont Special Collections.)

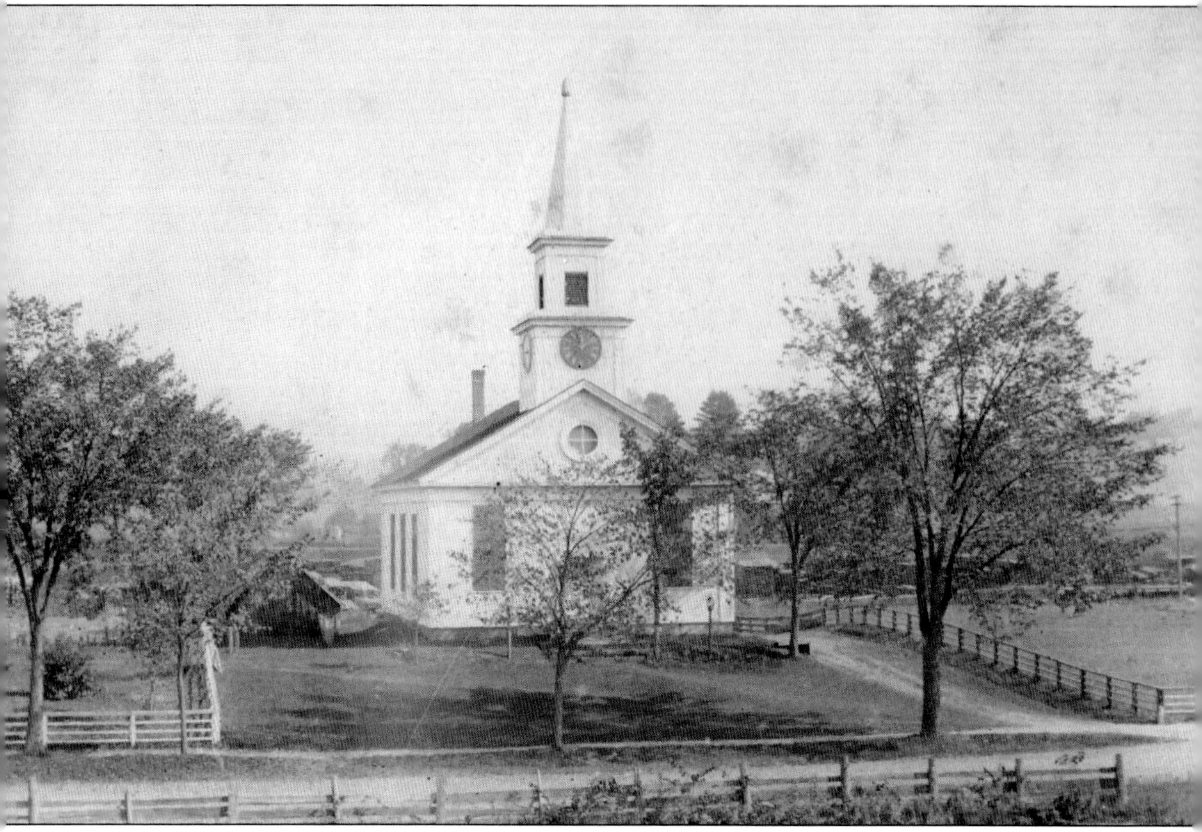

Look closely—the 1860 North Thetford Federated Church (now the United Church of Thetford) has a pineapple atop the steeple. It represents friendship, symbolizing the partnership from 1860 to 1913 when the church hosted Methodist Episcopal and Congregational services on alternate Sundays.

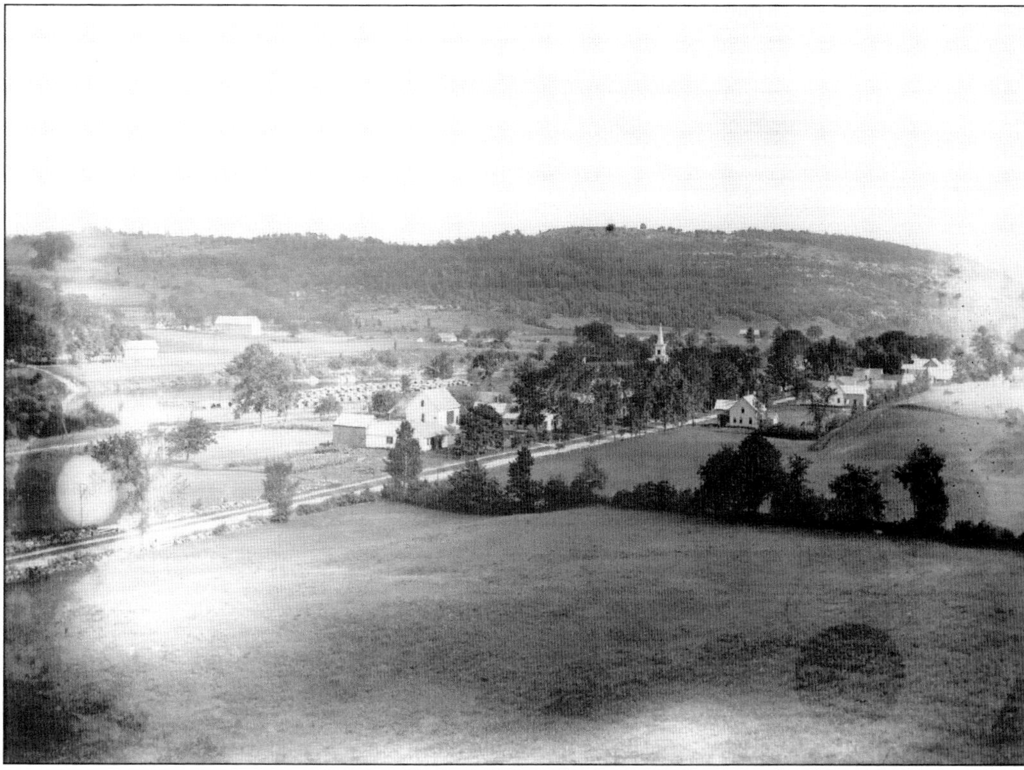

This undated photograph is a bird's-eye view of North Thetford looking southeast. (Courtesy of Lyme Historians.)

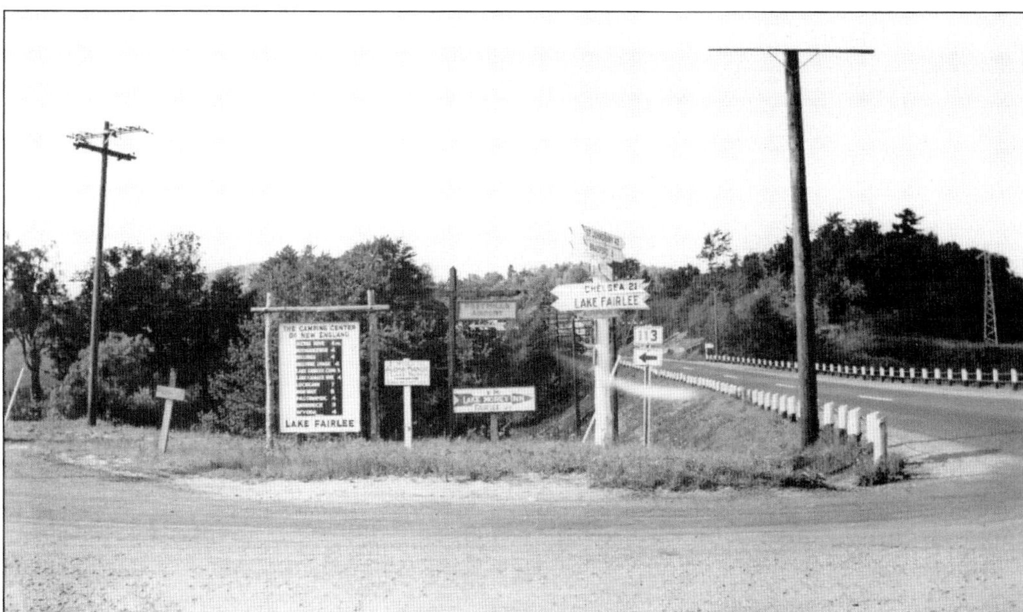

The crossroads at the corner of Routes 244 and 5 was an important intersection when Route 5 was eastern Vermont's main road for tourists and campers from points south.

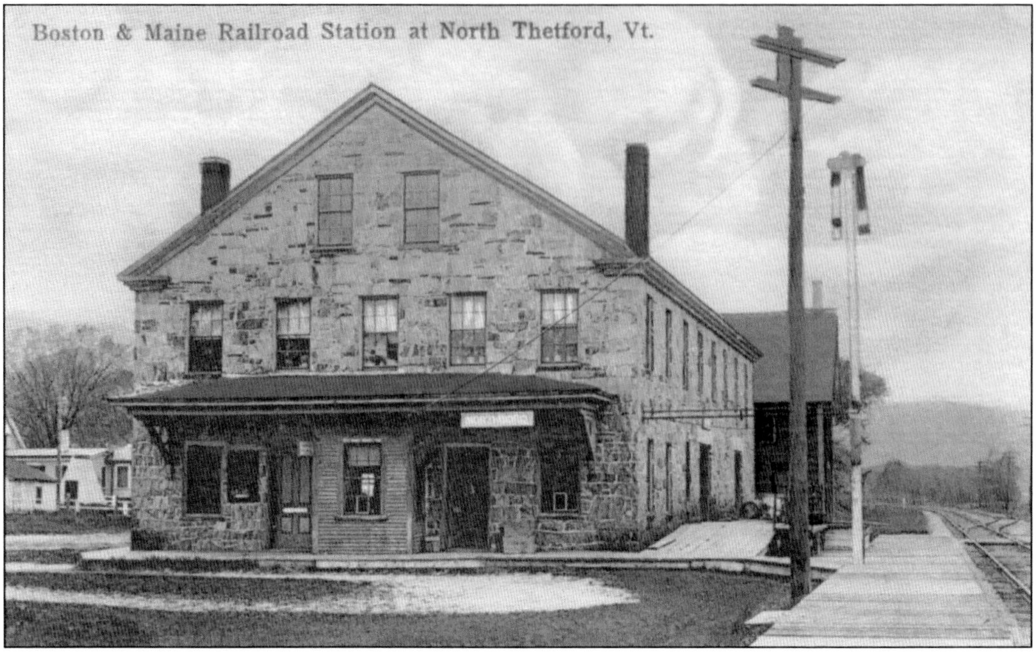

The depot in North Thetford was once made of stone, with separate waiting rooms for men and women. It was first served by the Connecticut and Passumpsic Railroad, running from White River Junction to Quebec. The station burned in 1915.

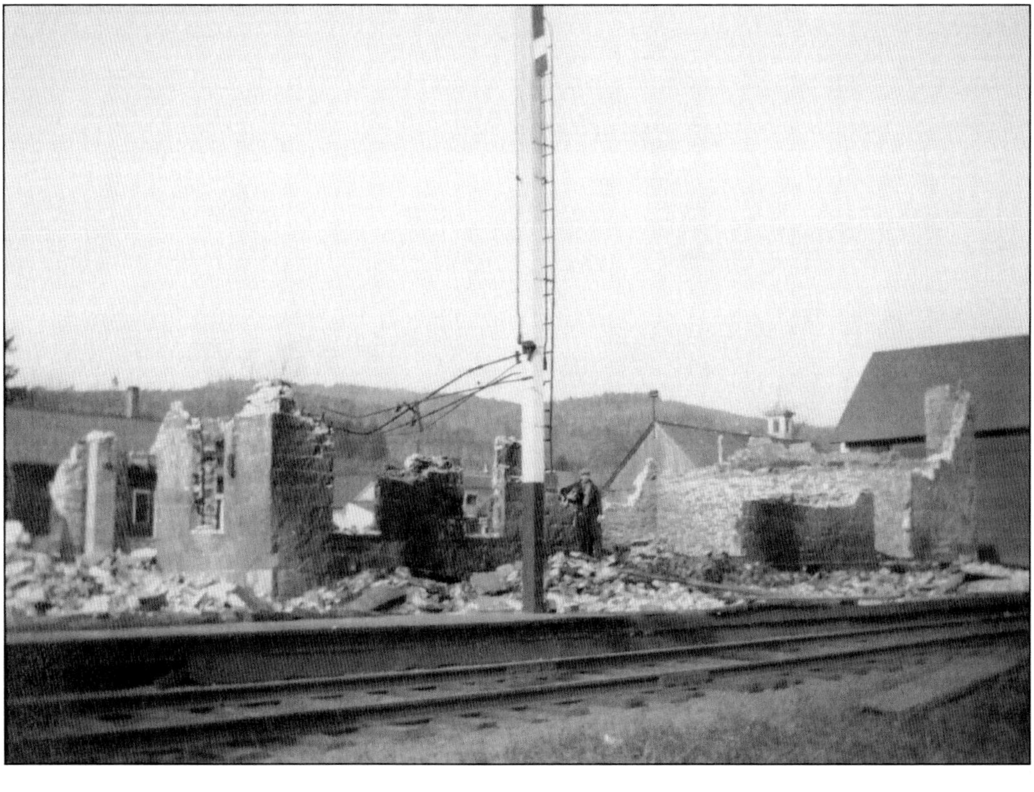

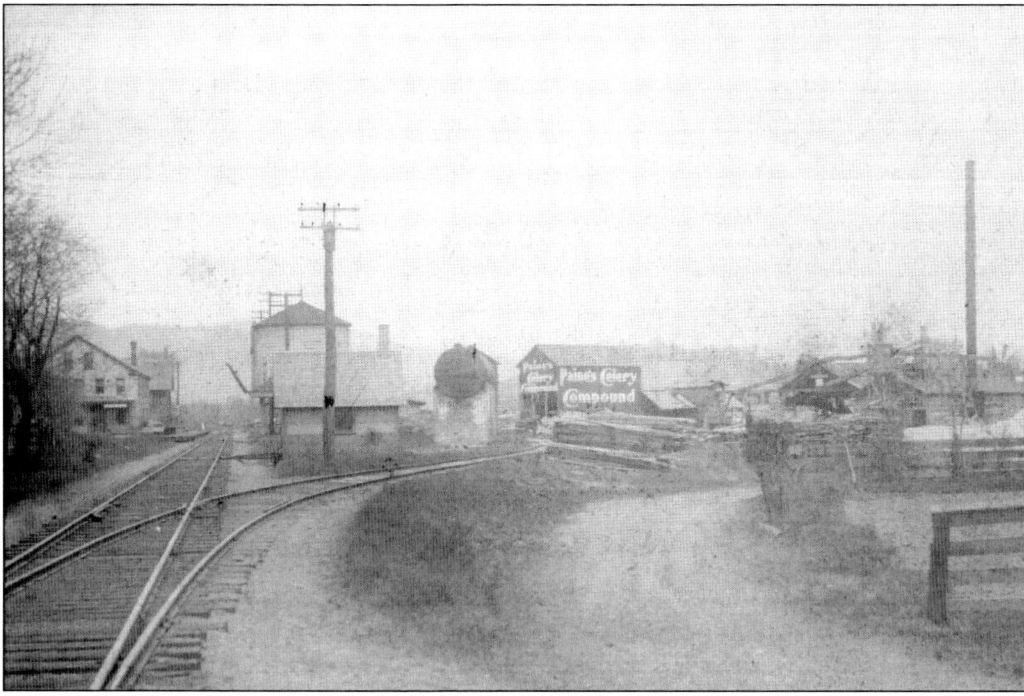

This photograph shows North Thetford's railroad station (known as Northboro), the water tank, the oil tank, and Ladd's sawmill.

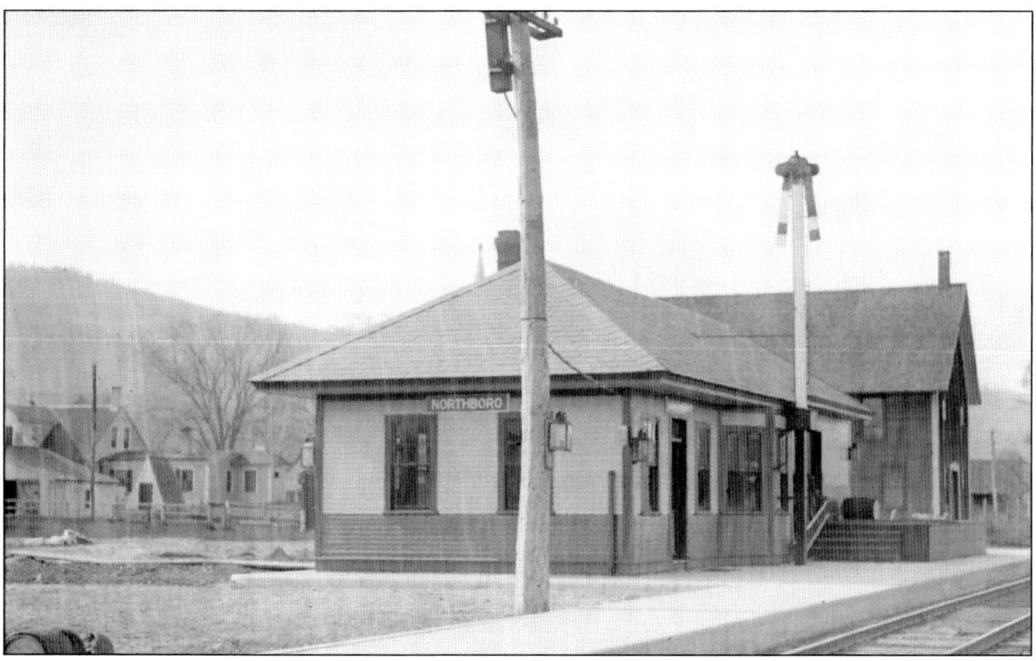

Pictured here is Northboro's second train station. Before the railroad came to town, riverside villages like North Thetford were dependent on Connecticut River traffic for trade and growth. (Courtesy of Frank J. Barrett Jr.)

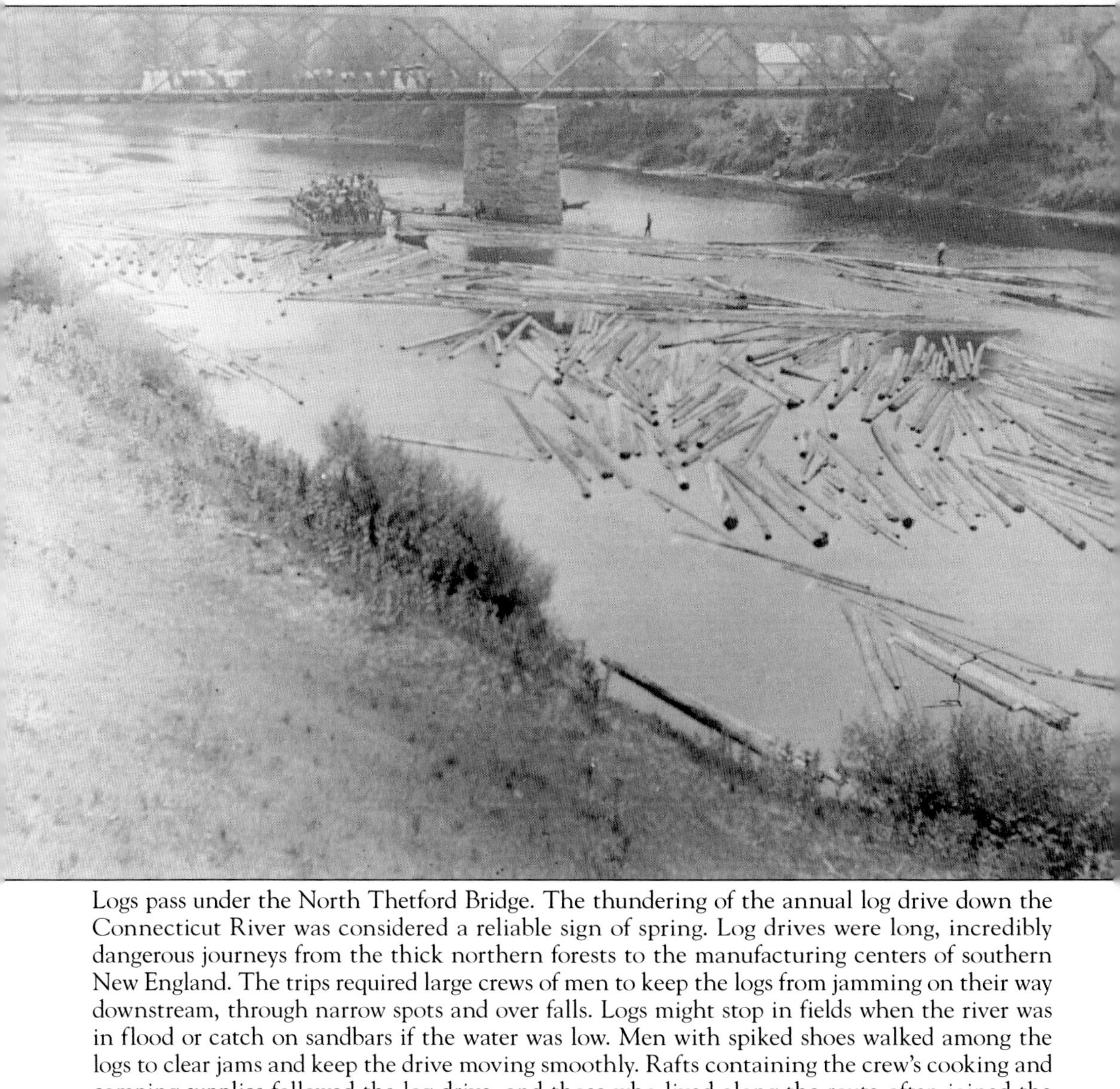

Logs pass under the North Thetford Bridge. The thundering of the annual log drive down the Connecticut River was considered a reliable sign of spring. Log drives were long, incredibly dangerous journeys from the thick northern forests to the manufacturing centers of southern New England. The trips required large crews of men to keep the logs from jamming on their way downstream, through narrow spots and over falls. Logs might stop in fields when the river was in flood or catch on sandbars if the water was low. Men with spiked shoes walked among the logs to clear jams and keep the drive moving smoothly. Rafts containing the crew's cooking and camping supplies followed the log drive, and those who lived along the route often joined the crew for meals.

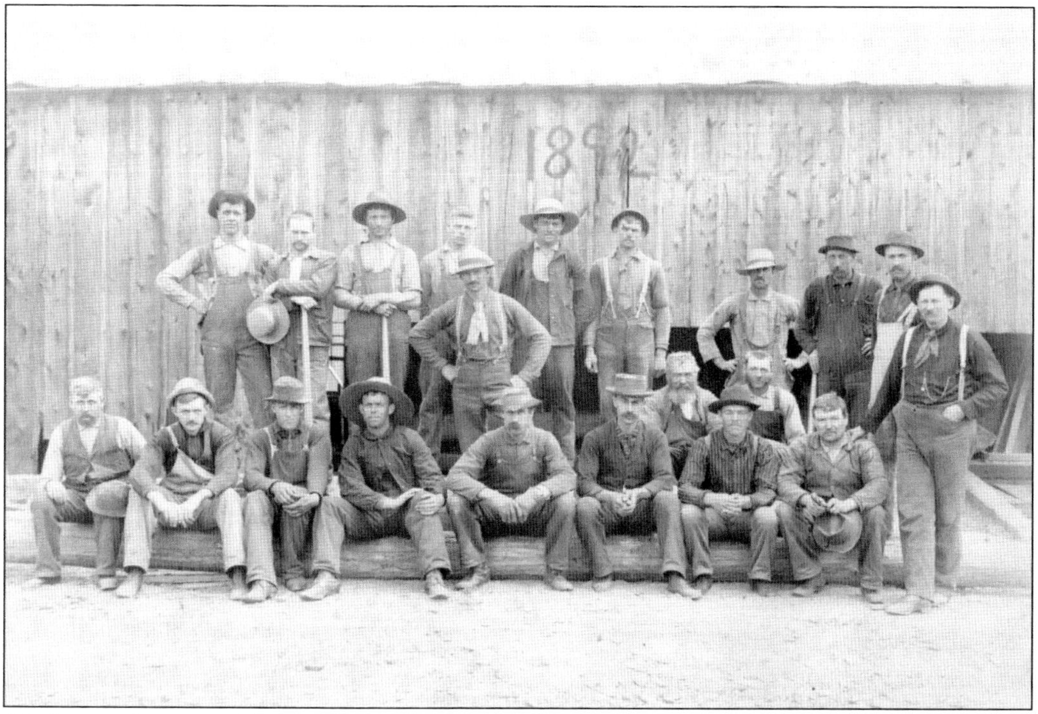

Workers gather at Ladd's saw, grist, and shingle mill. It was originally located in Post Mills but was moved to North Thetford to be closer to the railroad. It was rebuilt after burning in 1886.

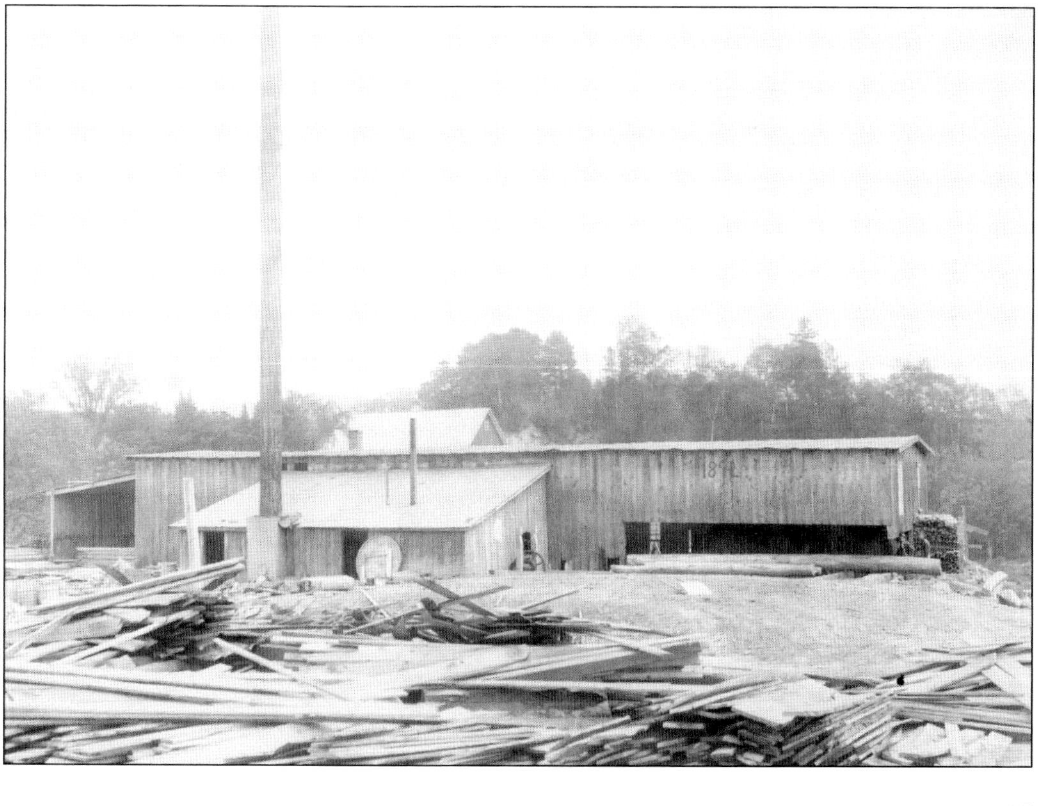

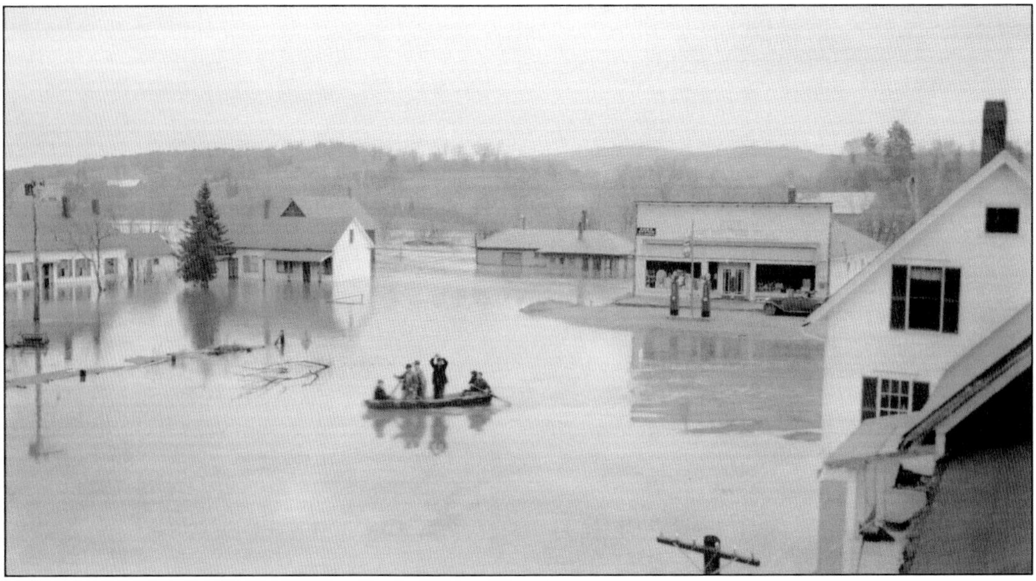

A combination of rapidly melting snow and heavy rains in March 1936 made for a historic flood across New England. North Thetford was inundated, and the only way to get around was by boat.

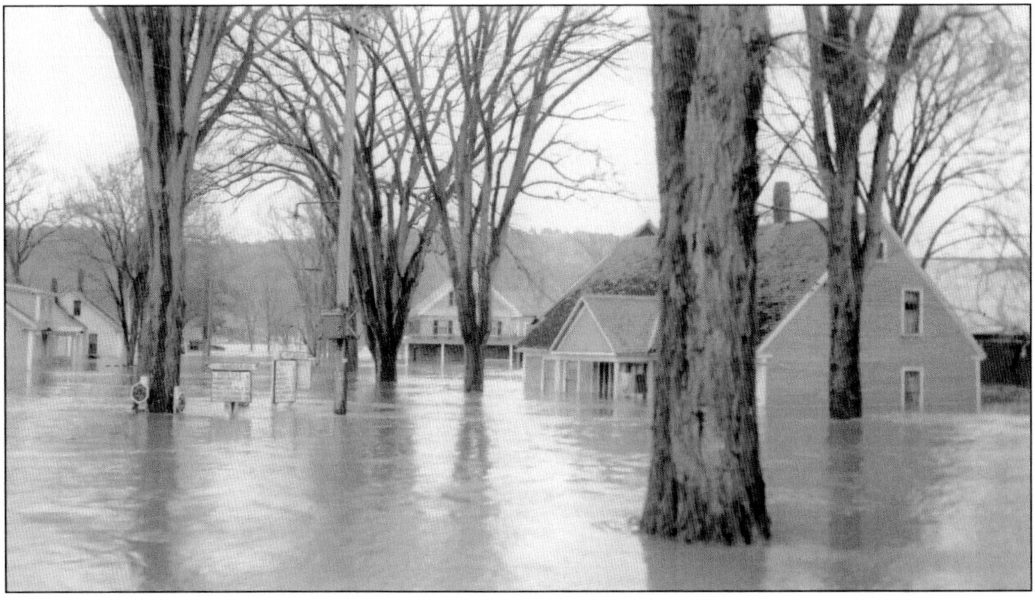

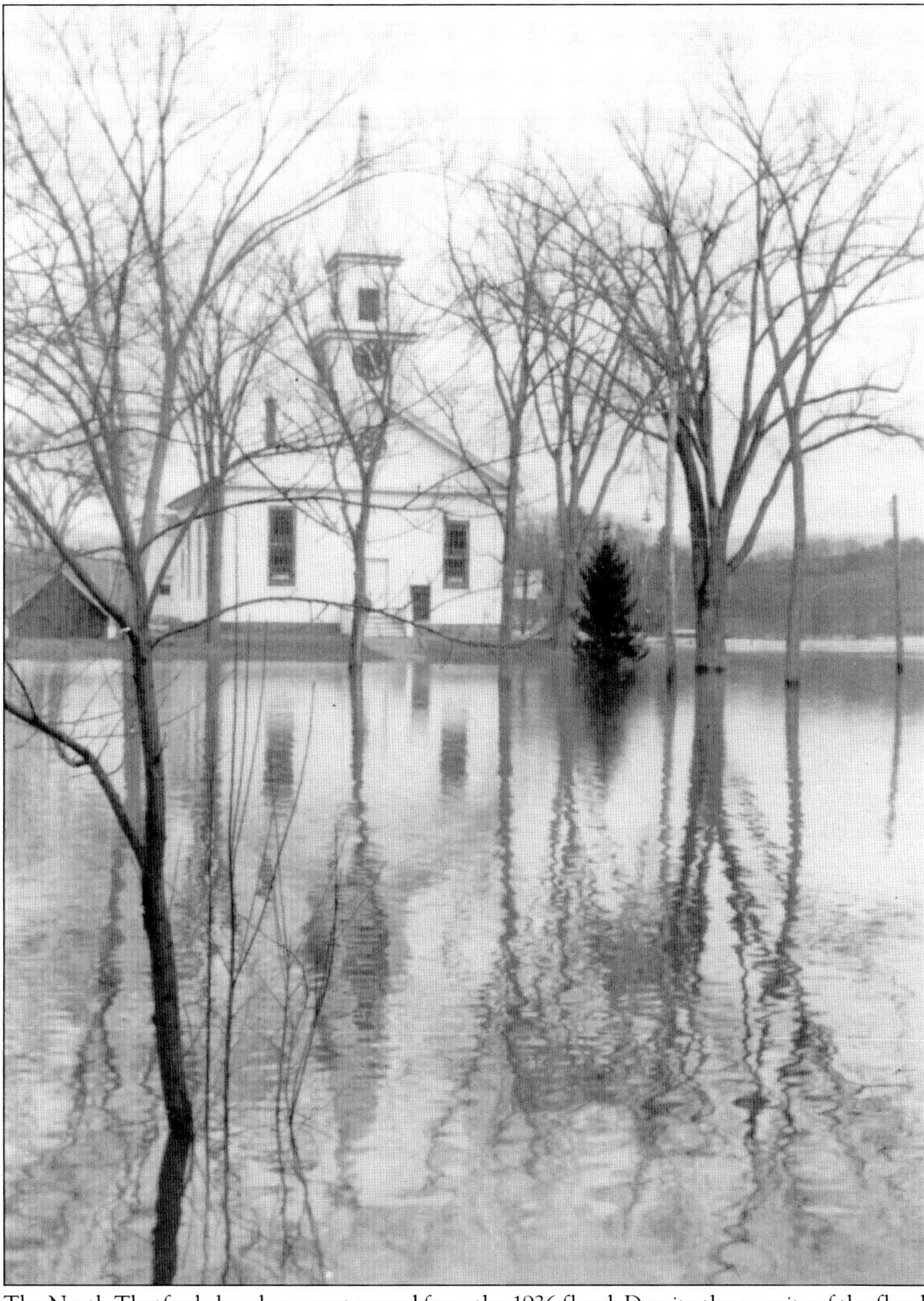

The North Thetford church was not spared from the 1936 flood. Despite the severity of the flood, the town did not sustain severe damage. Across New England, over two weeks, up to 30 inches of rain and snow fell, causing up to 200 deaths. That same year, Pres. Franklin D. Roosevelt signed the Flood Control Act of 1936 that led to the construction of the Union Village Dam in the 1940s.

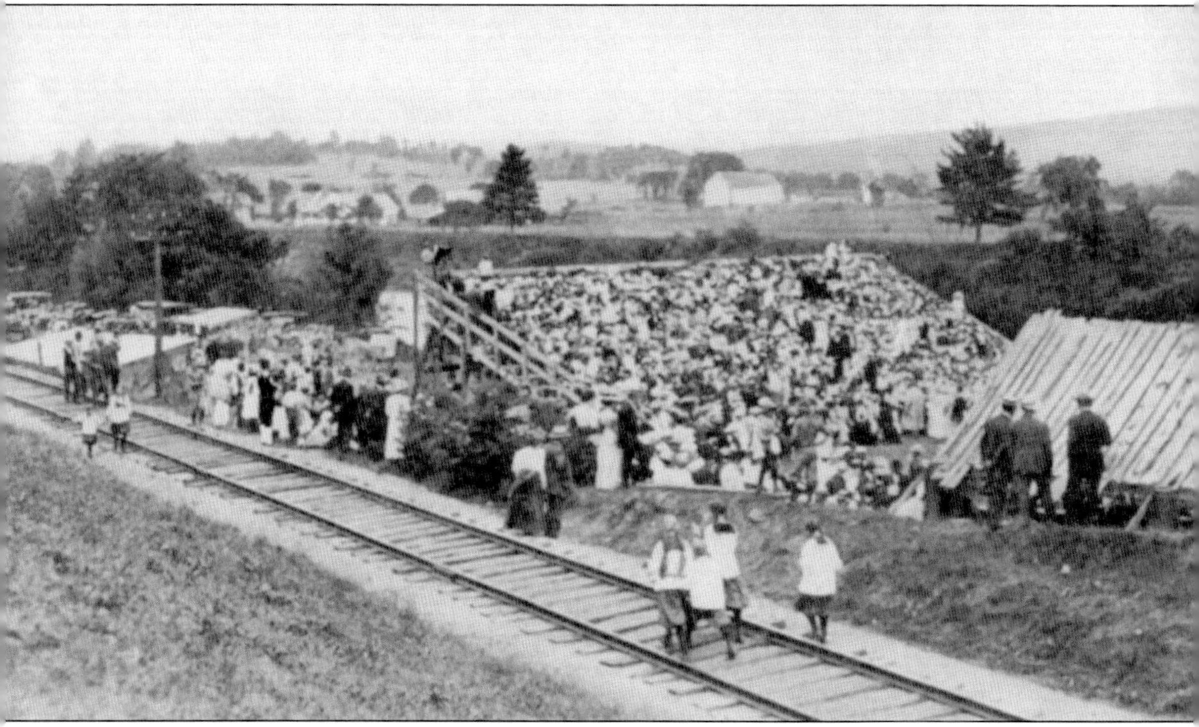

The August 1911 Thetford Pageant, which took place on the banks of the Connecticut River, celebrated the town's 150th anniversary. It was a four-day event with a cast of 500 including skits, dancing, and songs. Part history lesson, part entertainment, and part civic boosterism, it was spearheaded by pageant promoter William Langdon. The pageant was one of many in New England at the time whose purpose was to educate citizens, restore community spirit, and help focus a town's energy towards solving its problems. The Russell Sage Foundation, seeing the potential for community revitalization, gave Langdon a grant "to demonstrate whether or not the pageant may be used successfully as an agent in social advancement." The pageant was held within walking distance of the North Thetford railroad station, and special trains were arranged just for the event. That ease of access helped bring as many as 5,000 people to the pageant.

Each of the 12 episodes (and three musical interludes) told a story from Thetford's past but also imparted a lesson. Thetford suffered a marked decline in population and industry as America's business centers concentrated in cities, and farming shifted west. Symbolizing these changes in Episode 9, the character Lettie Davis begs Joe Edwards not to leave Thetford to find his riches elsewhere. (Alas, he does.)

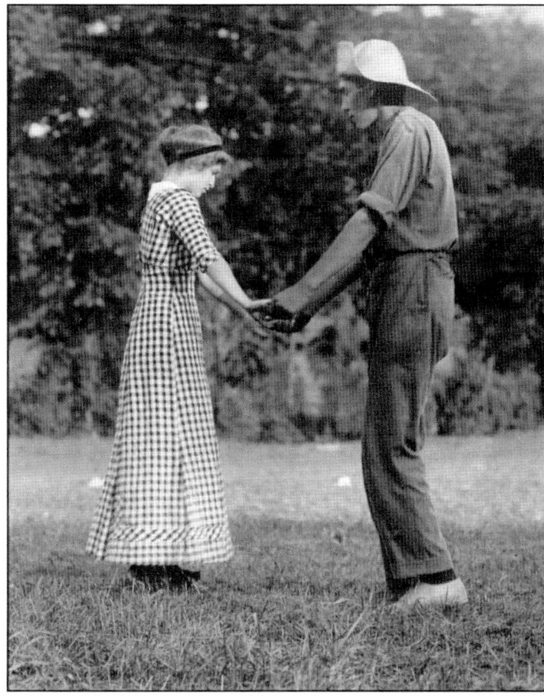

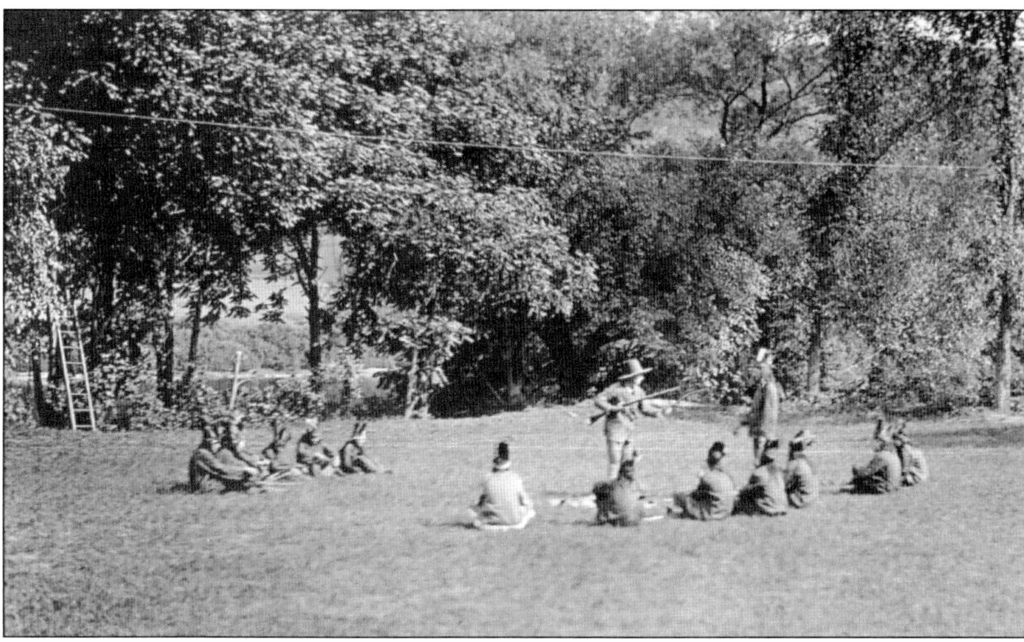

The history lessons were rife with questionable story lines and the prejudices of the times. "Quail" John Chamberlain, Thetford's first settler, is portrayed in Episode 1 acquainting himself with the local Native Americans. According to the story described in the pageant program, Quail John surprises a band of Indians in the woods. After pointing his gun at them, he makes the peace sign and shares his dinner and a pipe with them. The chiefs inform him that he may live on one side of the river but not the other, and Quail John convinces them to carry his things to his new home.

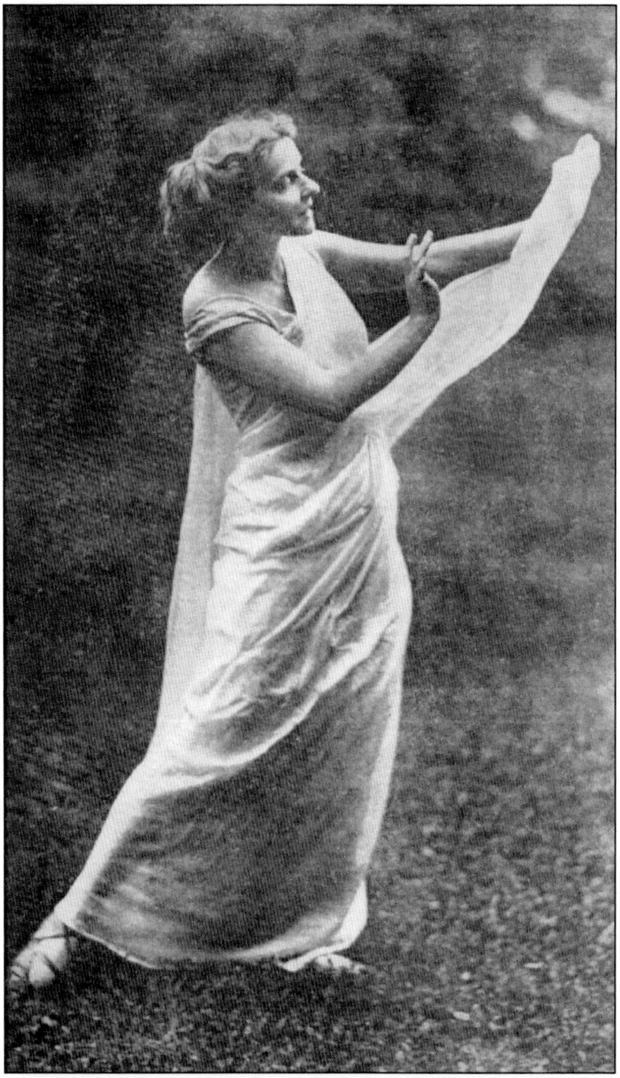

For the musical interludes, renowned dancer Virginia Tanner taught local girls and those from Thetford's summer camps to dance in the avant-garde style of Isadora Duncan. The girls were robed as nature spirits and left their hair long and flowing. Their dances told stories and served to reinforce the pageant's themes.

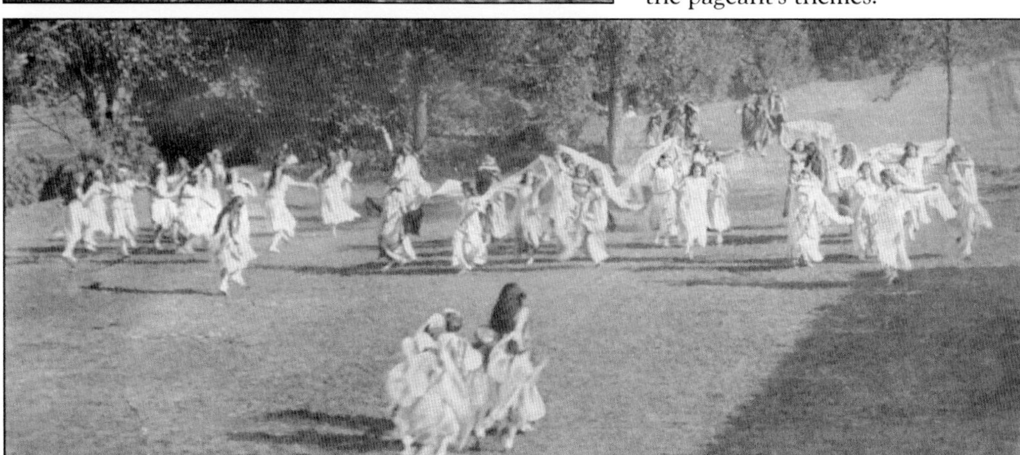

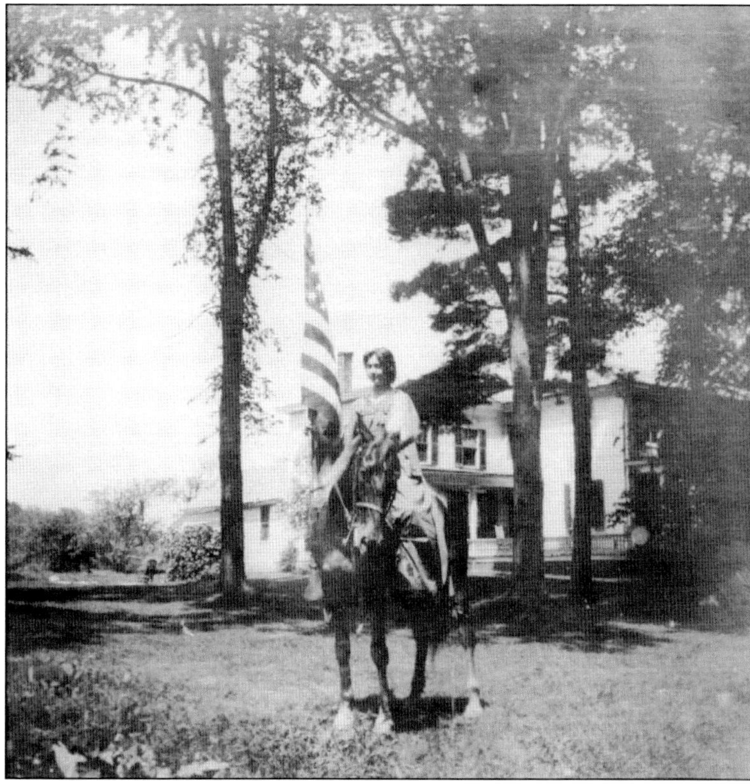

Katharine Vaughan, playing the Spirit of Vermont, sits astride a horse, complete with shield and flag. (Courtesy of University of Vermont Special Collections.)

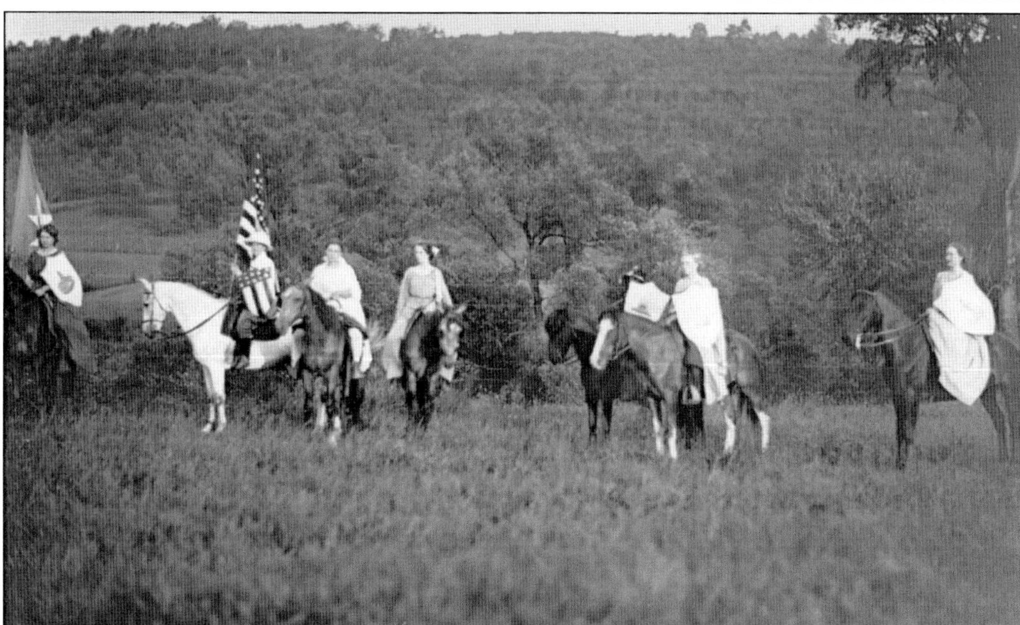

Other women played the spirits of America, Thetford, and nearby states in the finale, symbolizing Thetford's bright future with the help of the larger community. By the time the pageant was performed, Thetford was experiencing an increase in summer tourism (such as at Camp Hanoum, which supplied many of the pageant's dancers).

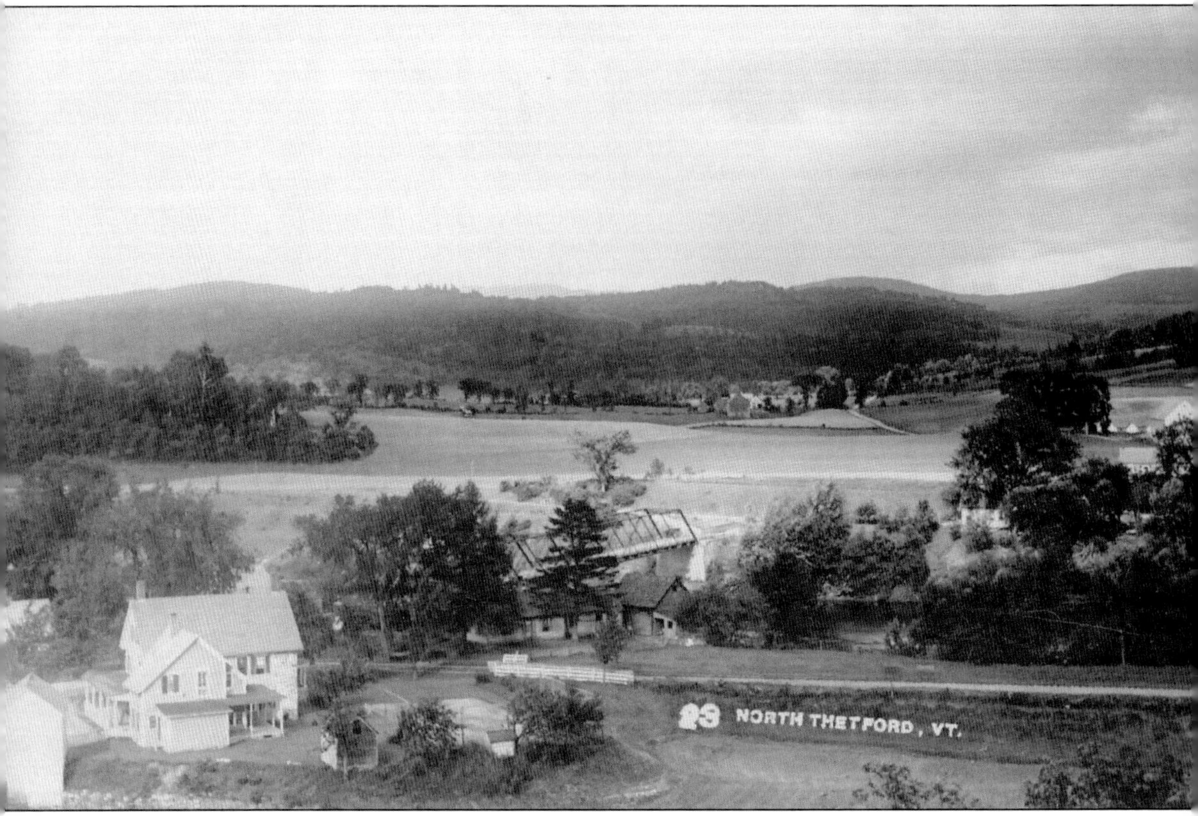

This photograph shows North Thetford, at left, looking across the Connecticut River to Lyme. (Courtesy of Lyme Historians.)

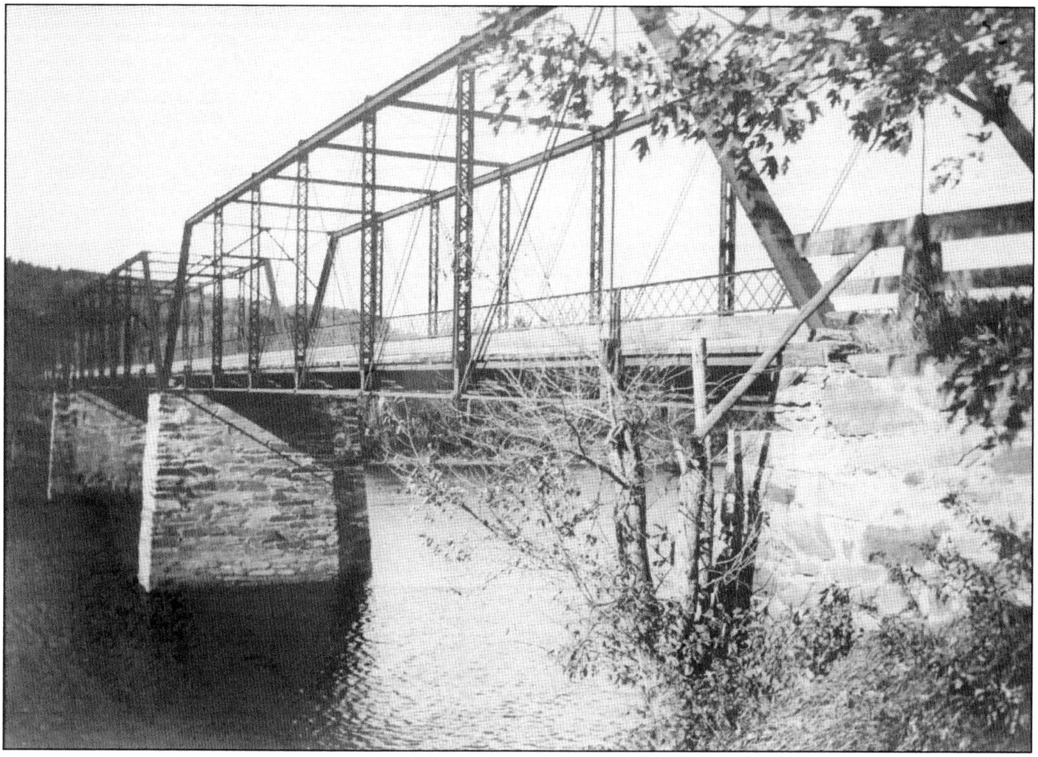

The North Thetford Bridge has been a Connecticut River crossing since a ferry route started around 1780. An 1896 flood destroyed the covered bridges at both North and East Thetford, and both were replaced with iron bridges.

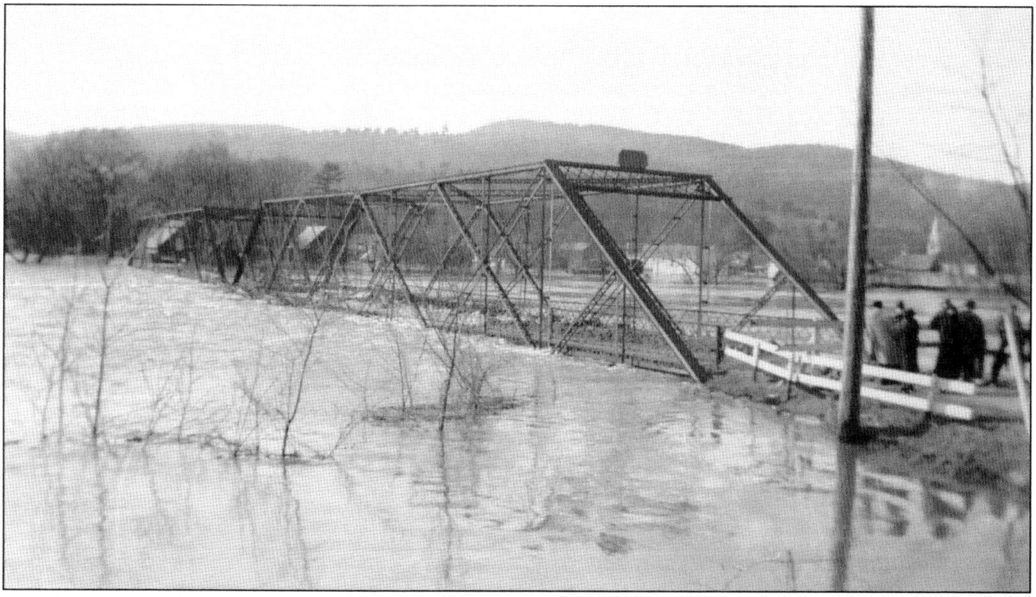

The North Thetford Bridge washed out in the flood of 1936 but was rebuilt. In 1959, an overloaded truck damaged the bridge; it was never repaired and was removed in the 1970s. (Courtesy of Lyme Historians.)

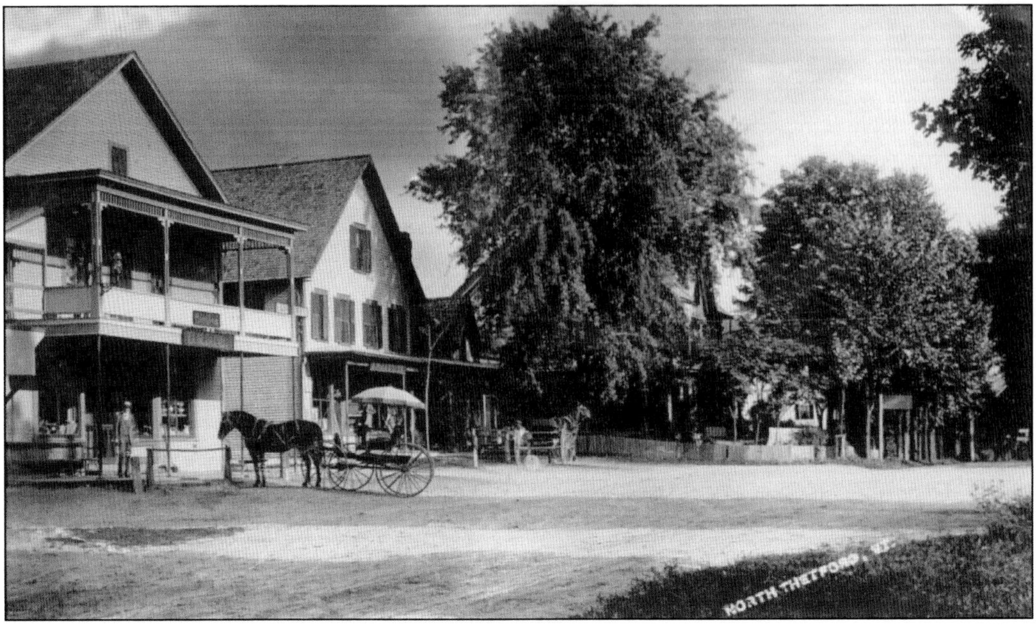

This is North Thetford's main street, with Bond's store at left. Jacquith's Hotel is next door. Arthur Jacquith also ran a general store near the bridge to Lyme.

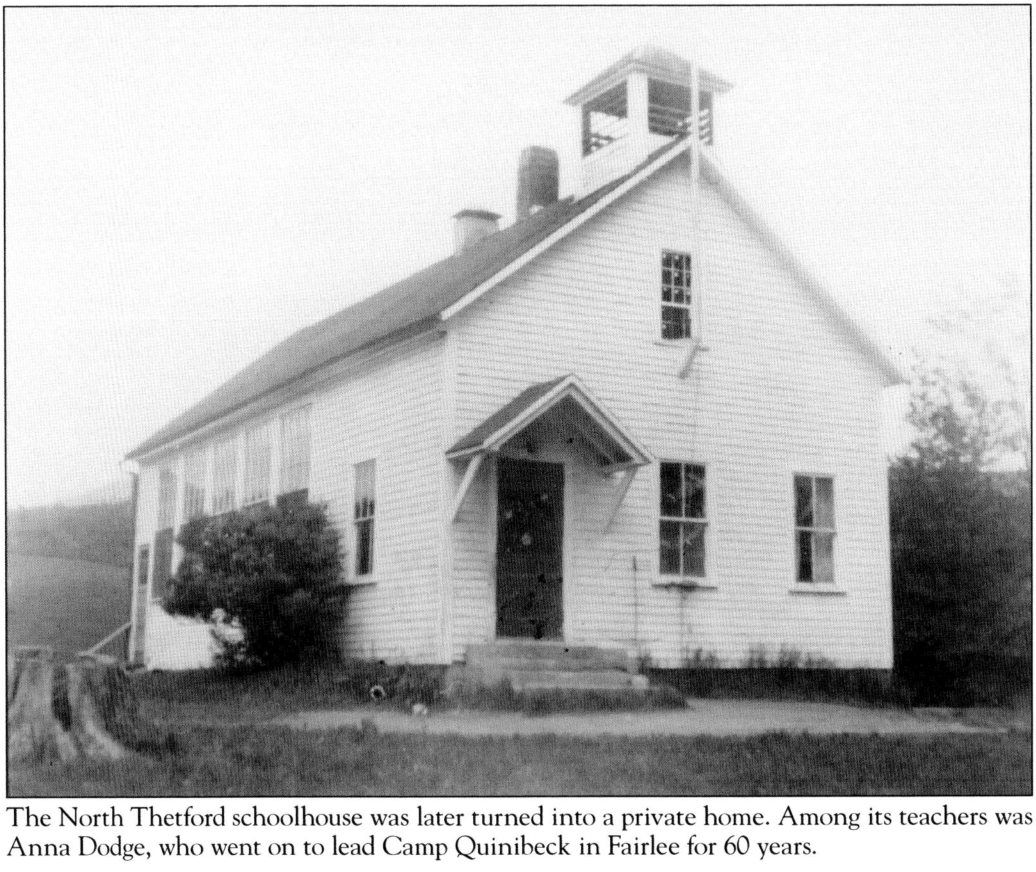

The North Thetford schoolhouse was later turned into a private home. Among its teachers was Anna Dodge, who went on to lead Camp Quinibeck in Fairlee for 60 years.

Six

East Thetford

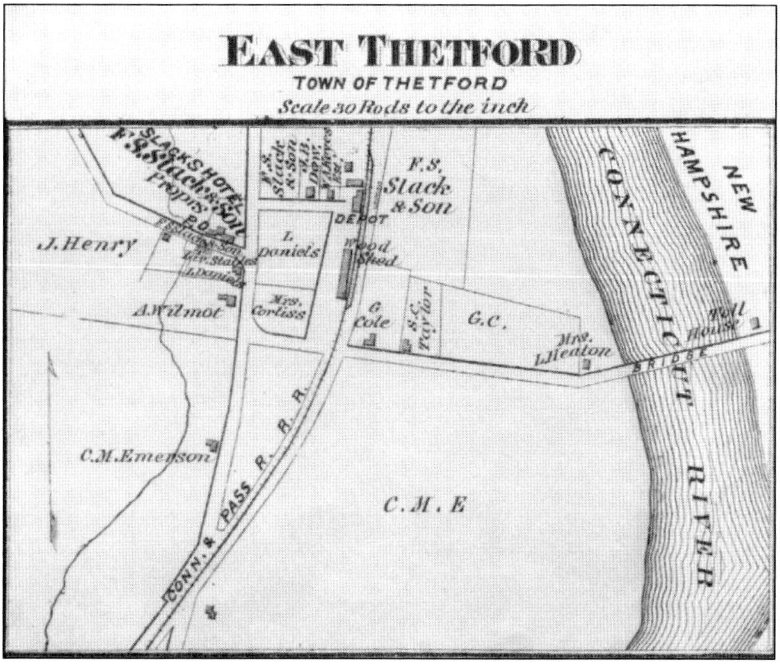

This map shows East Thetford as it was in 1877. East Thetford is home to Child's Pond, an interesting landmark because it is very deep, has no inlet or outlet, its level never changes through the seasons, and it is situated nearly 150 feet above the Connecticut River. Thetford's first schoolhouse, a small log cabin, was in East Thetford. (Courtesy of University of Vermont Special Collections.)

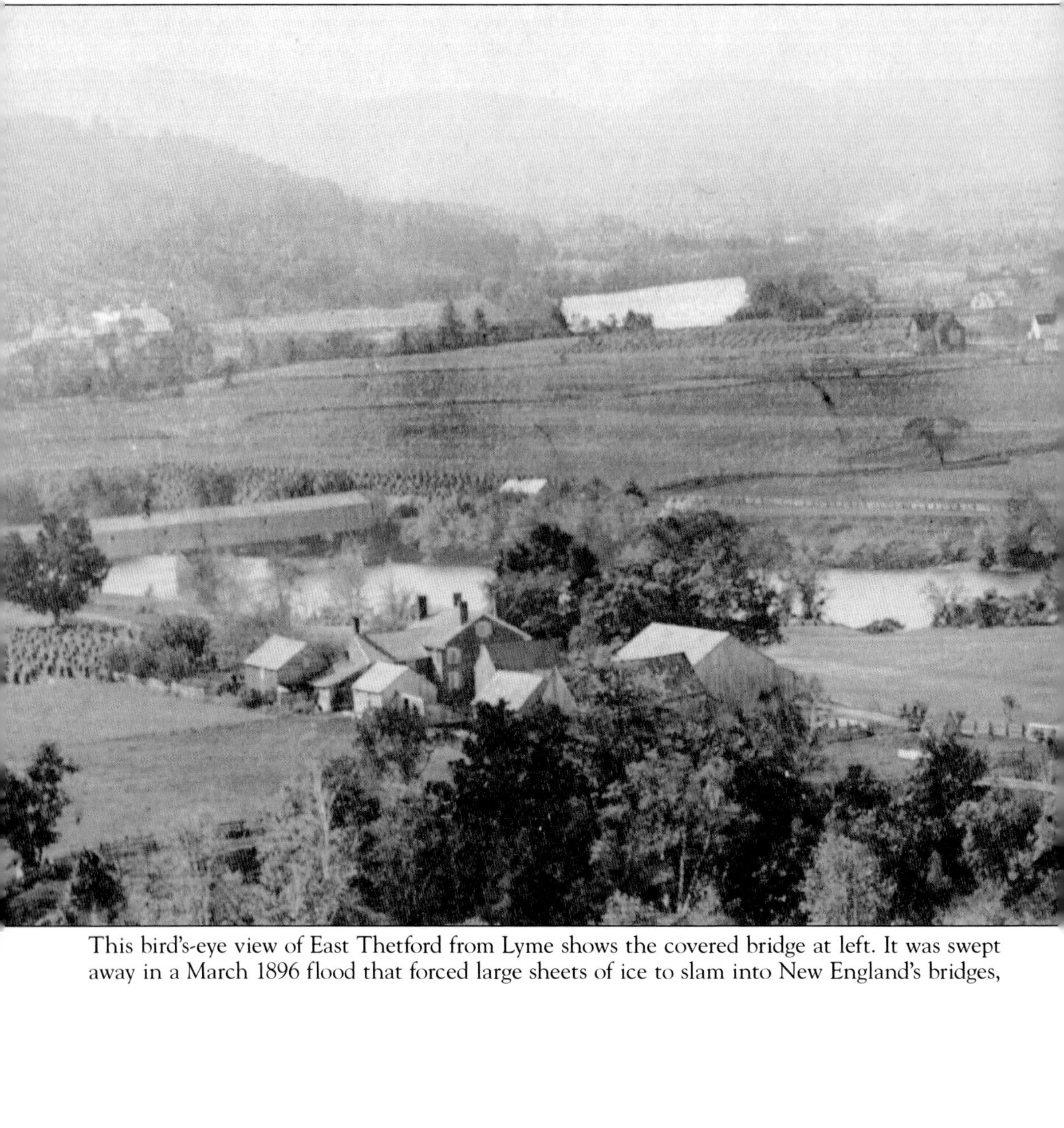

This bird's-eye view of East Thetford from Lyme shows the covered bridge at left. It was swept away in a March 1896 flood that forced large sheets of ice to slam into New England's bridges,

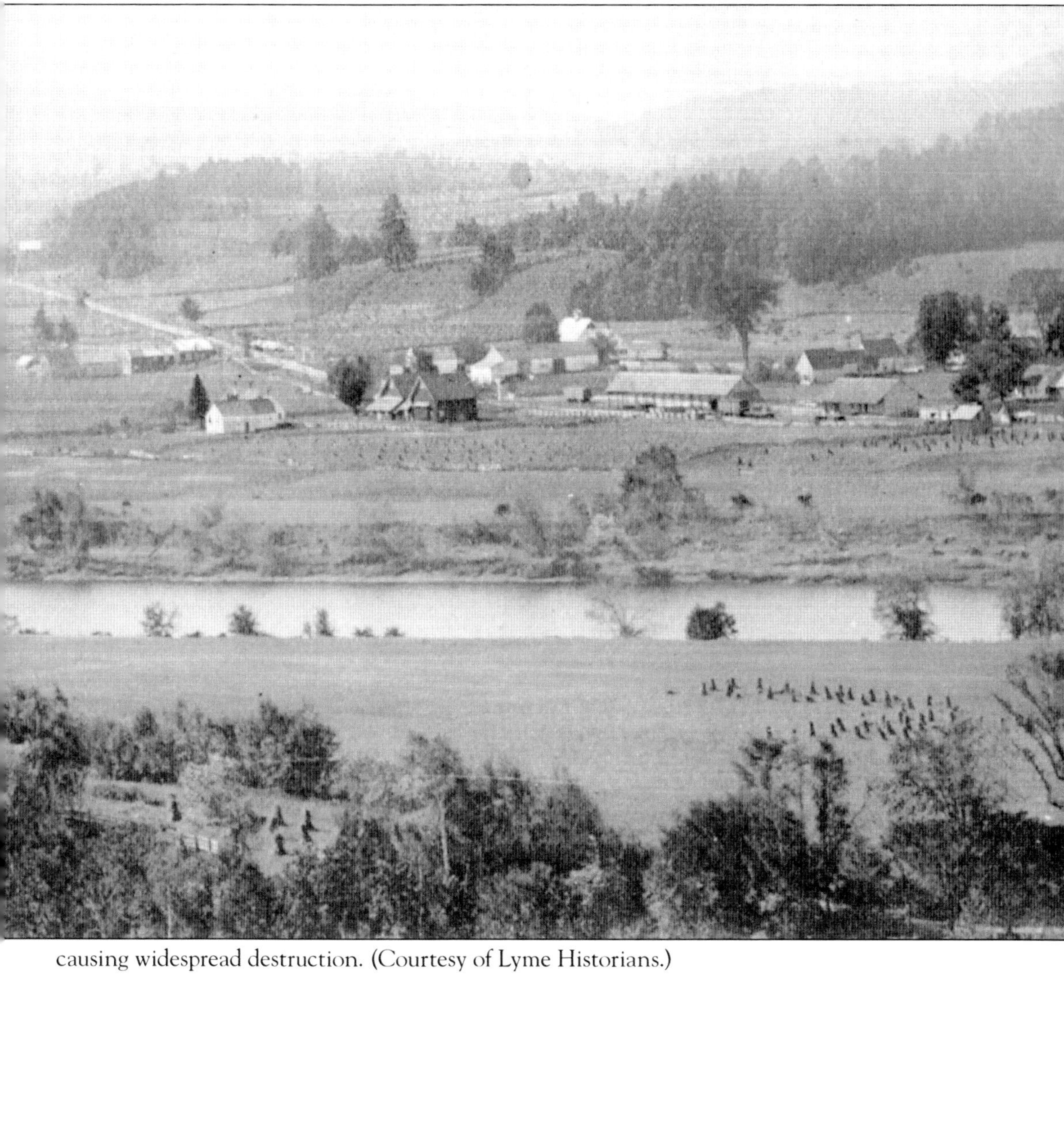
causing widespread destruction. (Courtesy of Lyme Historians.)

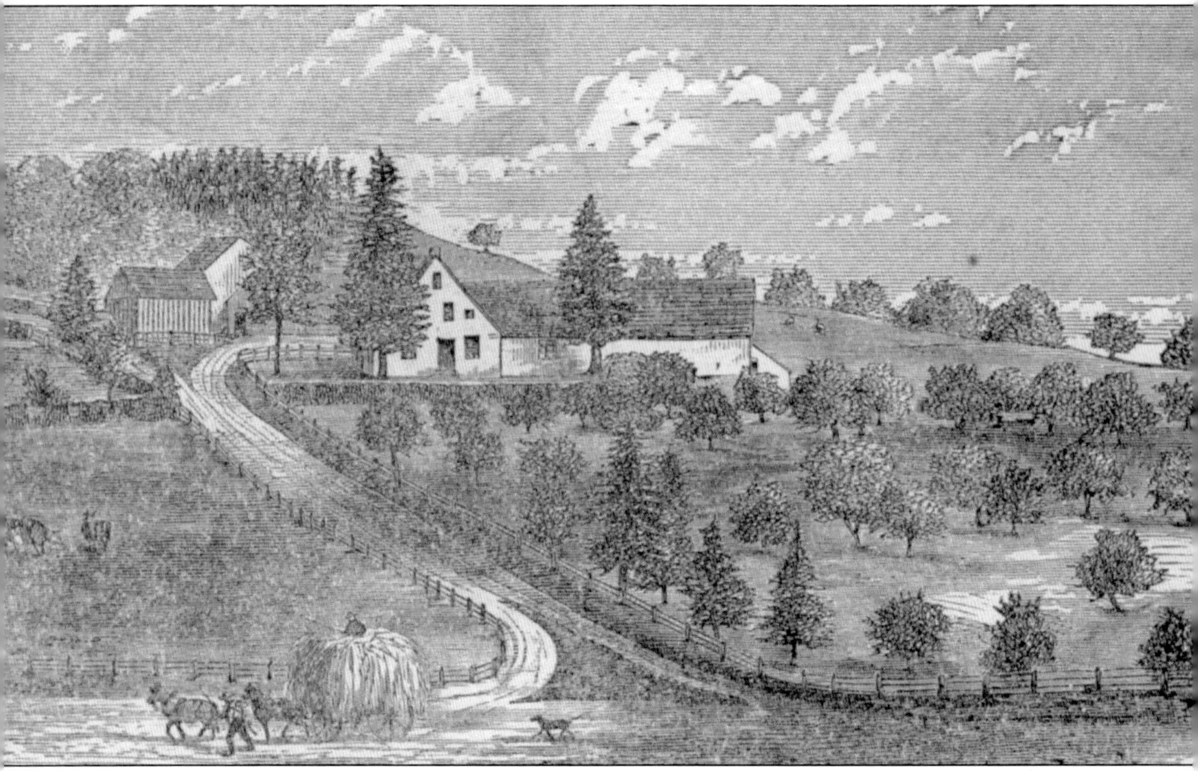

Asa Burton, second pastor for Thetford and one of its most prominent citizens, lived in the parsonage in the west end of the village. Upon his arrival in Thetford in 1779, the congregation gave him 50 acres, £50 for building a house, and the promise of £85 as an annual salary. Burton was raised in Norwich, Connecticut, and was a 1777 graduate of Dartmouth College. (Courtesy of University of Vermont Special Collections.)

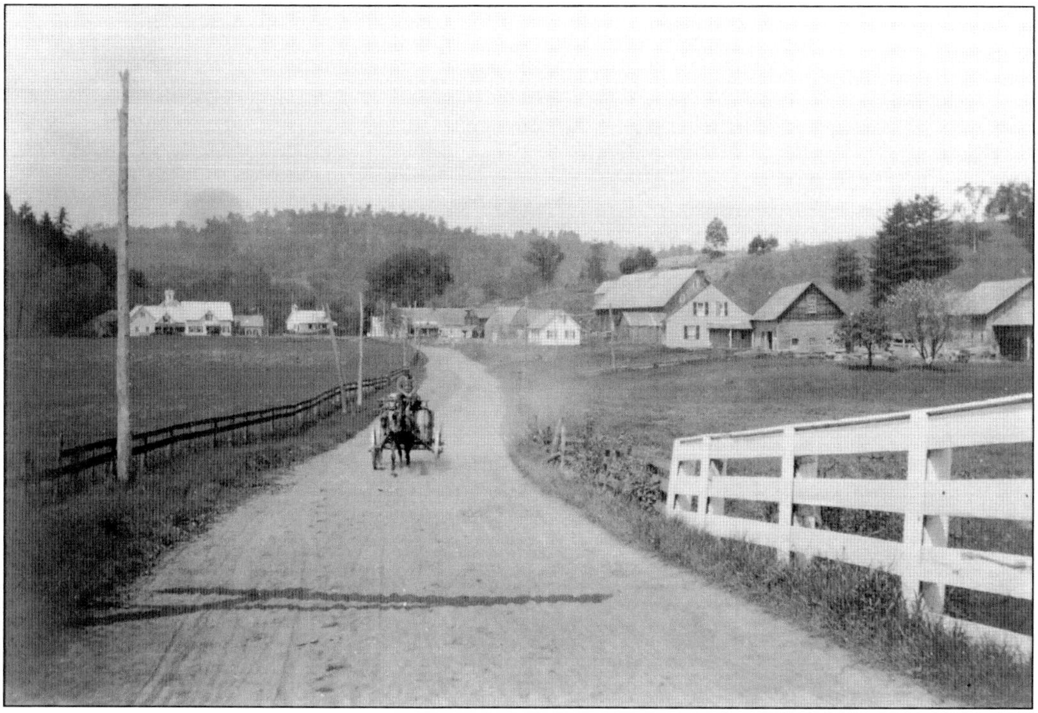

Route 5 was straightened in the 1930s to improve the road as the main north-south corridor through eastern Vermont and eliminate the many railroad crossings along the way, such as this one at what is now Pavilion Road (below). Ely Road (not shown) is also a remnant of the old Route 5.

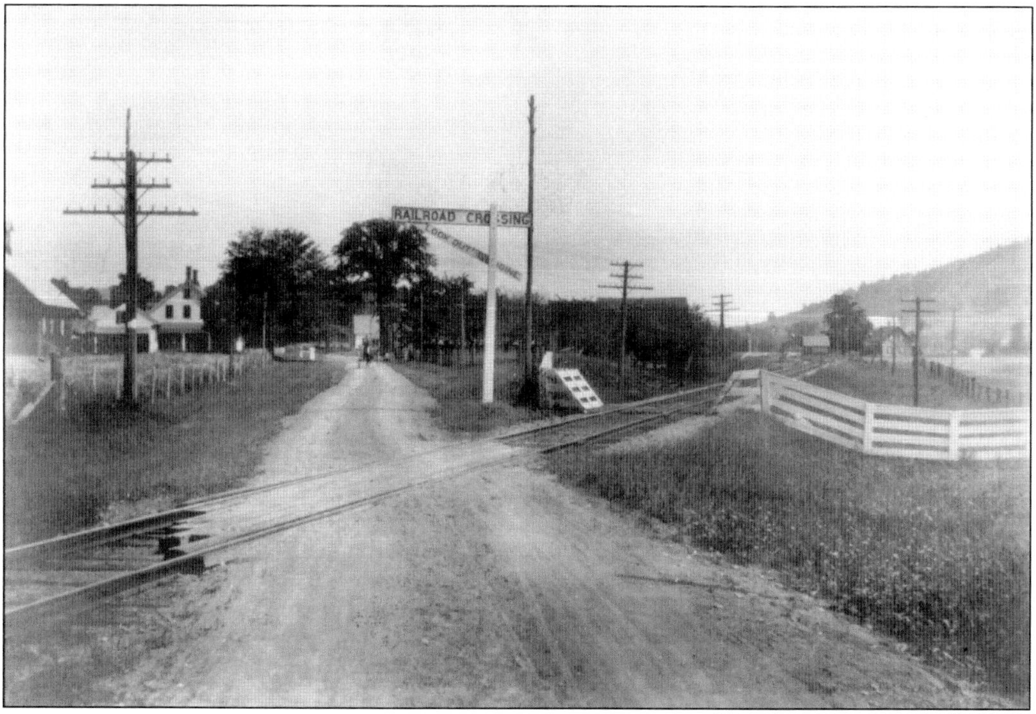

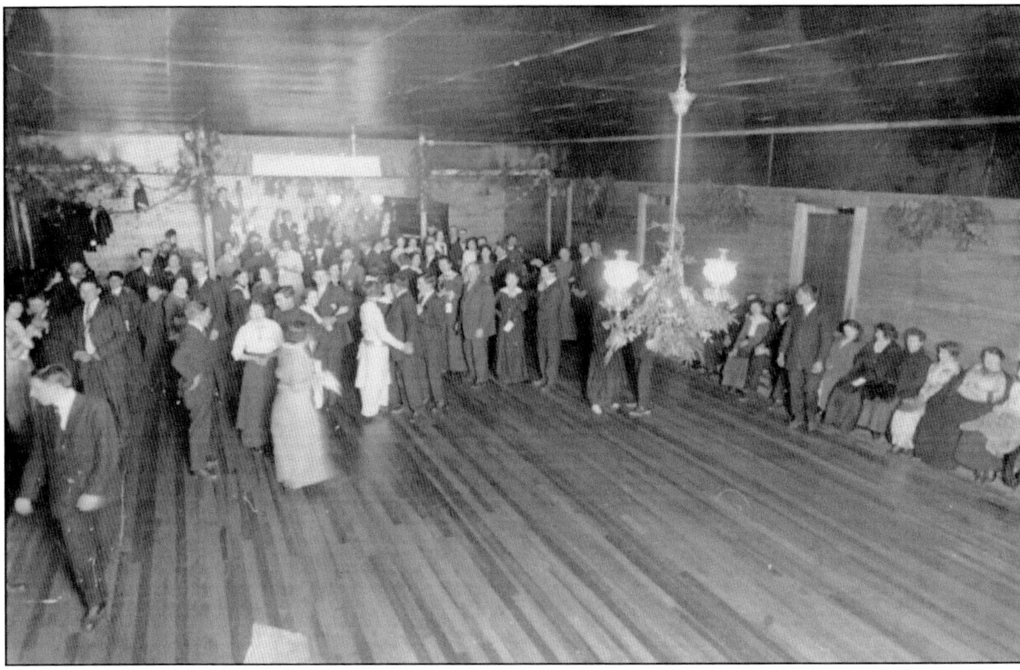

Couples dance at the Pavilion, owned by John Huntington, around World War I. Thetford used to have several dance halls; dances also took place in barns and taverns.

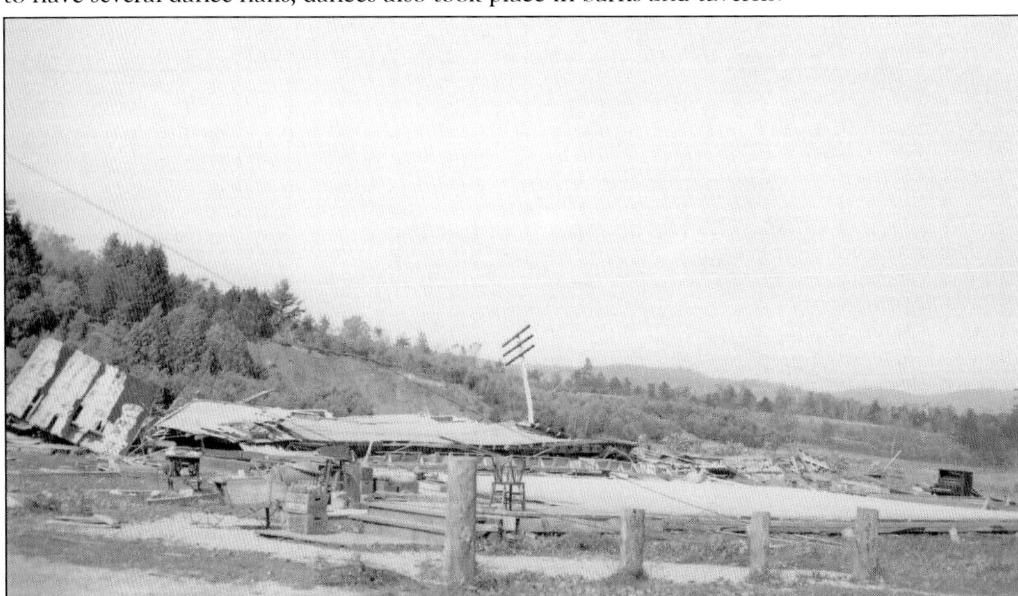

Huntington's Pavilion was hit hard in the hurricane of 1938. "The most spectacular thing at East Thetford was, of course, Huntington's Dance Hall, turned into a woodpile on the railroad tracks," reported Thetford resident Rosetta Estabrook in a letter to her sister Gladys. "The only whole thing there was the floor and that was warped. Possible one could do the Big Apple, but we didn't try. . . . The piano still plays although the woodwork was mostly blown off." The photograph's caption states that the floor itself was moved nine feet. The pavilion was rebuilt but closed in the 1950s. (Courtesy of the Vermont Historical Society)

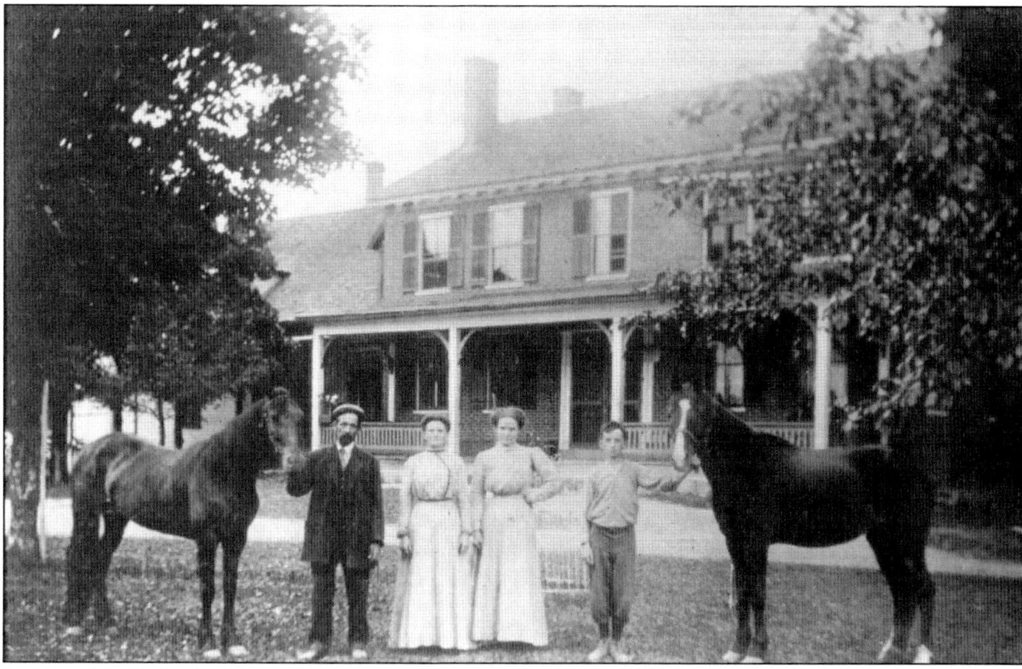

Frederick Slack's hotel, built soon after the railroad came to East Thetford, used to be at the intersection of Routes 5 and 113. The hotel was popular with traveling salesmen who got off at the depot across the street, checked into the hotel, and plied their trades in the area. The arrangement worked well for the Slack family; Frederick ran the hotel, and his brother Wilbur was station agent. (Courtesy of University of Vermont Special Collections.)

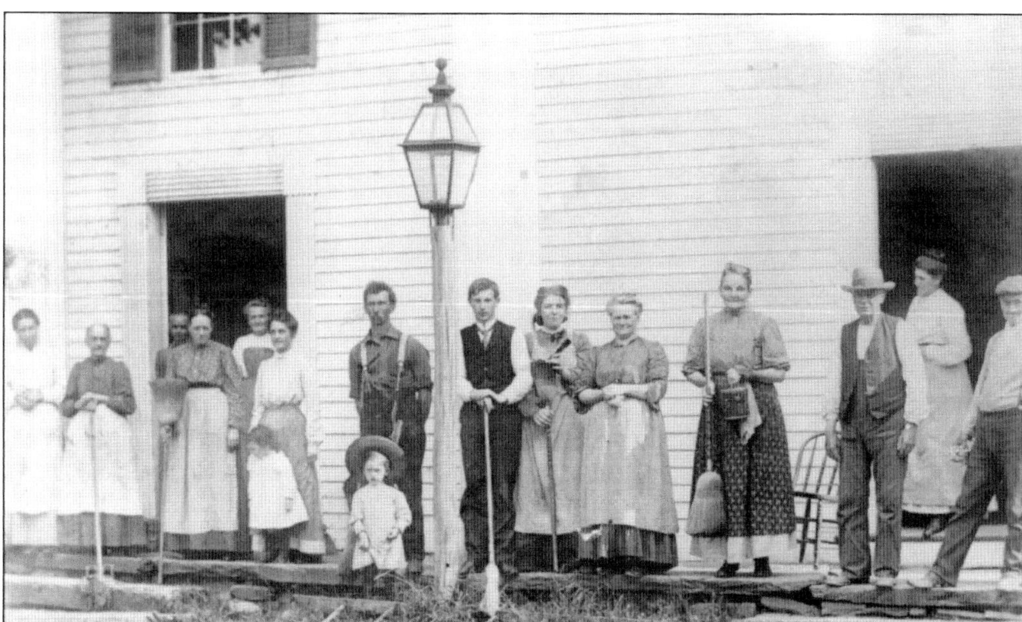

Before it was moved to East Thetford in 1984, the Thetford Baptist Church was the Cambridgeport Meeting House near Bellows Falls. This is spring cleaning day in Cambridgeport in 1910.

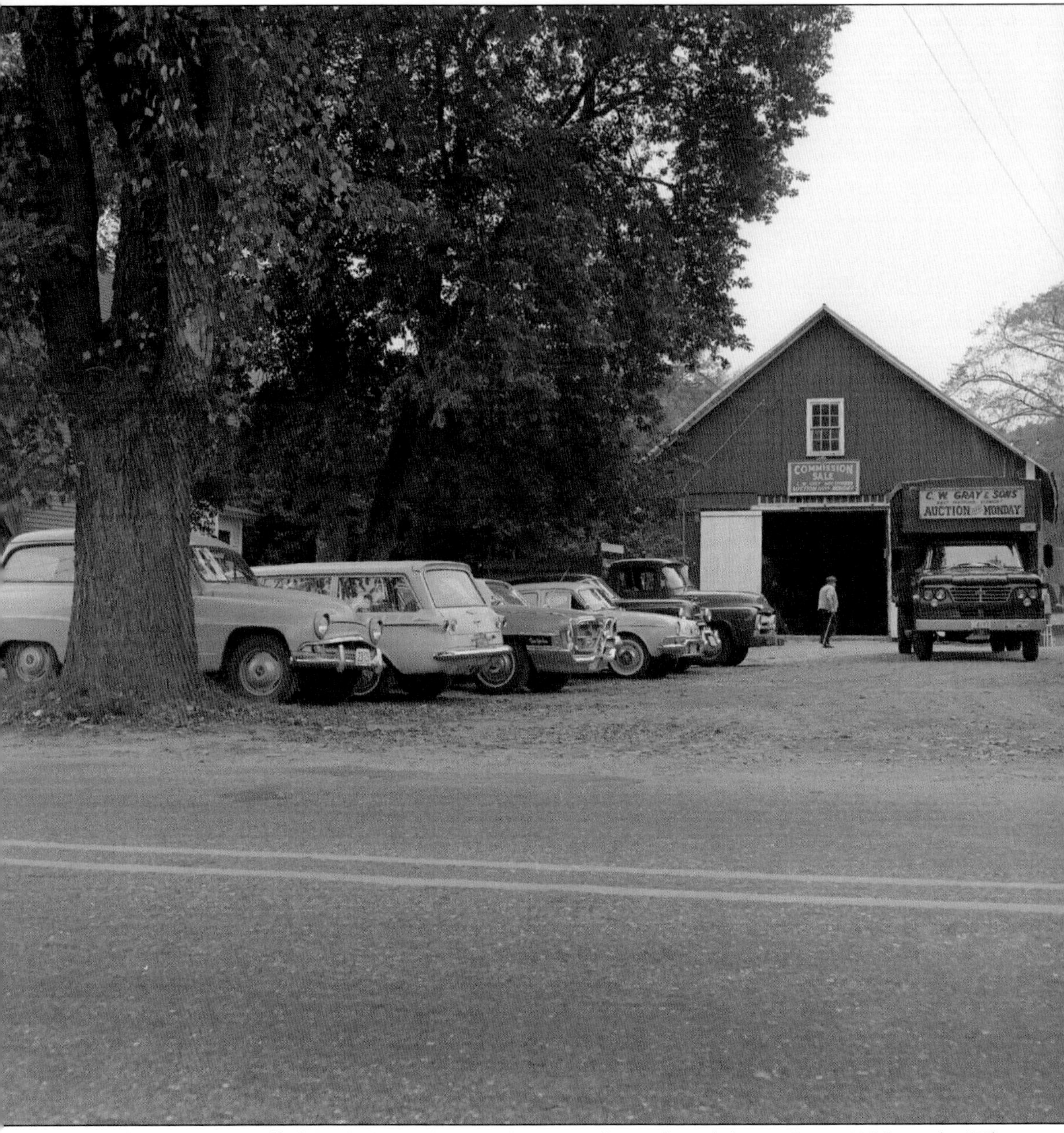

Yankee magazine called C.W. Gray's Auction House "a form of rural theater" in a 1976 article. "The grounds are crowded and assume the appearance of a small-scale country fair: trucks and cars parked everywhere and at every angle; people scattered about eating, drinking and socializing. Friends that haven't seen each other since the preceding Monday catch up on the week's happenings." (Courtesy of the Vermont State Archives and Records Administration.)

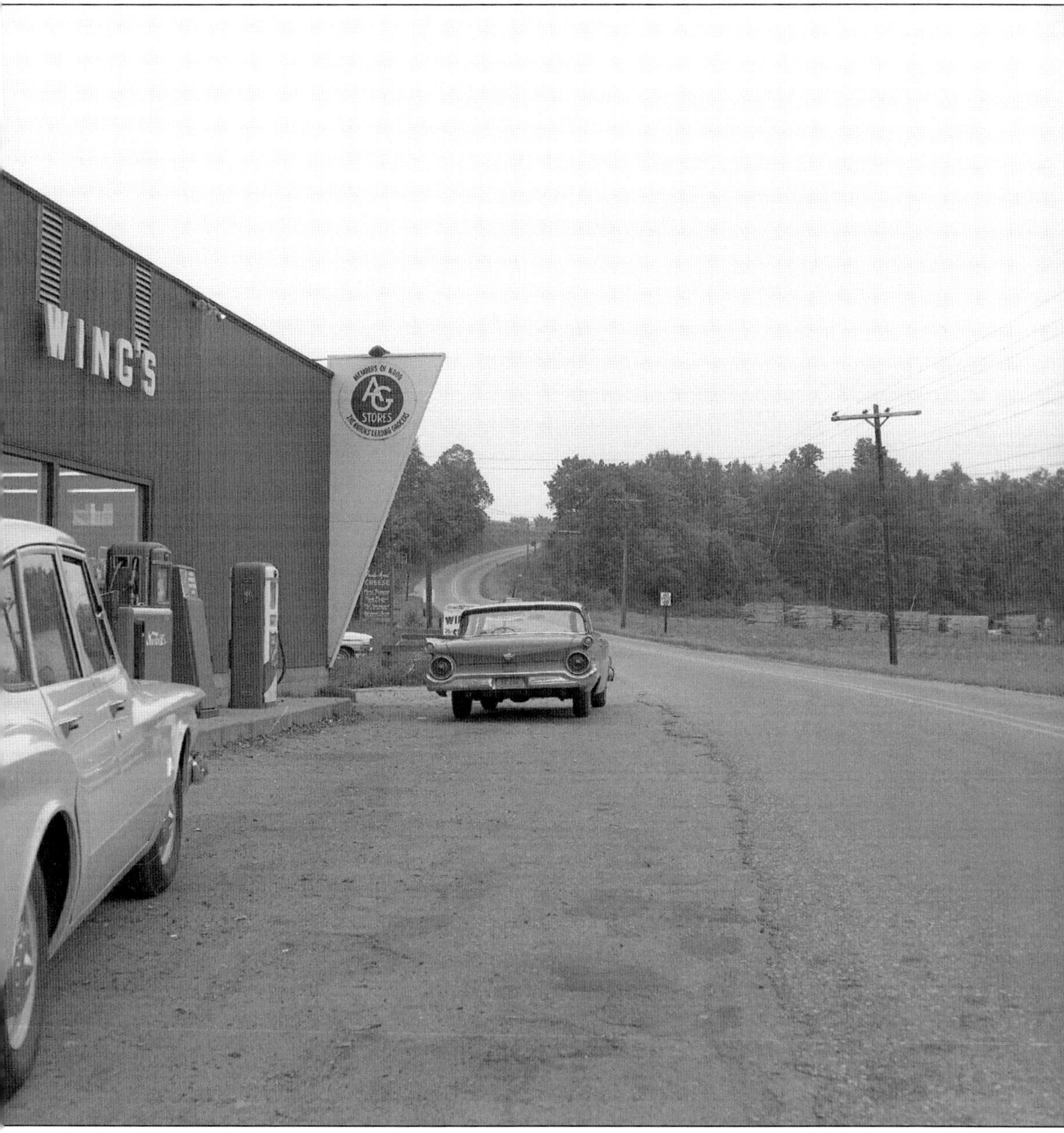

Stanley Wing's Market is not the first business to occupy this spot. McNight's blacksmith shop once stood here; it was later a service station. (Courtesy of the Vermont State Archives and Records Administration.)

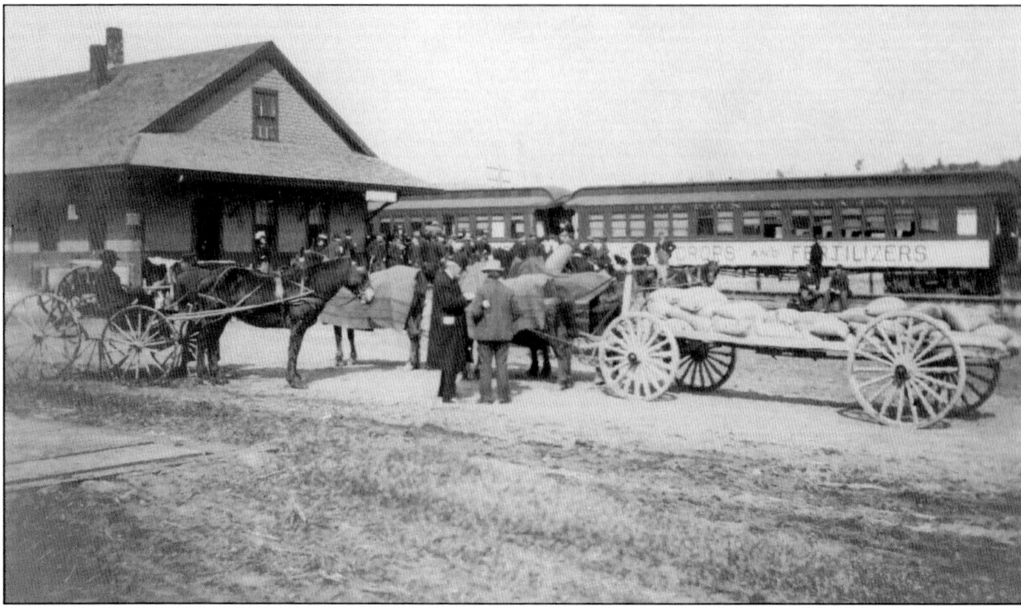

The railroad came to Thetford in 1848, and with it, a new kind of commerce. Farmers and small business owners were able to get their wares to a broader market, and the Ely mine sent its copper ore to southern New England to be refined. Later, as tourism boomed throughout Thetford, all three of Thetford's railroad villages thrived on business from summer tourists.

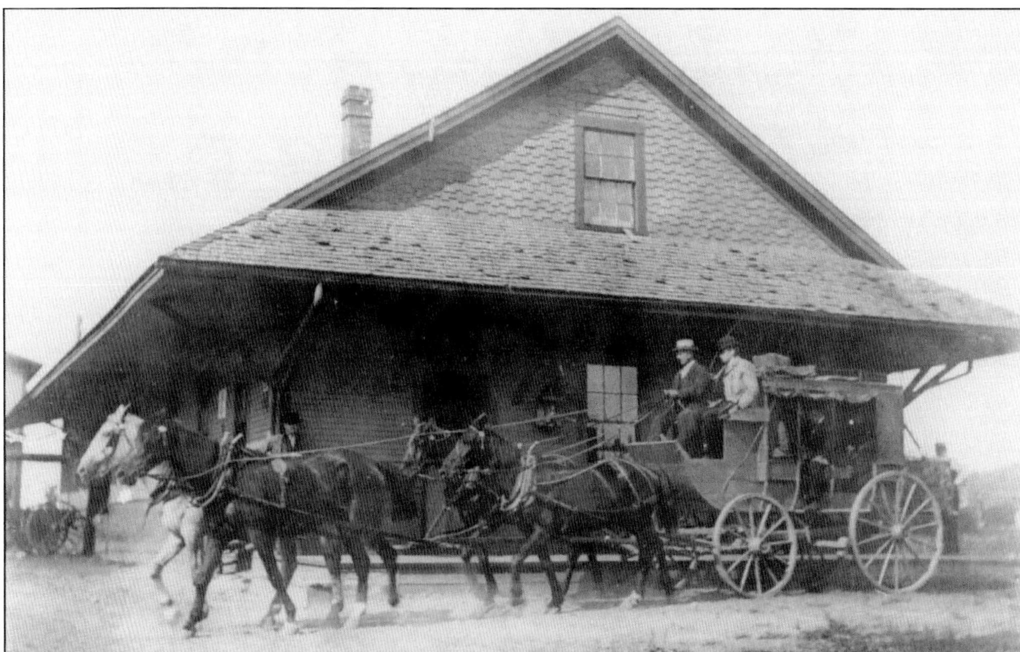

Soon after the railroad pushed its way into the Upper Valley, there were three stagecoach routes through Thetford: one from Boston, Concord, and Hanover into Thetford, then on along the Ompompanoosuc River to Strafford and Montpelier; one from the Norwich village of Pompanoosuc through Union Village, Rice's Mills, Sawnee Bean, Post Mills, West Fairlee, and Chelsea; and one from East Fairlee to Thetford Hill and Post Mills.

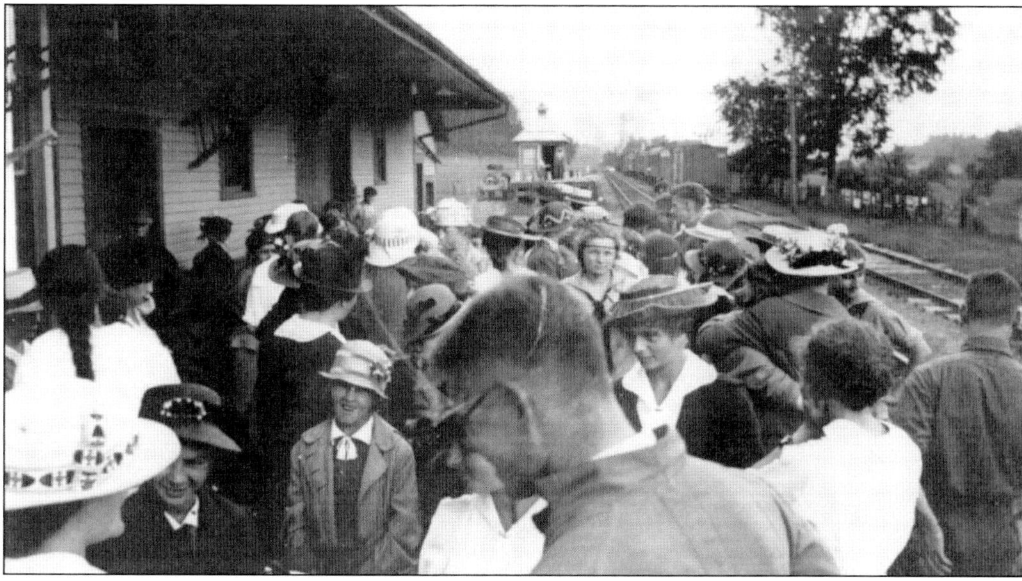

Campers wait for a train in East Thetford in 1915. Taxis to and from Thetford's camps were a common sight in summer, full of young people destined for Camp Hanoum (below) or the camps on Lake Fairlee. When girls (and later boys) arrived and left from Thetford's camps every four weeks or so, the depots in East Thetford, Ely, and North Thetford were awash with masses of young people, and the parking lots were full of hired cars waiting to transport them.

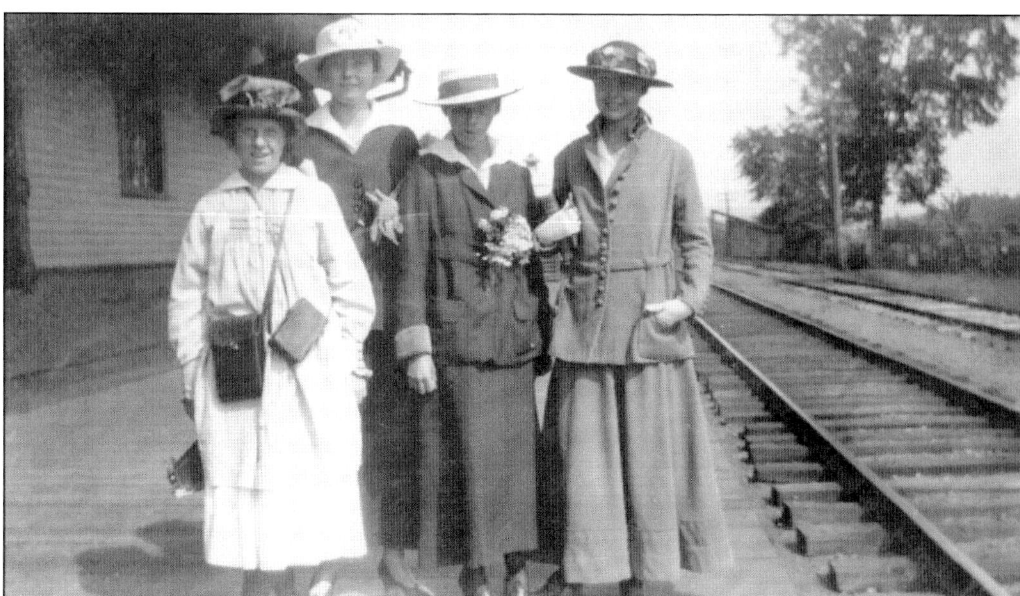

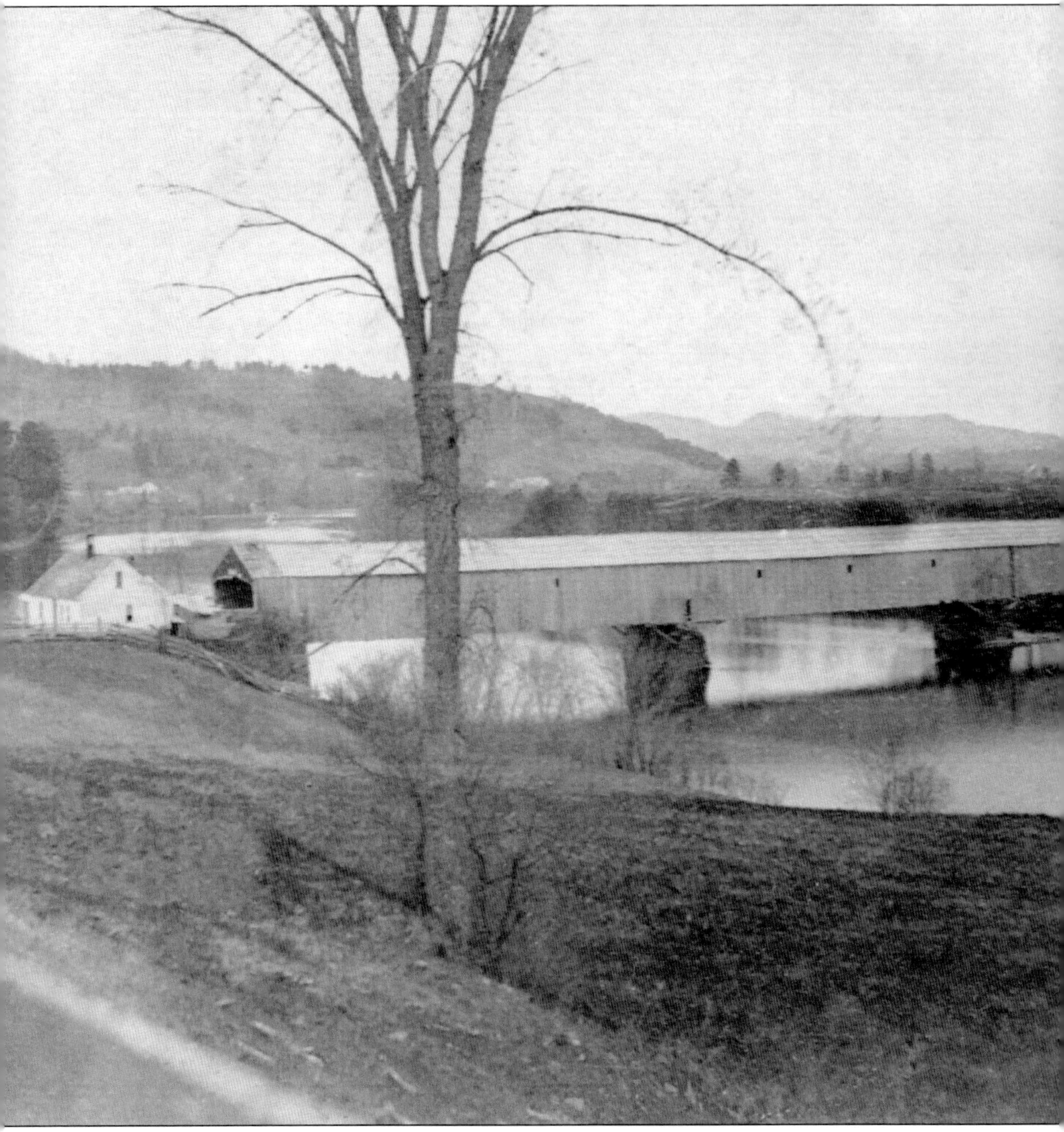

There has been a bridge in East Thetford since 1839 (and ferries before that since at least 1786). The 1839 covered bridge washed away in 1896, but the house from its toll bridge days still stands on the Lyme side. (Courtesy of Lyme Historians.)

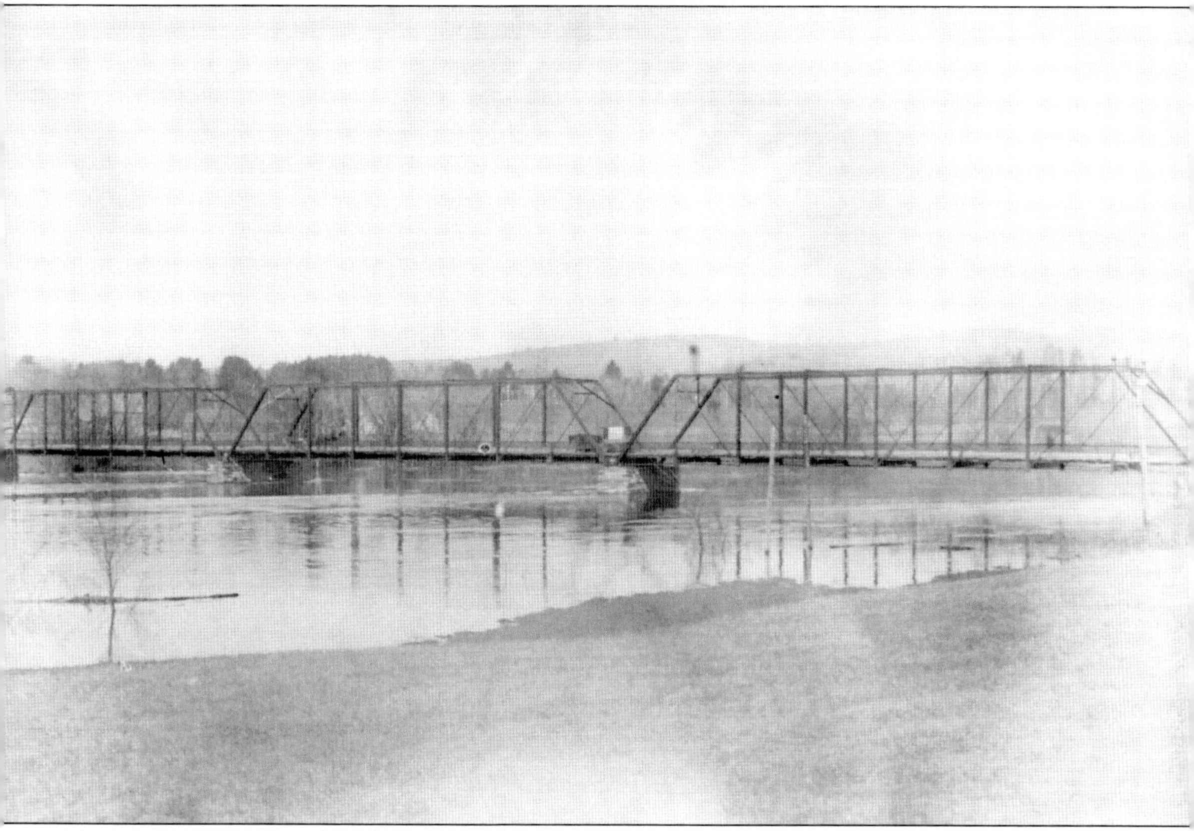

The iron bridge that replaced the covered bridge was destroyed in the flood of 1936 and replaced by the present structure.

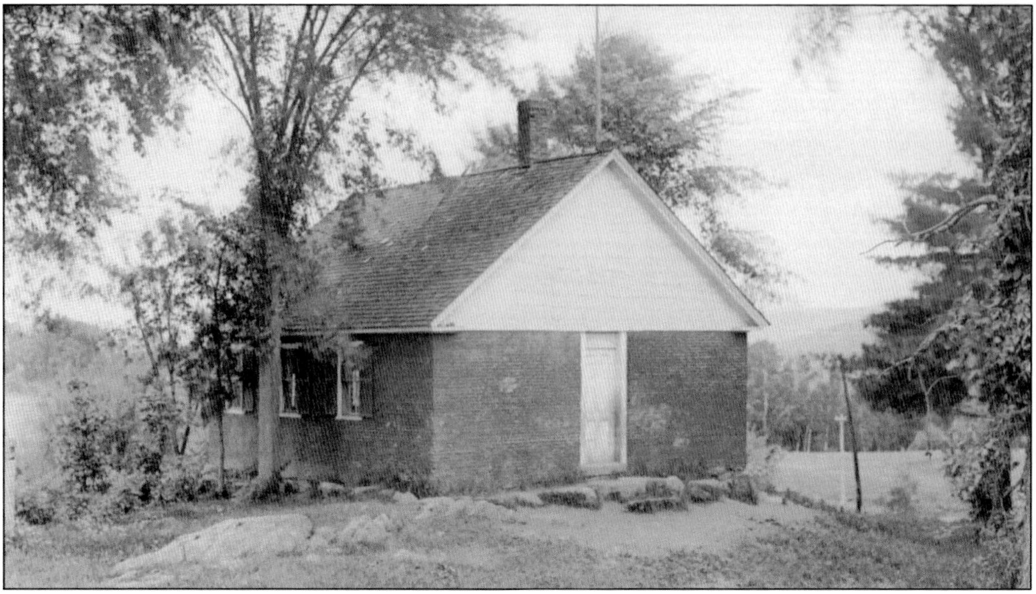

The 1803 schoolhouse in East Thetford sat on the eastern side of Route 5. It was East Thetford's second schoolhouse; the first one was in existence as early as 1773.

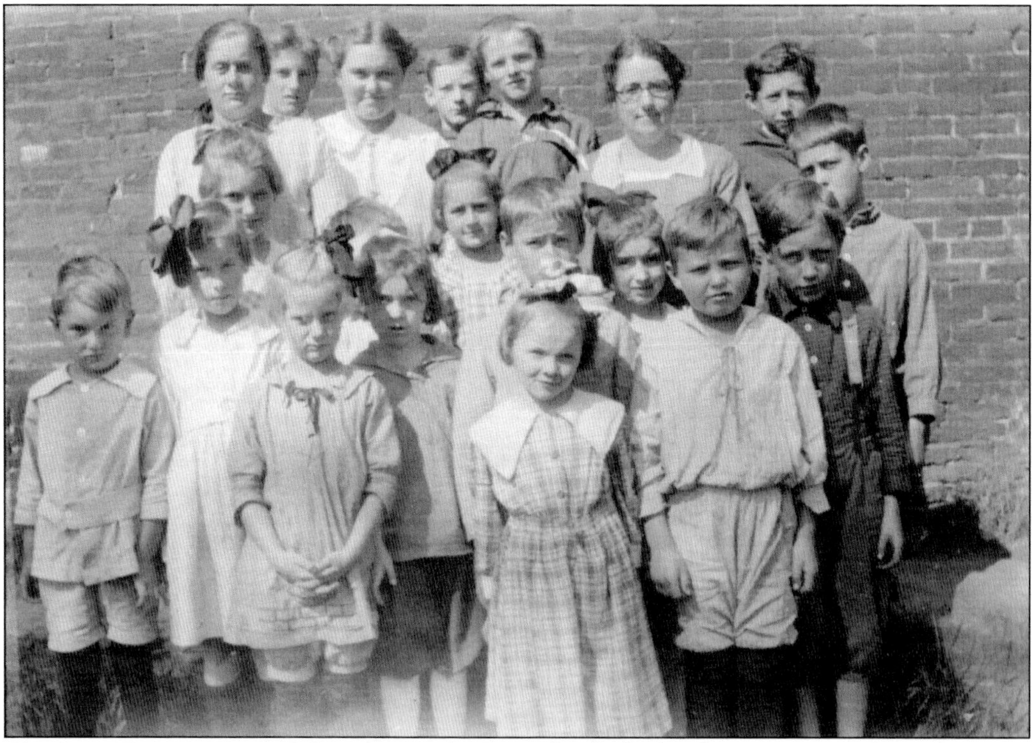

Charlotte Turner poses with her class at the East Thetford school, sometime in the early 1900s. As the 20th century progressed, it became harder to maintain district schools in the face of a declining population and stricter state standards. Some small schools would close for years on end, and their students would be sent to a nearby schoolhouse until their district's numbers increased again. After 1962, all students were sent to the elementary school in Thetford Hill.

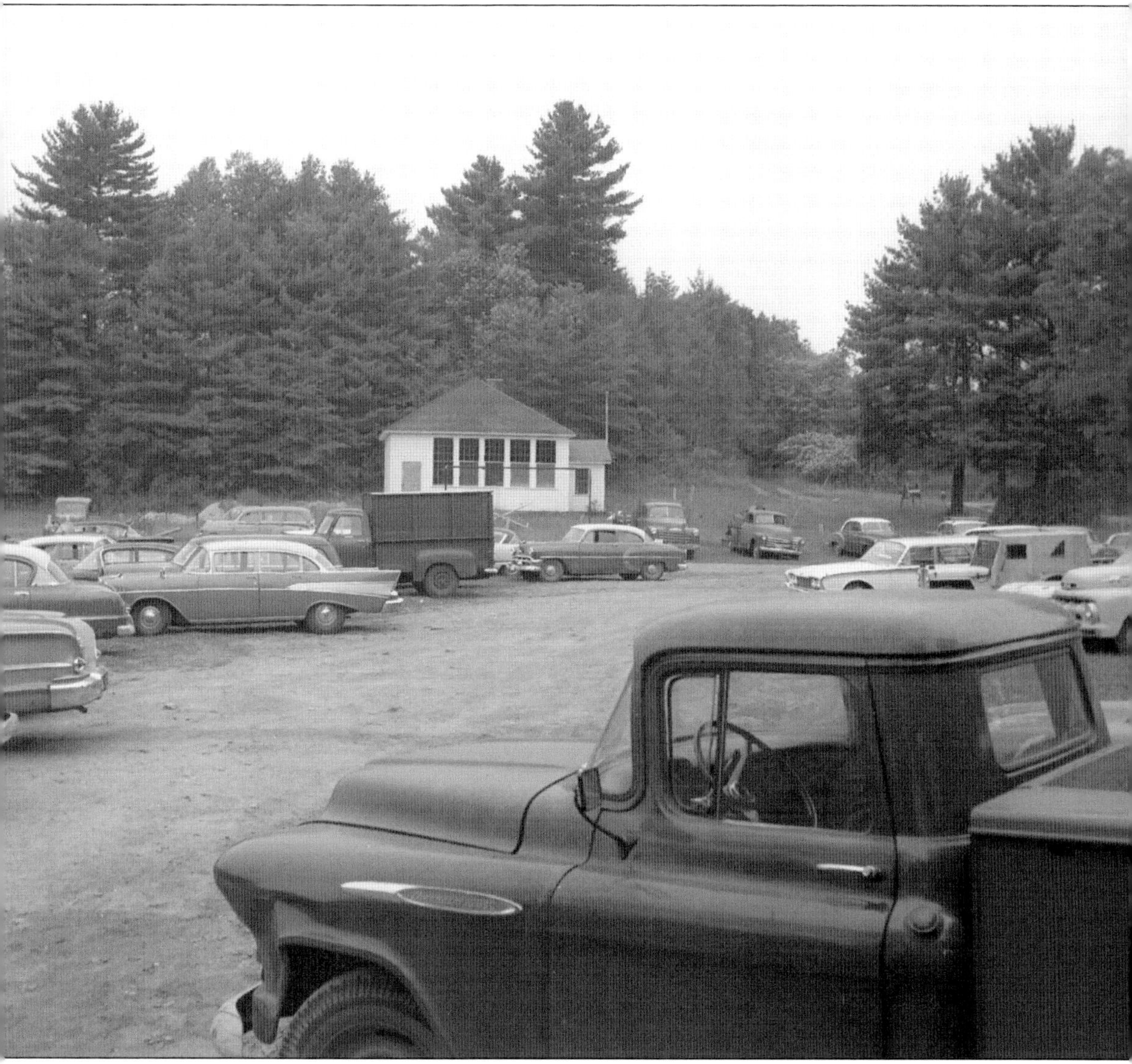

The East Thetford schoolhouse is pictured here behind cars and trucks parked for an auction. In 1927, it replaced the 1803 schoolhouse across Route 5. (Courtesy of the Vermont State Archives and Records Administration.)

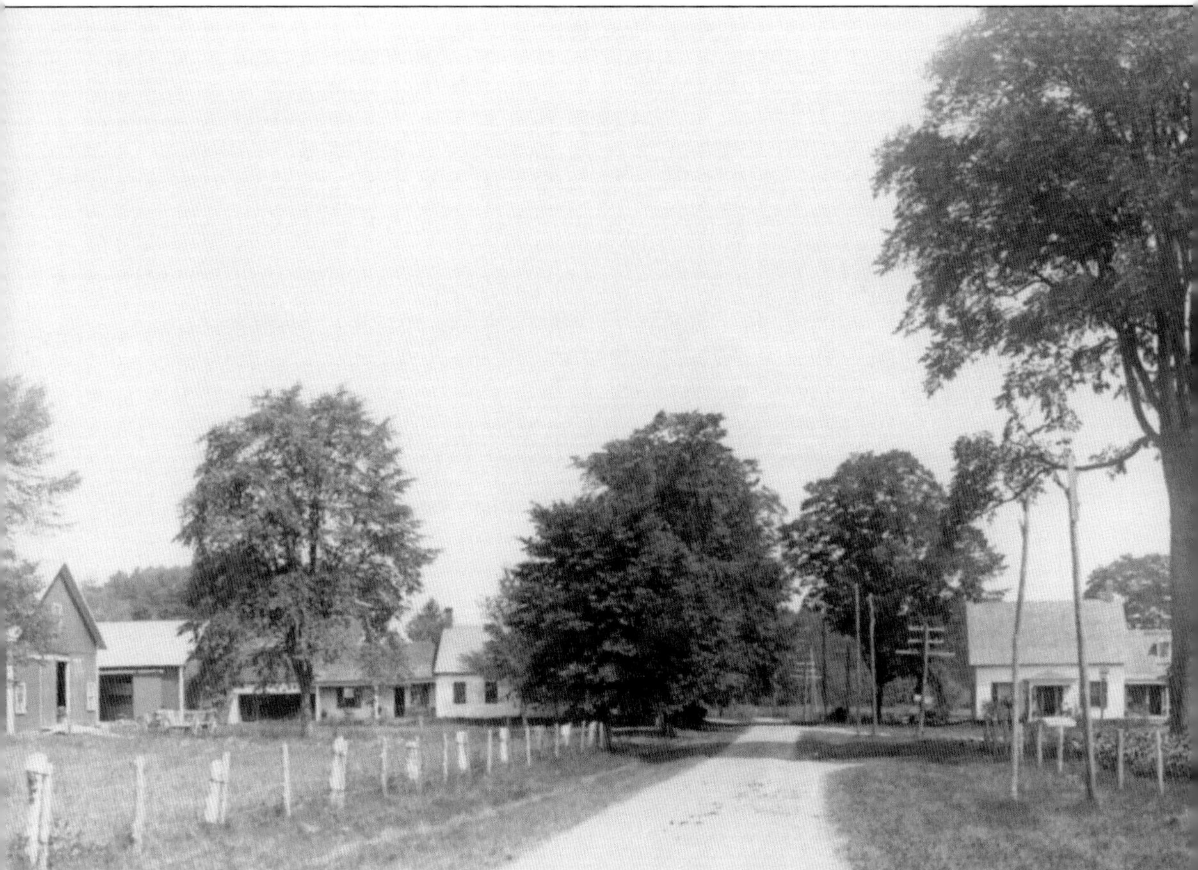

Looking north along Route 5, Gray's Auction House is at left, and the road to Lyme is in front of the house at right. In Thetford's early days, Route 113 crossed Route 5 from Lyme and continued straight up the hill, past Asa Burton's house and into Thetford Hill. It was moved north to its current location for unknown reasons in the early 19th century.

Seven

UNION VILLAGE

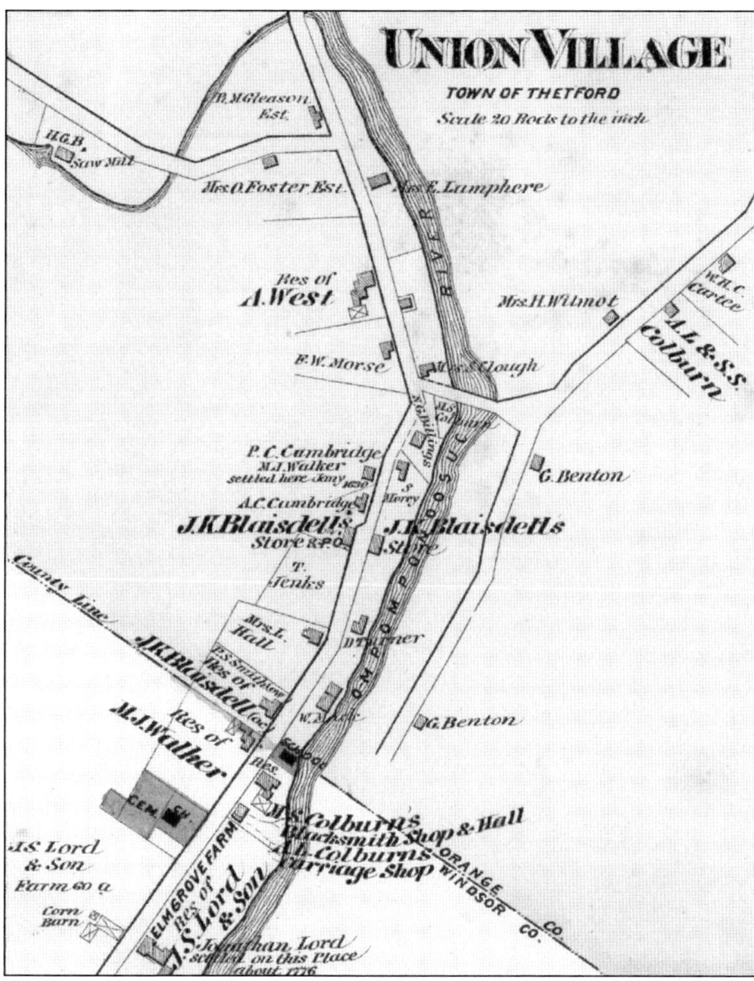

This map shows Union Village as it was in 1877. Union Village is so named because the village lies partly in Norwich and partly in Thetford. It was first settled by Samuel Locke and his family, who built mills on the Ompompanoosuc River and gave the village its original name of Locke's Mills. (Courtesy of University of Vermont Special Collections.)

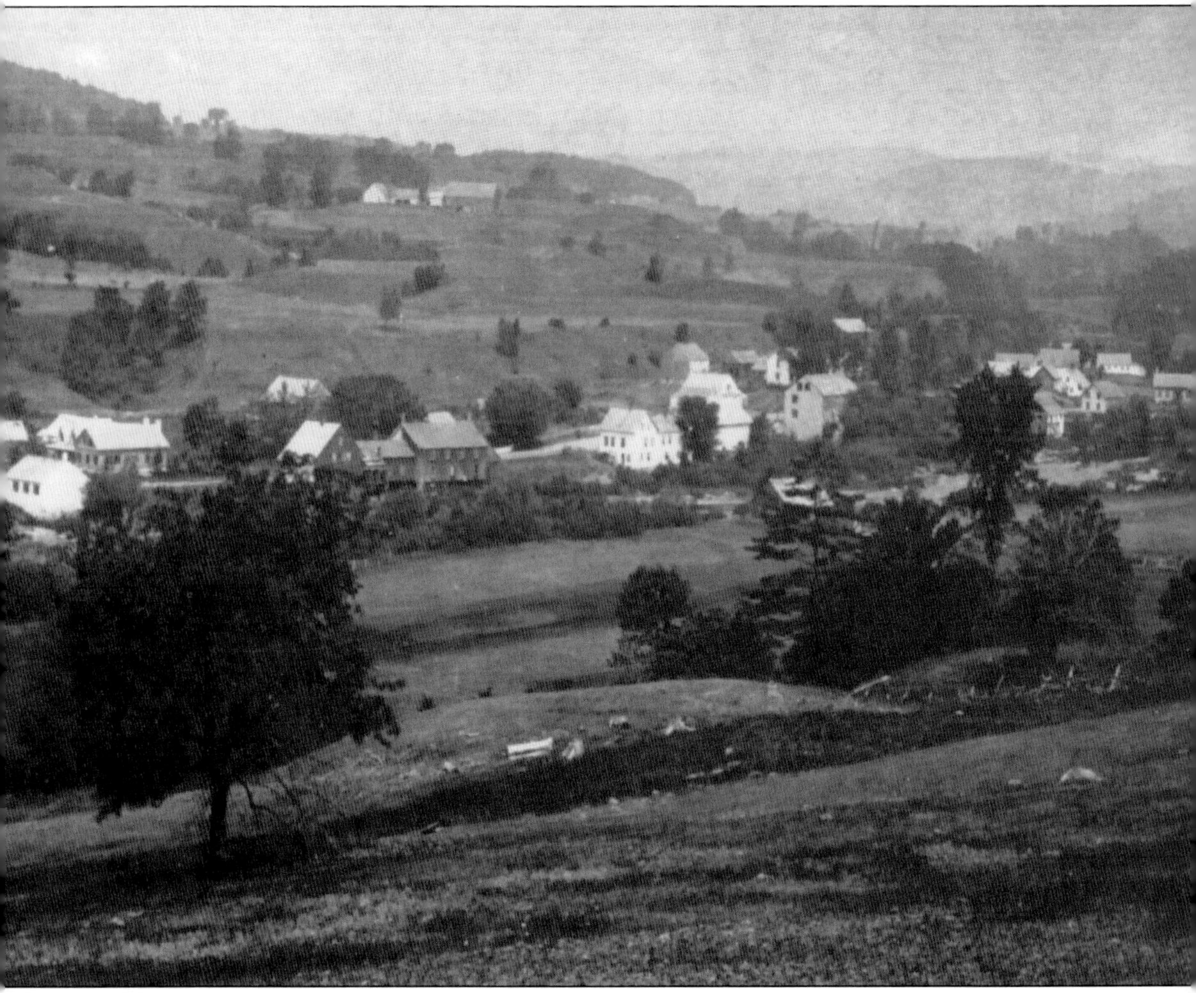

This photograph looks southwest across Union Village. The community has undergone more change in its history than most of Thetford's other villages. When the federal government built a flood control dam just upriver from Union Village in the 1940s, it changed the landscape in a long process of buying properties, removing buildings, contouring the land, and building new roads. Many farms and homesteads in both Union Village and Thetford Center were demolished, as were several covered bridges. Twenty years later, more land was taken over for Interstate 91, a project that also deeply affected East Thetford and North Thetford.

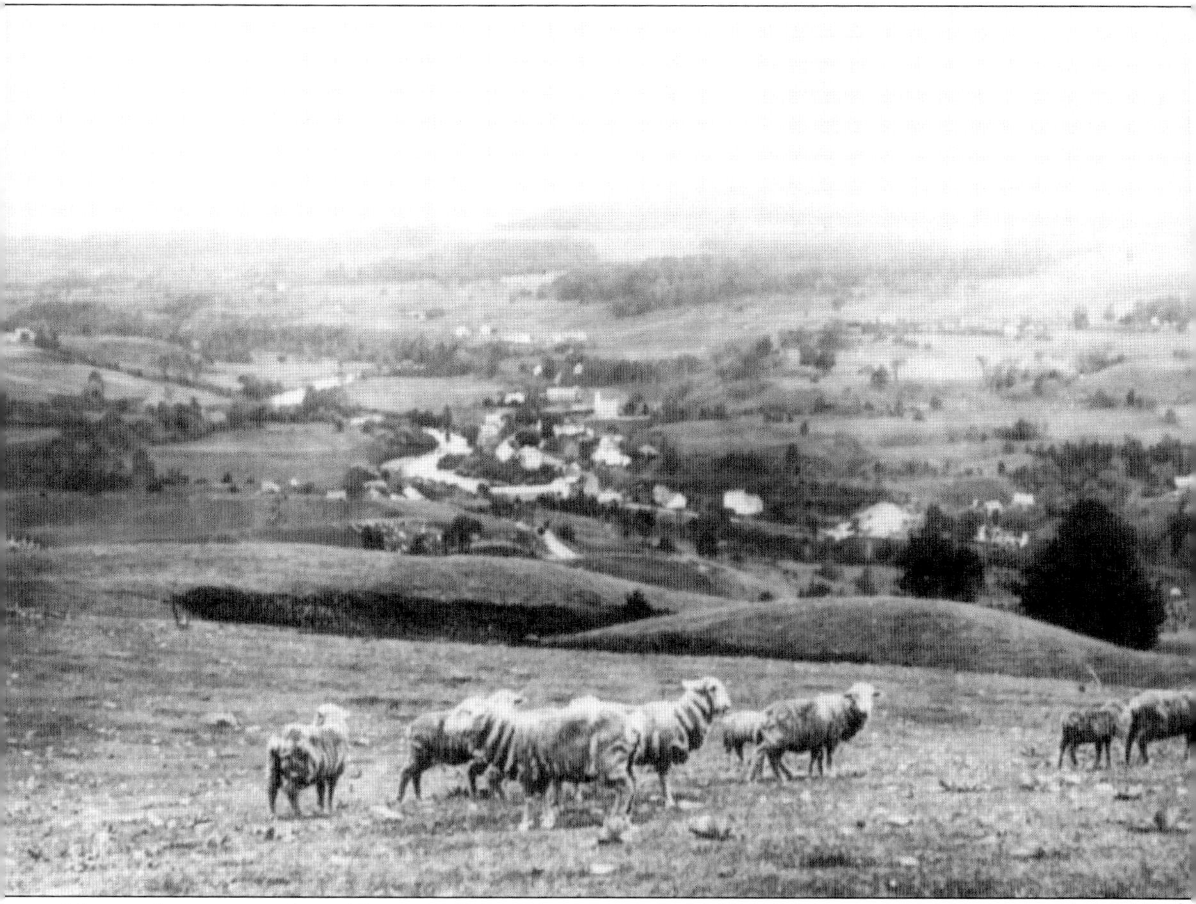

Merino sheep graze above Union Village. There was something of a craze for raising merinos in New England after the Spanish lifted the blockade on merino exports. The sturdy sheep thrived in poor soil and had fine wool. There were more than 13,600 merinos in Thetford in the 1840s (and one million merinos in Vermont). However, the market was flooded and cheaper western competition quickly undercut prices.

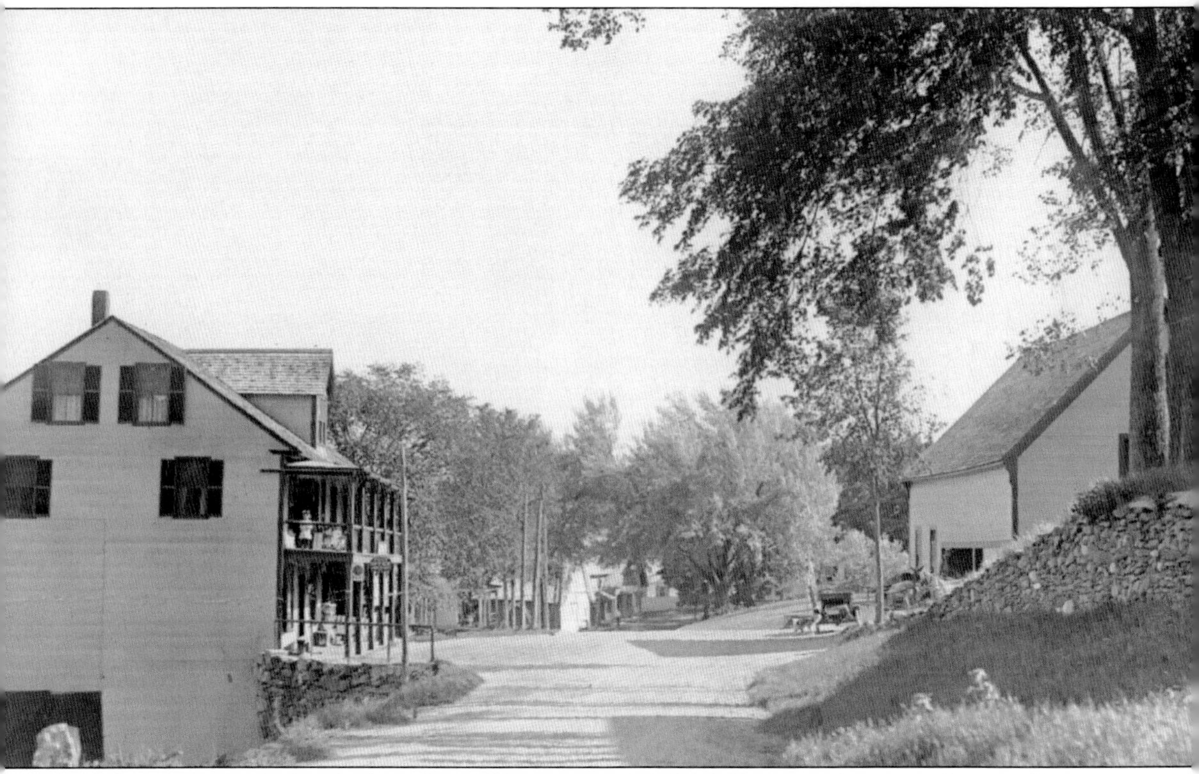

This image looks south along Main Street around 1920. The general store and post office is at left. (Courtesy of University of Vermont Special Collections.)

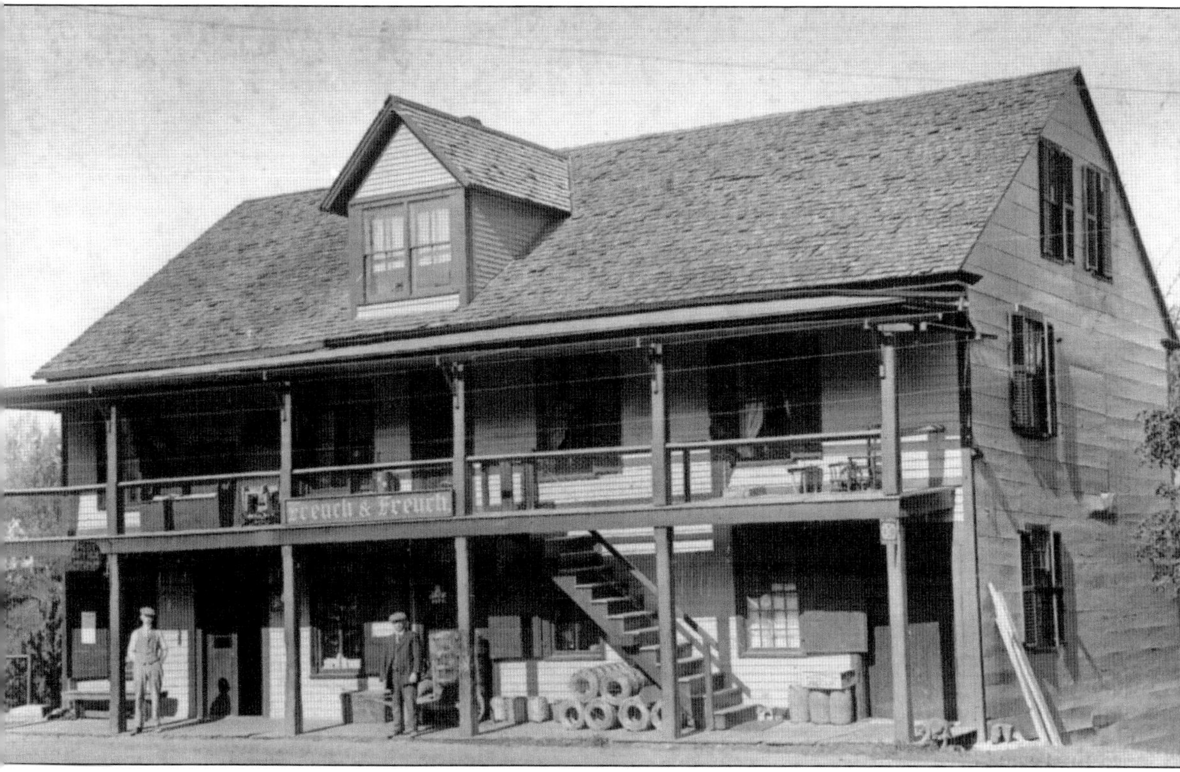

This is Henry and Joseph French's general store, which burned in the 1950s. (Courtesy of the Norwich Historical Society.)

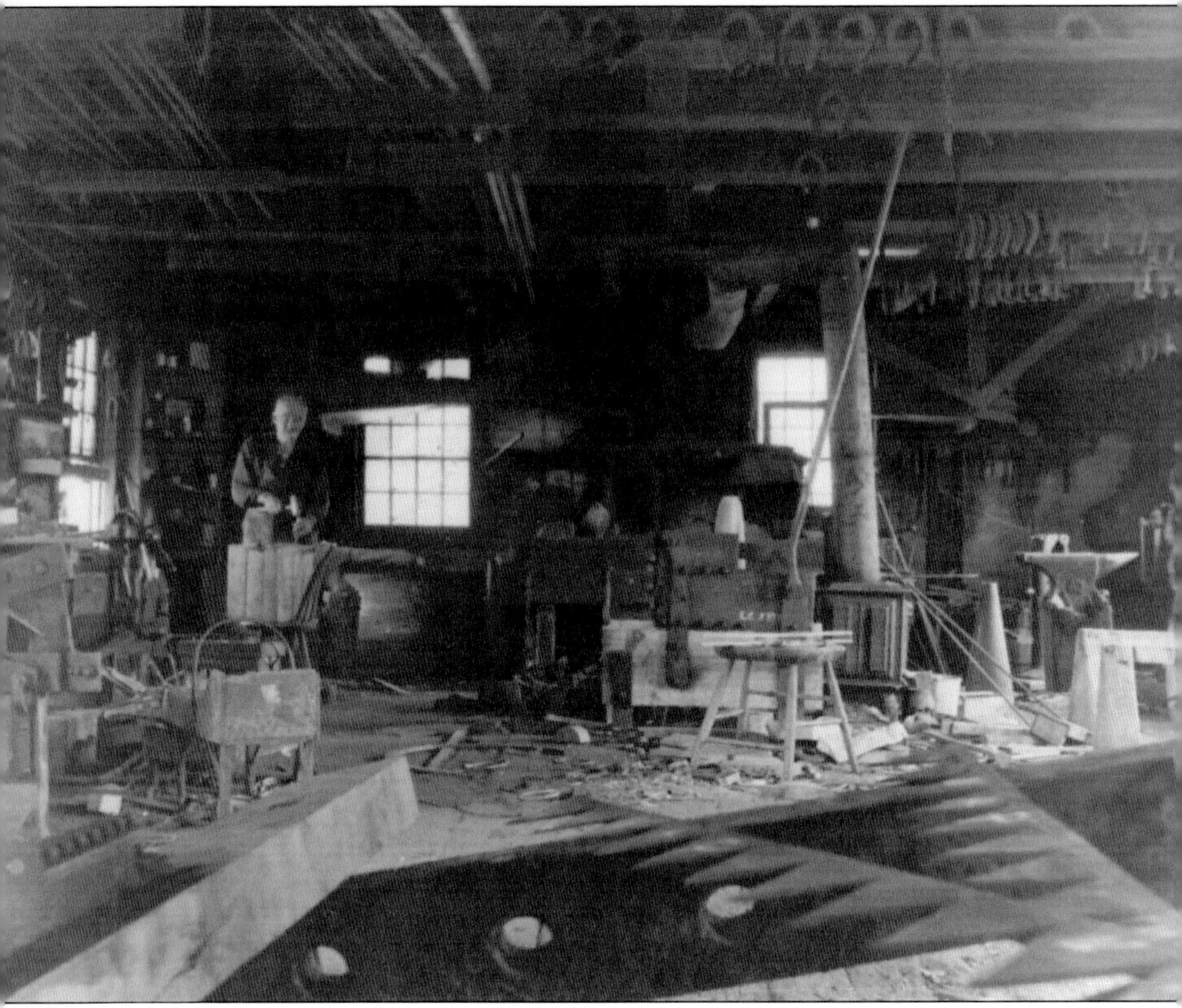

Thetford photographer Gladys Estabrook captured on film the interior of Myron Colburn's blacksmith shop, preserving a dying art that was once a crucial part of life. Until blacksmiths arrived in Thetford, farmers had to make their own nails and mend their own horseshoes, wheels, and sleigh runners. The ironwork of the blacksmith was once essential to the functioning of any village, but cheaper, mass-produced steel eventually overtook the market. Many blacksmiths eventually converted their shops into automobile garages. After all, they had been repairing vehicles for quite some time already.

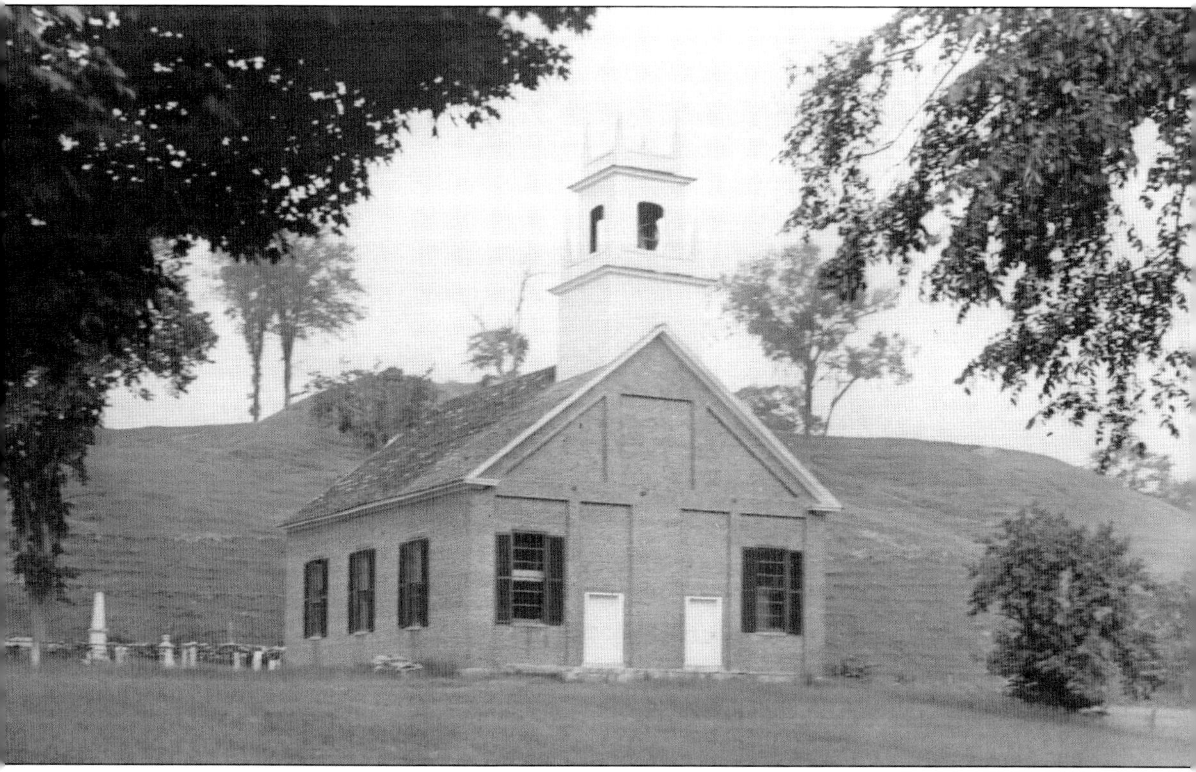

The Methodist Episcopal Church, built in 1836, sits on the Norwich side of Union Village.

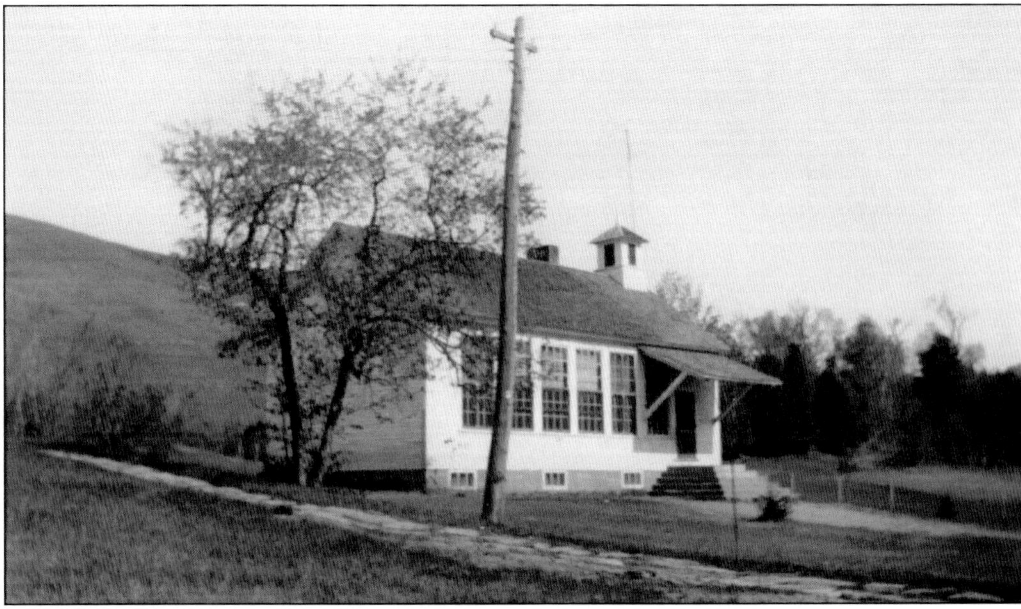

The Union Village schoolhouse was moved across the street in 1925 to give the children more room and bring it away from the river. It was closed in 1962 when the district schools were consolidated in Thetford Hill.

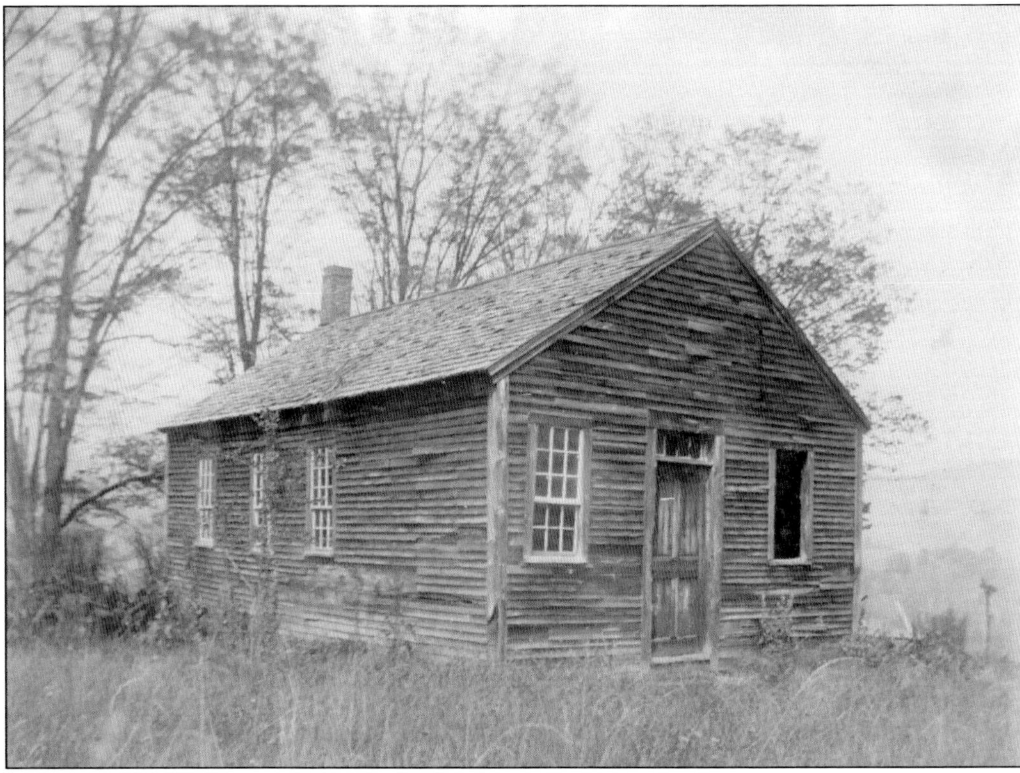

The tiny Cream Street school, located at the corner of Route 132, ceased operation in 1894 because of its poor condition and lack of students.

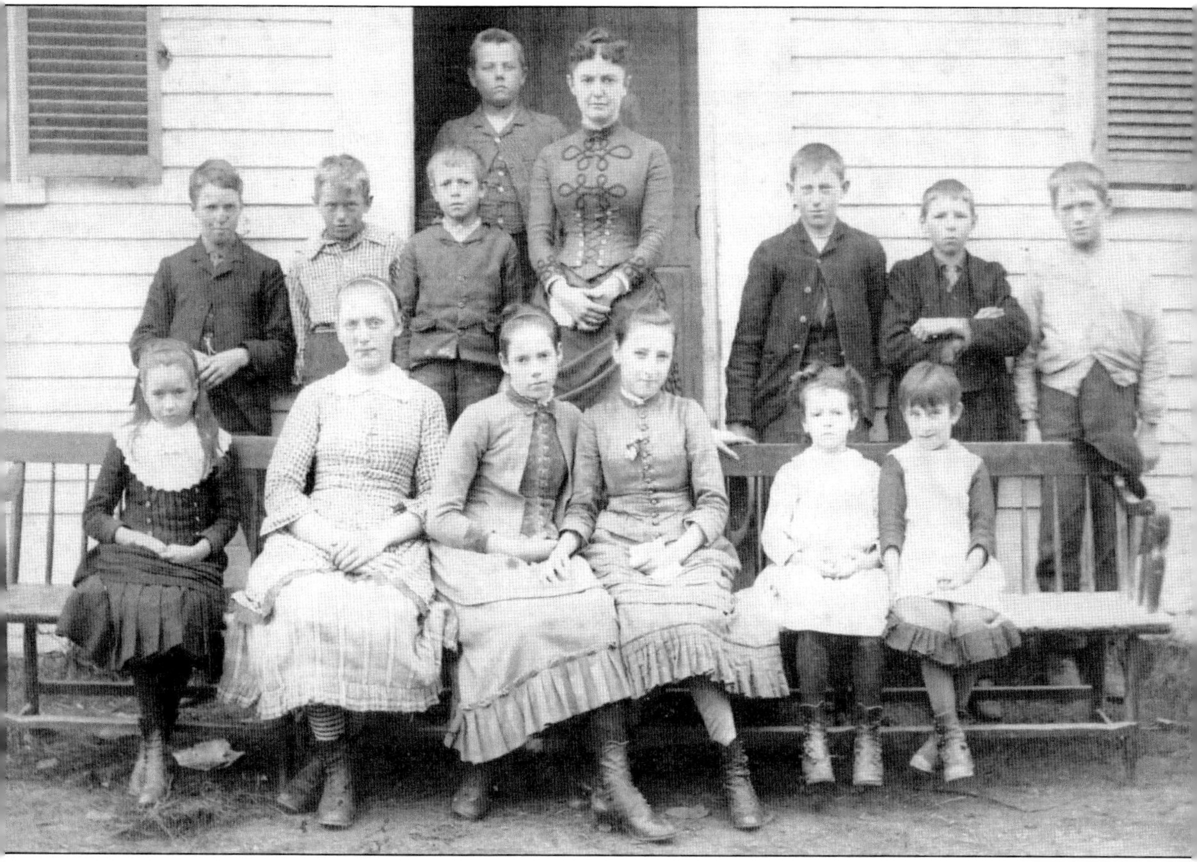

Alice Jenks poses with her class of Union Village students in 1887. Alice taught at Union Village for seven terms in a row—quite a rare occurrence. For much of the 19th century, most teachers only taught for one term and then were replaced with another. It is unknown why this was so, since school board reports regularly complained of the practice.

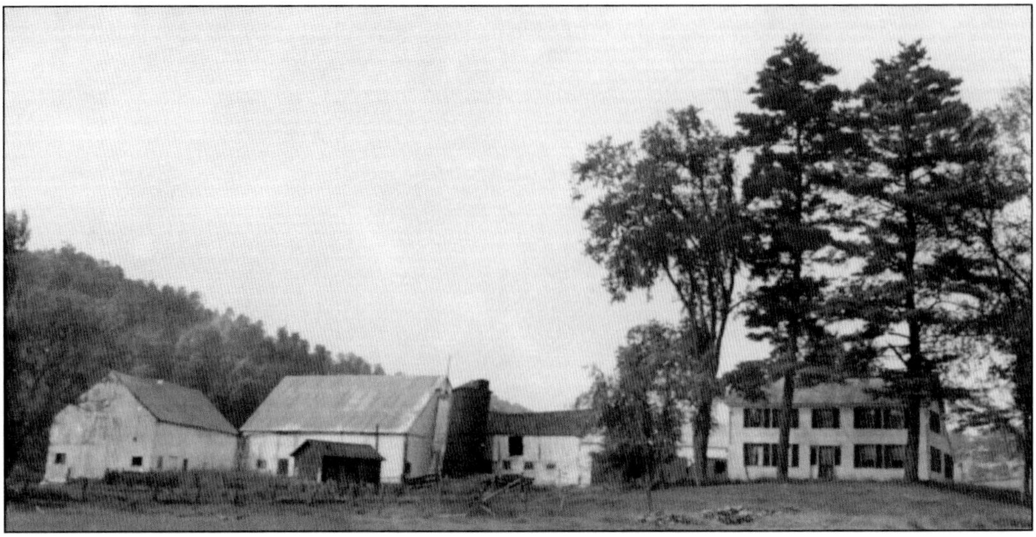

Charles Cook's farm was one of several in Union Village and Thetford Center that were demolished when the Union Village Dam was constructed over the Ompompanoosuc River in the late 1940s. After the floods of 1927 and 1936 and the hurricane of 1938, the federal government built 16 such flood control dams and reservoirs in New England to let water back up in Connecticut River tributaries, preventing major flooding downstream. "[I]t was a long-term plan; it was nothing that came up all of a sudden," recalled Kermit Cook, who worked on the dam and lived on this farm. "Most of us knew they were planning to take the land." The farm was demolished in 1946.

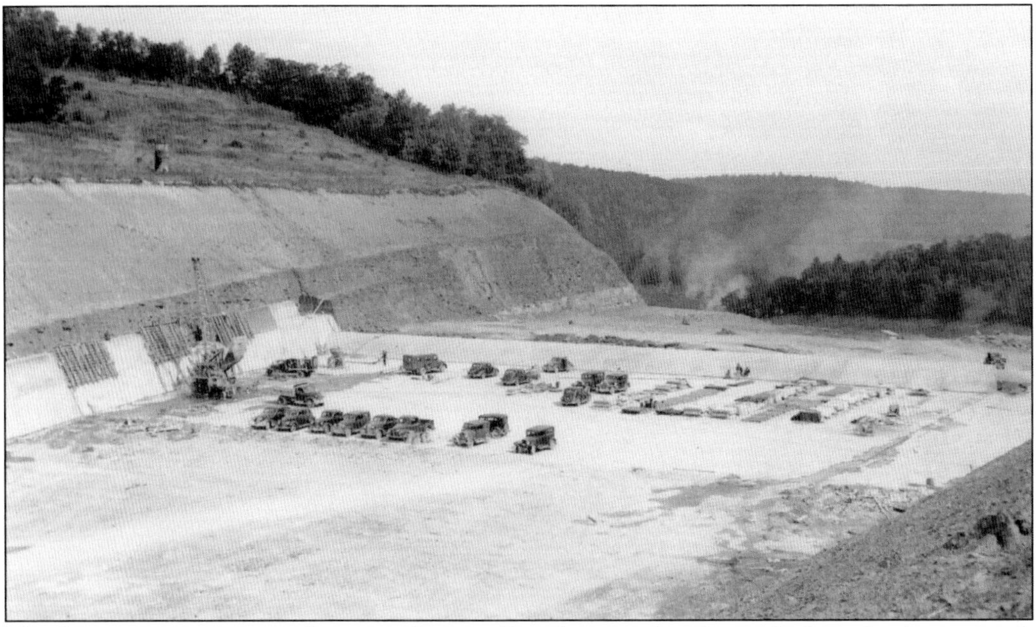

The dam was a massive gravel mound whose spillway burrowed underneath through a long tunnel, connected to a tall inlet tower. The river continued its daily course through another outlet. If filled, the reservoir area would cover 720 acres. (Courtesy of the Norwich Historical Society.)

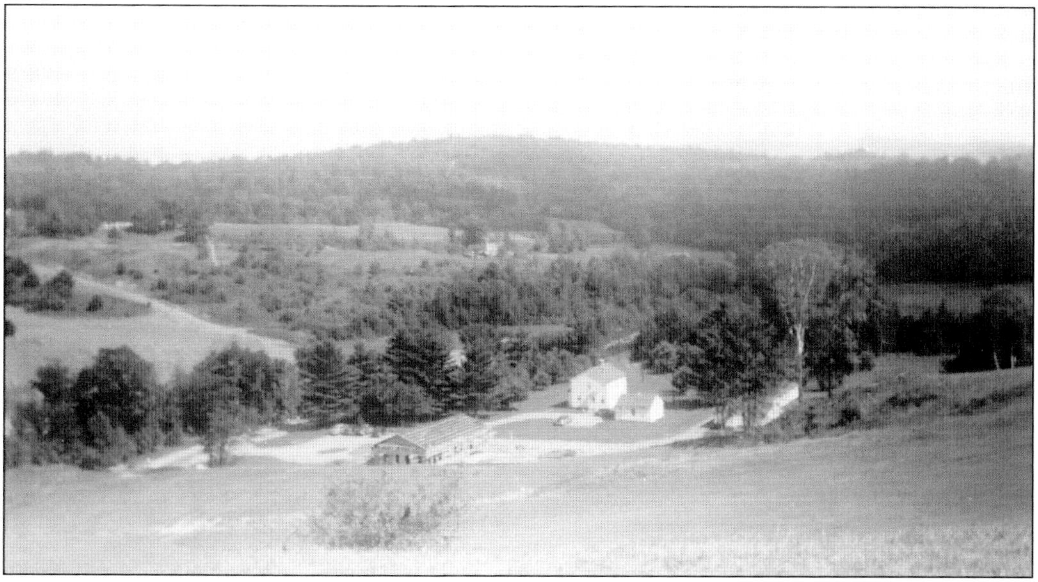

This is a view of the dam caretaker's house and outbuildings. (Courtesy of the Norwich Historical Society.)

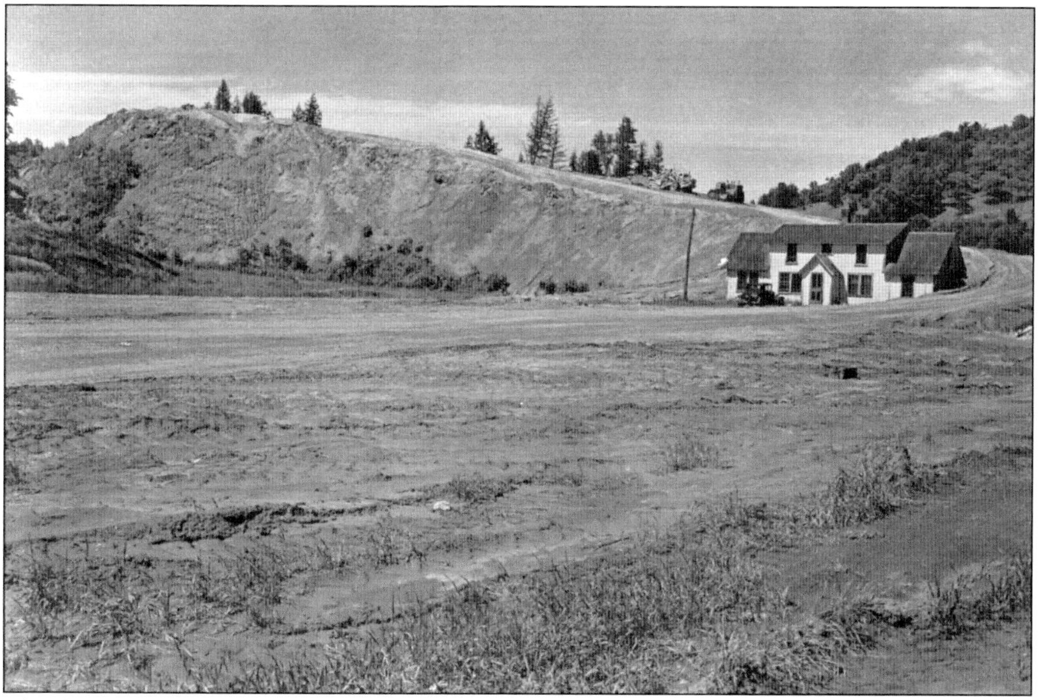

Thetford Academy principal Dwight Goddard had turned this house into a Buddhist monastery, but during dam construction, it was used as a field office before being demolished. The gravel hill behind the house was completely removed for fill. Goddard was one of the earliest Americans to bring Buddhism to this country. He had been a Christian missionary in China and spent a year living in a Japanese monastery. His attempts to create an American monastic community were unsuccessful, but he found great success when he wrote *A Buddhist Bible* in 1932 with D.T. Suzuki.

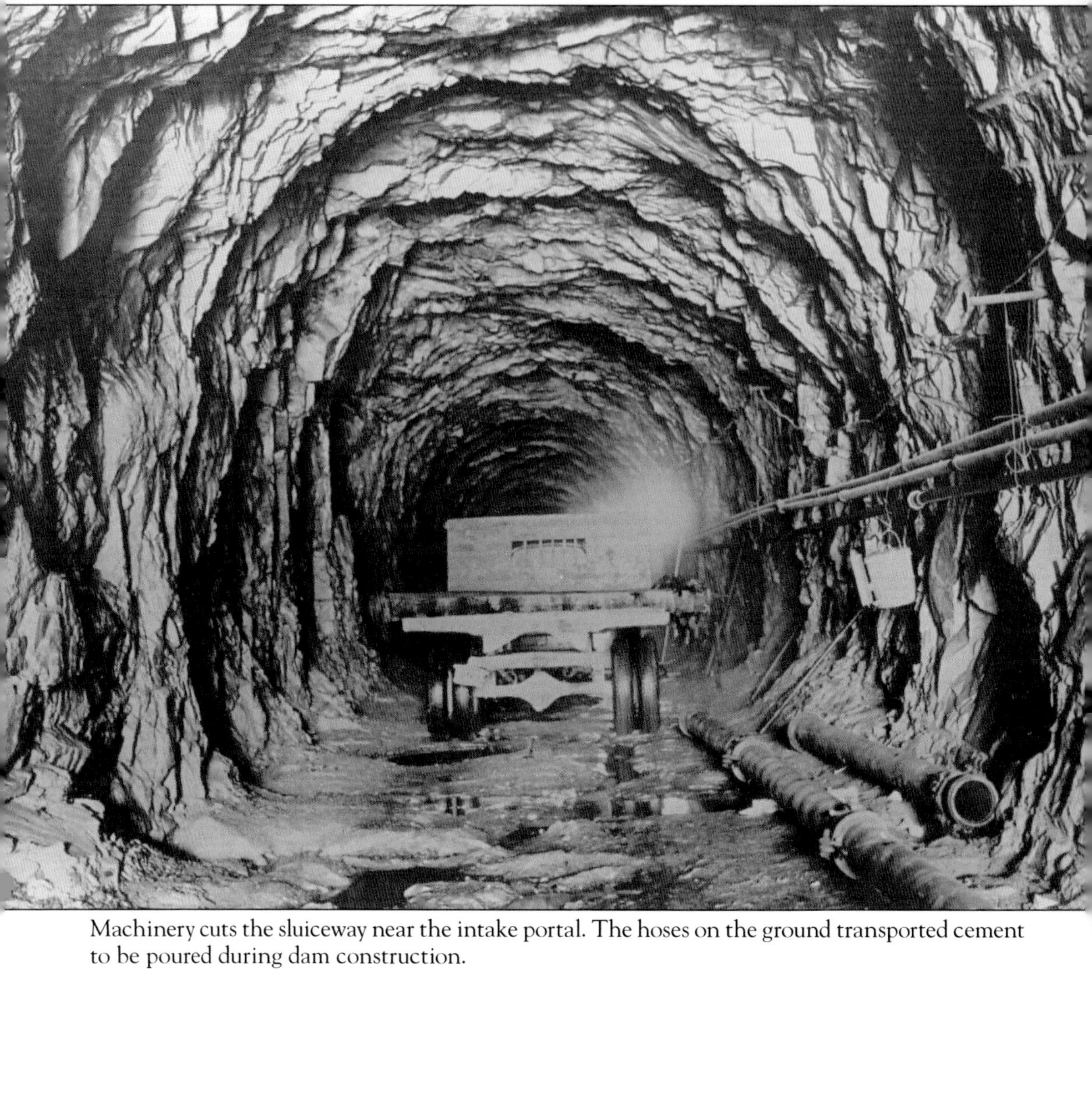

Machinery cuts the sluiceway near the intake portal. The hoses on the ground transported cement to be poured during dam construction.

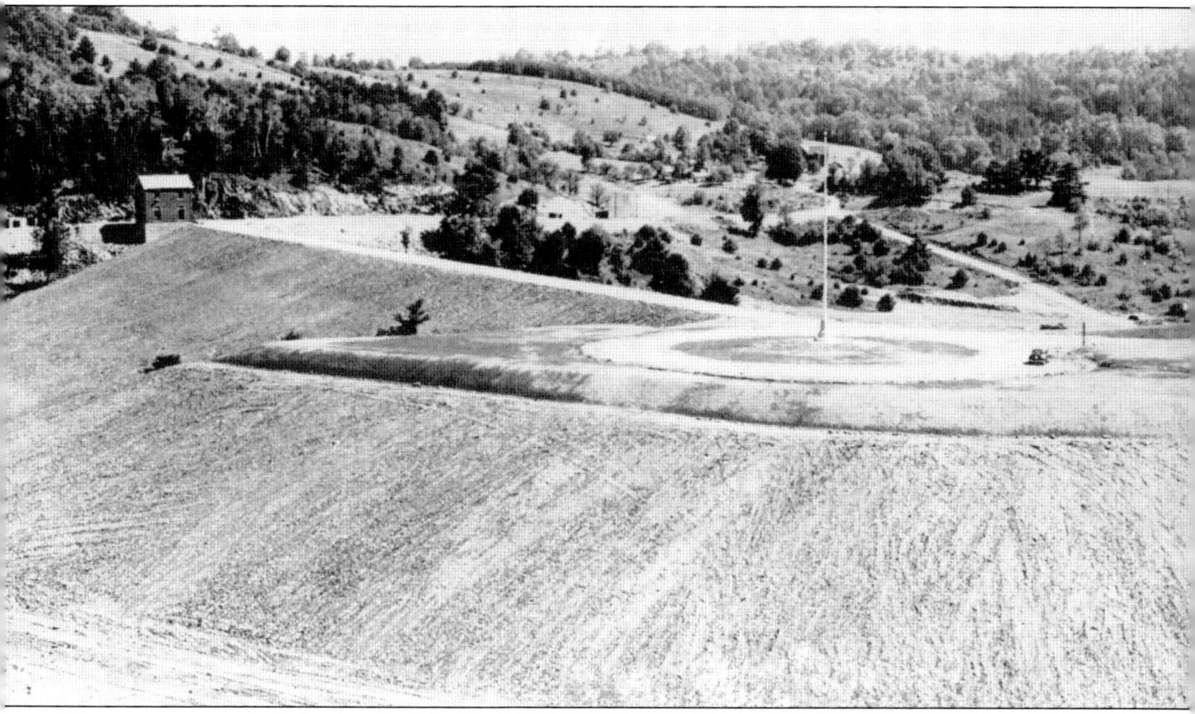

This is a postcard of the finished 1,100-foot dam. The Army Corps of Engineers maintains the site as a recreational area. (Courtesy of University of Vermont Special Collections.)

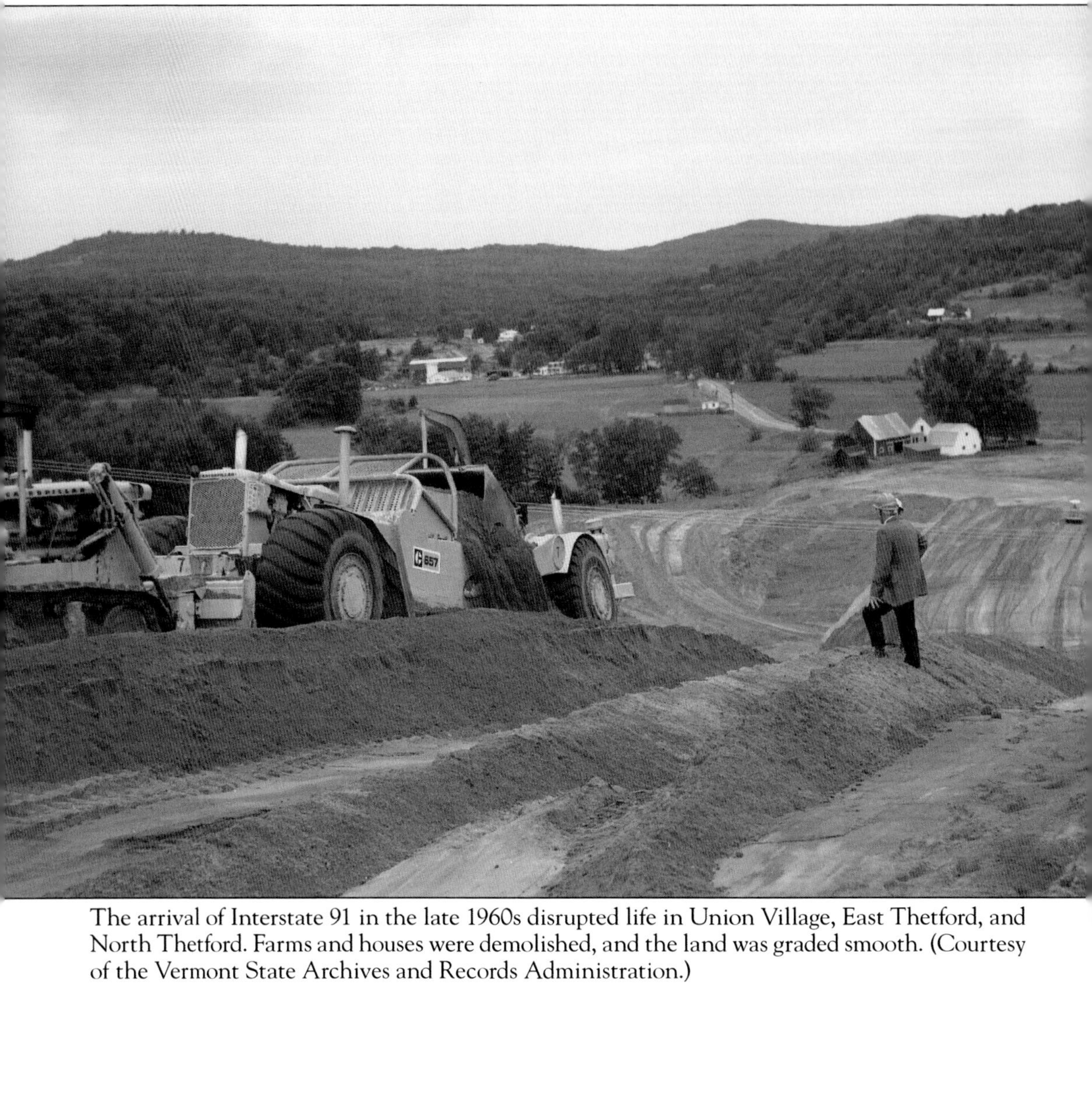

The arrival of Interstate 91 in the late 1960s disrupted life in Union Village, East Thetford, and North Thetford. Farms and houses were demolished, and the land was graded smooth. (Courtesy of the Vermont State Archives and Records Administration.)

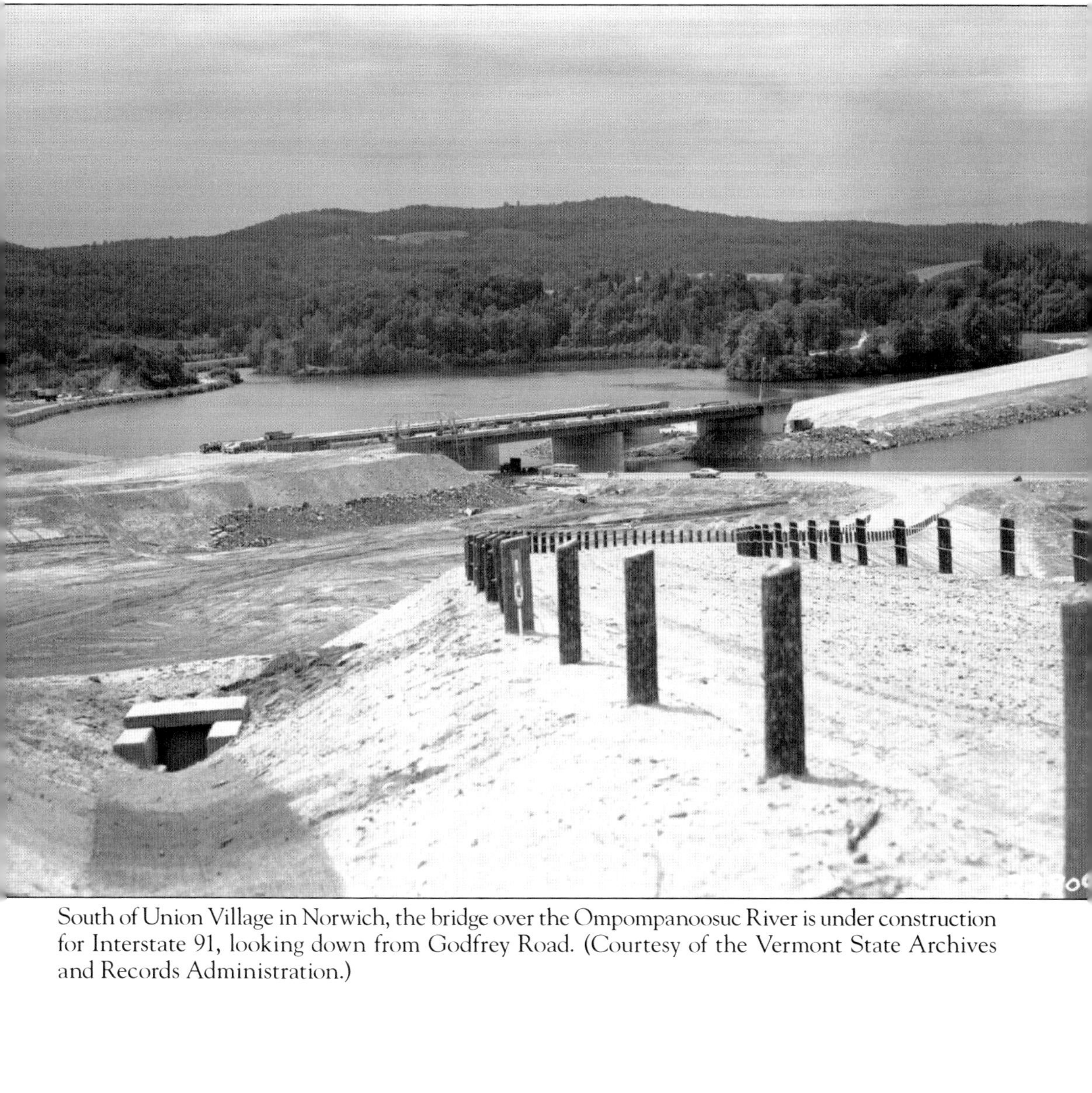

South of Union Village in Norwich, the bridge over the Ompompanoosuc River is under construction for Interstate 91, looking down from Godfrey Road. (Courtesy of the Vermont State Archives and Records Administration.)

Bibliography

Child, Hamilton. *Gazetteer of Orange County, Vermont*. Syracuse, NY: Syracuse Journal Co., 1888.

Glassberg, David. *American Historical Pageantry*. Chapel Hill, NC: University of North Carolina Press, 1990.

Hemenway, Abby Maria. *The Vermont Historical Gazetteer*. Burlington, VT: 1871.

Hughes, Charles W. *The Mills and Villages of Thetford, Vermont*. Thetford, VT: Thetford Historical Society, 1992.

Langdon, William C. *Book of Words for the Pageant of Thetford*. White River Junction, VT: Vermonter Press, 1911.

Latham, Charles Jr. *A Short History of Thetford, Vermont, 1761–1870*. Thetford, VT: Thetford Historical Society, 1972.

McCartney, Charlotte. Once Upon a Town. Self-published, 1985.

Paris, Leslie. *Children's Nature: The Rise of the American Summer Camp*. New York, NY: New York University Press, 2008.

Peters, Jeanne. "Thetford, Vermont: The changing dimensions of a New England hill town." Senior thesis for Middlebury College. Middlebury, VT, 1971.

Russ, Ruthe R. District Schools of Thetford, Vermont. Unpublished manuscript, 1963.

Slade, Mary B. *Thetford Academy's First Century*. Thetford, VT: Thetford Academy, 1956.

Thetford Historical Society. *Fifty for 250*. Thetford, VT: Thetford Historical Society, 2011.

Town of Thetford. Annual Reports, 1878–1975. Thetford, VT.

INDEX

Consistent with our mission to preserve history on a local level, this book was printed in South Carolina on American-made paper and manufactured entirely in the United States. Products carrying the accredited Forest Stewardship Council (FSC) label are printed on 100 percent FSC-certified paper.

MADE IN THE USA